THE
INSULAR
TRADITION

SUNY Series in Medieval Studies
Paul E. Szarmach, editor

THE
INSULAR
TRADITION

EDITED BY
Catherine E. Karkov
Michael Ryan
Robert T. Farrell

STATE UNIVERSITY OF NEW YORK PRESS

Published by
State University of New York Press, Albany

© 1997 State University of New York

For information, address the State University of New York Press,
State University Plaza, Albany, NY 12246

Production design by David Ford
Marketing by Patrick Durocher

Library of Congress Cataloging-in-Publication Data

The insular tradition / edited by Catherine Karkov, Robert Farrell,
   and Michael Ryan.
        p.   cm. — (SUNY series in medieval studies)
     Includes bibliographical references (p.   ) and index.
     ISBN 0-7914-3455-9 (alk. paper). — ISBN 0-7914-3456-7 (pbk. :
alk. paper)
     1. Art, Anglo-Saxon.   2. Art, Celtic—Ireland.   I. Karkov,
Catherine.   II. Farrell, Robert T.   III. Ryan, Michael, 1947–   .
IV. Series.
N6763.I58   1997
709'.41—dc20   96-38697
                                                              CIP

10 9 8 7 6 5 4 3 2 1

*This book is dedicated to our friend and colleague
Jim Lang, whose contributions to the study of
Anglo-Saxon sculpture have proven to be
of inestimable value.*

CONTENTS

ABBREVIATIONS

A.E.M.S.	American Early Medieval Studies
Ant.J.	*Antiquaries Journal*
Arch.J.	*Archaeological Journal*
Art Bull.	*Art Bulletin*
A.S.E.	*Anglo-Saxon England*
A.S.S.A.H.	*Anglo-Saxon Studies in Archaeology and History*
B.A.R.	British Archaeological Reports
B.B.C.S.	*Bulletin of the Board of Celtic Studies*
B.N.J.	*British Numismatic Journal*
Burl. Mag.	*Burlington Magazine*
C.B.A.	Council for British Archaeology
C.C.S.L.	Corpus Christianorum Series Latina
H.M.S.O.	Her Majesty's Stationery Office
J.B.A.A.	*Journal of the British Archaeological Association*
J.I.A.	*Journal of Irish Archaeology*
J.R.S.A.I.	*Journal of the Royal Society of Antiquaries of Ireland*
J.W.C.I.	*Journal of the Warburg and Courtauld Institutes*
M.A.	*Medieval Archaeology*
P.L.	Patrologia Latina
P.R.I.A.	*Proceedings of the Royal Irish Academy*
P.S.A.S.	*Proceedings of the Society of Antiquaries of Scotland*
R.C.A.H.M.S.	Royal Commission on the Ancient and Historical Monuments of Scotland
U.J.A.	*Ulster Journal of Archaeology*
Z.C.P.	*Zeitschrift für Celtische Philologie*

ILLUSTRATIONS

1. *The Bewcastle Cross*

2. *Symbols of the Passion or Power?*

3. *Worthy Women on the Ruthwell Cross*

4. *Survival and Revival in Insular Art*

5. King Oswald's Wooden Cross at Heavenfield in Context

PLATES

6. Daniel Themes on the Irish High Crosses

PLATES

7. The Tower Cross at Kells

PLATES

8. *Variations on an Old Theme*
FIGURES

9. *The Echternach Lion*
PLATES

10. *Recent Finds of Insular Enameled Buckles*
PLATES

12. The Menagerie of the Derrynaflan Paten

13. Innovation and Conservatism in Irish
Metalwork of the Romanesque Period

Robert T. Farrell

INTRODUCTION

Insular art, the art of the British Isles and Ireland during the early medieval period, is enjoying something of a renaissance. After a long period of relative neglect, the past few years have seen a remarkable growth in interest in the field, and a consequent growth in new information, discoveries, and approaches to the material. This is reflected in the present volume by the number of contributions from younger scholars, as well as by the number of new finds, new interpretations, and new ways of looking at Insular art that characterize all the essays.

The Insular Tradition, began as a symposium of the same name held as part of the Kalamazoo Medieval Congress in May 1991. The purpose of the symposium, and this volume, was and is to look at the various ways in which "tradition" becomes a part of Insular art and art history. The definition of tradition was deliberately left open to allow speakers to come up with their own traditions, as well as to allow them to deal selectively with the various traditions that form a part of Insular art and the study of Insular art. Chapters, therefore, deal with the Late Antique tradition and how it was preserved and modified by Insular artists (Ryan, Hawkes, Stalley); the "Celtic" tradition (Ryan, Ó Floinn, Henderson, Cramp), the "Anglo-Saxon" tradition (Cramp, Mac Lean, Lang, Farr, Karkov); the biblical tradition (Alexander, de Vegvar, Farr); methodological traditions (Stalley, Karkov,

Lang, Farr); technical traditions (Youngs, Whitfield); the overturning of
traditions (Farr, Hawkes, Stalley). It is obvious from this list that a number of
the papers deal with the assimilation of, rejection of, or conflict between
traditions. The papers represent a wide range of material and methodological
approaches to that material, and cover all the major areas of Insular art.

A primary concern of the contributors to this volume is the value of
interdisciplinary studies and the need for dialogue between scholars
working not only in different disciplines, but also in the different subfields of
archaeology and art history. We tend more and more to specialize in
manuscripts, metalwork, sculpture, burial archaeology, settlement archaeology, and so forth, with the result that we can sometimes lose sight of the
larger picture, and sometimes neglect evidence provided by other disciplines, media, and methodologies. *The Insular Tradition* conference and its
proceedings are both attempts to keep the dialogue open.

The essays that follow are grouped primarily according to media. The first
three chapters deal specifically with Anglo-Saxon sculpture, Catherine E.
Karkov's "The Bewcastle Cross: Some Iconographic Problems," Carol A.
Farr's "Worthy Women on the Ruthwell Cross: Woman As Sign in Early
Anglo-Saxon Monasticism," and Jane Hawkes' "Symbols of the Passion or
Power? The Iconography of the Rothbury Cross-head."

All the crosses are of great importance in the context of Insular stone
sculpture, but it is probably accurate to say that the Ruthwell and Bewcastle
crosses have received more attention than any others in the corpus.
Catherine E. Karkov addresses the problematic bottom panel on the principal (west) face at Bewcastle. The panel shows a man and a bird with a
large T-shaped object, probably a perch. There have long been two schools
of thought on this panel; one takes the human figure as secular, a layman
engaged in hunting, while the second identifies the panel as a portrait of
John the Evangelist with his symbol the eagle. Karkov proposes an interpretation in which a royal figure appears on the bottom of the cross,
separated from the sacred figures at the top by a commemorative inscription.
However, this is but one interpretation, she proposes for a monument which
is clearly multivalent, in the best tradition of Insular art.

Carol A. Farr starts her study of the Ruthwell cross by enumerating the
four panels on which women are depicted, and makes the observation that
scholarly discussion of the rich iconographic program on Ruthwell "almost
never considers, even in passing, the significance of these exceptional images
of women" (p. 47). The panel showing two confronted women grasping one
another in the cross-head sequence, above the fragmentary inscription
dominae is identified as Martha and Mary, but specifically "modeled upon
Visitation images creating a resonance with the story in which the Virgin

recites the canticle the *Magnificat*" (p. 49). Mary and Martha parallel the figures of Paul and Anthony on the lower part of the Ruthwell shaft, with both panels representing a monastic ideal. No one can doubt the importance of the large panel, which occupies a central position on the lower shaft of the cross, Mary Magdalene washing Christ's feet with her hair. Farr speculates "the image may have encouraged the personal devotions of an audience which at least included females, whose devotions were further directed or amplified by the other sculpted figures and the inscriptions" (p. 53).

The Rothbury cross, in its original realization, must have been close to the level of Ruthwell in complexity and richness of design. Jane Hawkes addresses the vexed question of the cross-head iconography. The obverse of the cross-head is so damaged at its center that the subject cannot be identified, though it has long been assumed to have held a bust of Christ. This supposition is bolstered by the long-held interpretation of the three remaining cross-arms as carrying the instruments of Christ's Passion. While instruments of the passion certainly show up in later Anglo-Saxon contexts, no early parallels are known. Hawkes rightly points out that the figures on the cross-arms seem to be venerating Christ and presenting him with the objects they hold.

Hawkes questions the nature of the objects as well. The upper figure in fact holds rods or scepters of power, similar to those on the Alfred jewel or the Fuller brooch, though these ninth-century versions in metal work and enamel are more decorative. Similar iconographies are found in manuscripts such as the Lichfield Gospels and Kells, though the ultimate source seems to be the insignia in late imperial diptychs. The figure on the right lateral arm at Rothbury supposedly holds *two* crowns of thorns. Hawkes rightly points out how this is in itself contradictory, because the crown was *unique*. Once again, later imperial tradition provides an answer, in that circular objects are crowns of victory, which were common on coins in both late imperial and Early Christian contexts. The figure on the lower arm, who—in the *earlier* interpretation—held nails for the Crucifixion, Hawkes sees as carrying tubular objects or folds of cloth very much like the *mappa circensis*, the napkin lowered to mark the beginning of the games. She cites numerous examples of consular diptychs being used in early Insular liturgy. While there is still at least a chance for the traditional interpretation of this enigmatic panel, it must be said that there is a great deal of suasion in the evidence presented here.

A group of five chapters broadens the picture to include Irish and Pictish art, largely sculpture: James Lang's "Survival and Revival in Insular Art: Some Principles," Douglas Mac Lean's "King Oswald's Wooden Cross At Heavenfield in Context," Shirley Alexander's "Daniel Themes on the Irish

High Crosses," Roger Stalley's "The Tower Cross At Kells," and Isabel Henderson's "Variations on an Old Theme: Panelled Zoomorphic Ornament on Pictish Sculpture At Nigg, Easter Ross, and St. Andrew's Fife, and in the Book of Kells."

James Lang broadens our picture of Insular art by examining the use of style in Anglo-Saxon and Irish sculpture. This chapter is concerned with native Anglo-Saxon and Irish styles, rather than the Late Antique. Lang explores the "problem" of why some stylistic traits remain popular throughout the Insular period, as well as why certain styles are deliberately revived by individual artists, schools, and patrons, or on individual works. This essay nicely demonstrates the way style itself rapidly becomes politicized in both Anglo-Saxon and early Irish sculpture.

Douglas Mac Lean addresses the intriguing question of how a Christian cross would have functioned for a newly converted Anglo-Saxon army. Bede tells us that King Oswald had his army kneel before the monument at Heavenfield and pray for victory. Mac Lean poses two questions unanswered in Bede's account: where did Oswald get the idea of a cross, and why did the army kneel? As to the first question, Mac Lean makes a convincing case to show that Oswald both learned the faith, and acquired a knowledge of wooden crosses, at Iona. He turns to two excavated royal sites, Yeavering and Cheddar, for a pre-Christian context for wooden crosses, *suggesting* a continuity between pagan and Christian practice. In Mac Lean's view, the importance of the wooden cross at Heavenfield cannot be overstated. "In choosing to kneel before Oswald's wooden cross, the Anglian army of Bernicia inadvertently paved the way for Oswald's foundation of Lindisfarne, the evangelization of much of England, the architectural patronage of St. Wilfrid and Benedict Biscop, and the development of the Insular freestanding sculptured stone cross" (p. 92).

Shirley Alexander surveys the meaning and function of Daniel scenes on the Irish high crosses. Daniel iconographies are of prime importance in Early Christian contexts, and Ireland follows this trend. Alexander notes that on Irish crosses Daniel panels are most frequently associated with the Fall. The sources for these Daniel iconographies, we are told, most often are third- and fourth-century Roman catacomb paintings. Alexander's principal interest is "the meaning of the Daniel theme on the Irish crosses, and the clues the sculptors have provided for the interpretations of the subject" (p. 100). She tells us that in the visual arts the meaning of the image, and the message of the monument are constructed by the viewer (p. 107). Several Irish crosses are then reviewed, and both the Daniel panels and the scenes against which they are juxtaposed are analyzed.

Roger Stalley studies the best preserved of the monuments at Kells, the Tower cross. Stalley respectfully but resolutely challenges the long-held orthodox analysis of the orderly and typological development of Irish stone crosses which suggests "a Darwinian-like faith in the process of evolution" (p. 118).

The Tower cross is of great importance, but as the interpretation of the cross also involves *date*, great problems arise. If the cross is indeed related to the Book of Kells, the date (a *terminus post quem*) would be either 804/07, for those who believe the manuscript was made at Kells or brought there after the attack on Iona, or after 878 for those who believe it was brought over in that year with the other relics of Columba. After an analysis of five major dates of importance for Kells, Stalley turns to style and iconography, which he feels accord most closely between the Tower cross and the Scripture cross of ca. 900. He concludes by locating the cross firmly within the monastic politics of the late-ninth century.

Isabel Henderson examines Pictish art and its place within the Insular tradition. Her primary focus is on the zoomorphic ornament on the cross-head at Nigg, though her piece is much enriched by close study of similar ornament in the Book of Kells. In the course of a detailed study of the elements of the Nigg cross-head, Henderson finds a primary characteristic of "balanced asymmetry—a deceptive symmetry created by using the same motif within symmetrical constructions that support markedly varied internal arrangements" (p. 147). The notion that the Nigg slab is either isolated or atypical is challenged, with the St. Andrew's Sarcophagus as most in accord with Nigg. While the two panels of the sarcophagus do not match each other, Henderson believes that they have "exactly the same degree of similarity and difference as the pairs of decorative panels that flank the cross-shaft on the Nigg slab" (p. 149). While there is no evidence that the Nigg and St. Andrews sculptors borrowed directly from the Book of Kells, Henderson holds that the animal ornament in all of these contexts is in a similar stage of development. David Wilson long ago concluded that ornament in the St. Ninian's Isle treasure had parallels at Nigg, and Henderson reinforces that relationship in the last part of her study.

Carol Neuman de Vegvar's "The Echternach Lion: A Leap of Faith," continues the discussion of animal art, focusing specifically on one central image in the Insular manuscript tradition. Few would disagree with de Vegvar's claim that this beast is "one of the most compelling works in Insular art" (p. 167). Her study addresses the meaning of the image, and the "dynamic opposition of energies of figure and frame" (p. 167). De Vegvar provides ample evidence to show that the lion has a christological frame of reference in liturgy and commentary, which she caps by claiming a close association with the Athanasian Creed. She further cites the Homilies on Ezekiel of Gregory the Great and Latin hymns from the *Antiphonary of*

Bangor, "Turba Fratrem," and "Praecamus Patrem," which associate the lion with flame and/or light.

Four chapters are devoted to metalwork: Susan Youngs, "Recent Finds of Insular Enameled Buckles," Niamh Whitfield, "Filigree Animal Ornament From Ireland and Scotland of the Late-Seventh to Ninth Centuries: Its Origins and Development," Michael Ryan, "The Menagerie of the Derrynaflan Paten," and Raghnall Ó Floinn, "Innovation and Conservatism in Irish Metalwork of the Romanesque Period."

Susan Youngs studies fourteen objects, only four of which have been published, and three of which are new finds from Leicestershire and Lincolnshire. The recent finds came from the activity of metal detectorists. A number of these buckles are Irish, though their origin may perhaps be derived from the same model that underlies the seventh-century "dummy" buckle from Sutton Hoo, mound one. Youngs also explores the function of the buckles:

> The introduction of buckles as a new type of fastener in Ireland raises some interesting questions about function, whether decorated belt-buckles are evidence for a change in dress-style in the aristocratic, and therefore possibly more cosmopolitan section of Irish secular society. However the continued development of distinctive Celtic brooch forms, which included absorption of design elements from very different Germanic models, shows a strong and vigorous native dress tradition, an impression borne out by scraps of pictorial evidence from illuminated manuscripts and sculpture. (pp. 198)

Niamh Whitfield provides a closely detailed study of important *minutiae* in filigree animal ornament. Whitfield begins her essay by calling into question Michael Ryan's strong case for an Early Christian base for the Insular tradition. While it is right to see the Early Christian tradition as one aspect of the base, gold filigree ornament is very much influenced by Germanic traditions. The Hunterston brooch *clearly* parallels the filigree ornament on the Ålleberg, Möne, and Färjestaden collars, Swedish pieces dating to A.D. 450–500. While similarities exist, it is highly unlikely that the influence was direct, and Whitfield sees Anglo-Saxon England as the path of communication. It is now certain that there was continuous communication between Scandinavia and the North of England as John Hines' case in *The Scandinavian Character of Anglian England in the pre-Viking Period* (B.A.R. Brit. ser. 124 [1984]) is not to be ignored. Whitfield concludes that the Insular debt to Germanic goldsmiths is heavy indeed. On the inspiration of the Early Christian tradition for the Irish, Whitfield sees a "cousinly relationship . . . between motifs executed in different styles in different areas, making craftsmen who were familiar with one idiom receptive to designs executed in the other" (p. 225). Yet, in her conclusion, she stresses that none of these models was followed slavishly, rather all were transformed by the originality and technical virtuosity of Insular craftsmen.

No one can doubt the importance of the remarkable Derrynaflan hoard, unearthed in 1980, for the study of Insular art and archaeology. The wine strainer is of interest, the chalice a brilliant balance to Ardagh, but the paten—in design, methodology and execution—is unique. It was made in such a way that it could be disassembled and reconstructed without insuperable difficulty, and it is virtually certain that the piece had been taken down twice in antiquity. Michael Ryan tells us that the object is in the "mainstream of Irish style metalwork of the eighth century, and is to date the most elaborate and accomplished piece to come to light from that tradition" (p. 247). Of the twenty-four filigree ornaments that surround the rim, three are abstract, four show two kneeling men, and seventeen include animals. Paired arrangements are most common on the paten, either of men or beasts. Ryan has elsewhere made the case for the source of the human figures in Late Antique silver plates from which perhaps the paten itself was derived. Derrynaflan is the only large scale paten to have survived from early medieval western Europe. The remainder of the chapter is devoted to a discussion of the *possible* resonances and meanings of the paten and its ornament through a survey of parallel objects, exegetical texts, and especially liturgy. The reader is warned against any attempt to seek an all encompassing controlling order or sum of meanings in the piece, because "far too many certainties have been claimed in the field of early Irish art history" (p. 254).

Raghnall Ó Floinn's contribution opens with the observation that while the renaissance of the eleventh and twelfth centuries in architecture can be dated, the case for the dates of metalwork is not easily made. The later metalwork is distinctive in several ways: it is all ecclesiastical in nature; the objects survived mainly because they were in the keeping of certain families down to modern times; the late metalwork has parallels in earlier Irish forms, but these forms are largely unparalleled in Anglo-Saxon or continental metalwork. In a careful analysis, Ó Floinn draws out details which show these late pieces to be derived from work on the continent, most often Germany. These new forms include arm shrines, cross- or candlestick-bases, crucifixes and crucifix figures, as well as a hint of new techniques in metal working and decoration.

Rosemary Cramp concludes the volume with "The Insular Tradition: An Overview," itself a summary of the tradition based primarily on archaeological evidence. She boldly proposes that Insular material is absolutely distinctive, that with a few border exceptions no one could mistake a piece of sculpture from the continent as Insular, or vice versa.

Cramp's essay focuses on new research and new discoveries which have increased our understanding of "the social and technological processes which formed and developed the Insular traditions" (p. 283). She discusses the ways in which political and social contacts in the early Anglo-Saxon period encouraged artistic and cultural assimilation, but points out that distinctive styles and traditions remained. Cramp emphasizes that what we now call the "Insular tradition" is not "monolithic," but instead is characterized by a number of regional and cultural variations, "particularly between those who did and those who did not accept without adaptation Mediterranean traditions" (p. 295). She then discusses the forces that produced Insular culture, its many manifestations, and the problems it still poses for modern scholars. Cramp's essay not only serves as a response to the conference theme and the individual papers, but also emphasizes that the end is the beginning, and that new discoveries and interpretations will continue to alter and enrich our understanding of the Insular tradition.

CHAPTER ONE

Catherine E. Karkov

THE BEWCASTLE CROSS

Some Iconographic Problems

No two monuments of Anglo-Saxon sculpture have received more attention than the early eighth-century Bewcastle (Cumberland) and Ruthwell (Dumfriesshire) crosses, yet there are probably no two monuments about which so many questions remain unanswered. The two are frequently studied as a pair,[1] with the emphasis being on their stylistic and iconographic similarities. It is important to remember, however, that they are also very different, both in function and in iconography. The purpose of this paper is not to examine all the differences between the two, but to look in detail at the iconography of the Bewcastle cross, focusing on its one unique and pivotal panel, the panel displaying the standing figure of a man with a bird (pls. 1.1, 1.2).

The image of the man and bird is located at the base of the west face of the shaft. The man has long curling hair and stands turning slightly to the left. He holds a rod or stick (or possibly a cross) in his right hand, while a bird of prey balances on his extended left arm. There is a long T-shaped object, possibly a stand or perch below the bird. To put the panel in context, it appears just below a lengthy runic commemorative inscription; above the inscription are two panels with religious subjects, the first showing Christ over the beasts, and the second John the Baptist with the Agnus Dei.[2] The cross-head is now missing. The north face of the shaft is

Pl. 1.1. The Bewcastle Cross. Photograph by author.

carved with panels of plant-scroll, interlace and geometric ornament. The east face displays a continuous inhabited vine-scroll, while the south face is decorated with plant-scroll, interlace ornament and a sundial.

Pl. 1.2. Bewcastle Cross, detail of west face. Photograph by author.

The exact identification of the figure holding the bird on the west face of the cross is still very much a matter of debate. There are basically two schools of thought. The first sees the figure as the "portrait" of a layman—a suggestion first put forward in 1865 by William Nicolson in a letter to Obadiah Walker.[3] The second interprets the figure as a portrait of John the Evangelist with his symbol the eagle. It has been pointed out on a number of occasions, most recently by the editors of the second volume of the *Corpus of Anglo-Saxon Stone Sculpture*, that if the figure is an evangelist portrait it is a highly unusual one.[4] The most obvious problem with interpreting the panel as a portrait of John is that the appearance of the figure with his long curling hair, short garments, and large collar or ruff is more appropriate for a layman than for an evangelist. The figure is also shown without a halo, standing rather than seated, and with the bird perched on his outstretched hand rather than hovering above or alongside him (the latter arrangement is found in the panel with John and his eagle at Ruthwell). Moreover, nowhere else in Anglo-Saxon sculpture does a single evangelist appear in this position on a cross.

It has also been suggested, however, that it is the context of the panel which brings out its religious meaning. Éamonn Ó Carragáin, for example, believes that this face of the cross deals with the theme of recognition. He points out that the runic inscription between the upper two panels "+*gessus kristtus*" implies that Christ is to be recognized "*in propria figura*," as the beasts recognized him, and also as the Agnus Dei.[5] He then suggests that the "evangelist portrait" at the foot of the cross represents the scriptural authority for the Agnus Dei chant which had recently been introduced into the Roman liturgy of the mass, the chant being based on John 1:29.[6] He goes on to state that John's symbol, the eagle, was "more significant" than the other evangelist symbols. It was not only John's symbol, but also a symbol of the resurrected Christ, and the renewal of life through baptism.[7] It would, therefore, not be out of place appearing alone on such a monument.

This symbolism, however, centering on the idea of resurrection, is surely more appropriate for the head of a cross than for the base of its shaft. Evangelist symbols, when they do appear on Anglo-Saxon stone crosses, usually appear on the head or upper shaft, and it is certainly possible that the missing head of the Bewcastle cross contained portraits of the four evangelists and/or their symbols. On the Ruthwell cross, the evangelists and their symbols appeared at the top of the shaft and in the remaining three arms of the cross-head, with John and his eagle in the uppermost arm of the cross.[8] In the case of metalwork crosses, on which the four evangelist symbols are arranged in the terminals of the two arms and at the head and foot of the cross, the eagle, with or without John, appears most often, if not exclusively, at the top of the cross. This is the case on the Brussels reliquary cross, the Crucifixion reliquary in the Victoria and Albert Museum, and on an Anglo-Saxon processional cross now in Copenhagen, though all three of these examples are eleventh-century in date.[9]

A further problem with the interpretation of the figure at the base of the Bewcastle cross as John the Evangelist is that it is separated from the other two figural scenes on this face by a lengthy commemorative inscription. The inscription has sustained far too much damage to be reconstructed with any certainty, but it does begin with the sign of the cross and the words "*þis sigbecn*" (this victory beacon) and end with a form of the phrase "*gebidaþ þær sawle*" (pray for the soul). The prayer is intended for the soul of the individual (or individuals) whose names are recorded on the cross. Variations on this formula are common on Anglo-Saxon commemorative monuments.[10] It is possible that the name Alcfrith appears in the third line of the inscription—the letters *lcfri* survive. If the name is actually Alcfrith, it may refer to Alcfrith, sub-king of Deira and son of Oswiu, king of Northumbria and overlord of Mercia in the third quarter of the seventh century. This particular interpretation is supported by the fact that the name Kyniburg (also in runes) appears just above the lowest panel of the north face of the cross, and Alcfrith is known to have married a Mercian princess (Cyniburgh) of that name.[11] The most interesting parallel for the Bewcastle inscription is provided by a fragmentary cross-shaft at Urswick (Lancashire). The inscription is in runes and occupies the central panel of the main face of the shaft. It reads:

> +tunwinisetæ
> æftertoroჳ
> tredæbeku
> næfterhisb
> æurnægebidæs þe
> rs||au
> ||læ
> (Tunwine raised this cross in memory of his lord [or son] Torhtred. Pray for his soul.)

Beneath the inscription is a panel with two figures in secular dress with the artist's signature (Lyl [made] this) running across their torsos. Thus, the general composition of this face of the cross with apparently secular figures depicted beneath a commemorative inscription is very close to that of Bewcastle.[12] The date of the Urswick cross-shaft remains uncertain, though it has most recently been placed in the ninth century.[13]

In her discussion of the Bewcastle cross, Rosemary Cramp states that: "The figure carving at the base of the Bewcastle cross may have been a precocious essay in depicting a secular type, or a secular person." She goes on to add, however, that "it seems to have no development in surviving Anglo-Saxon art until the tenth century 'portraits' of such kings as Aethelstan and Edgar."[14] She therefore believes it "more prudent" to interpret the figure as John the Evangelist.[15]

Hunting and falconry, however, were noble pastimes, and hawks are found as attributes of nobility throughout the Anglo-Saxon world. Bird heads decorated high-status objects such as brooches. Birds of prey appear on a number of objects from the Sutton Hoo burial, most notably on the lyre, purse cover, gold buckle, drinking horns, and shield. A rider with a hawk does appear on a tenth-century cross-shaft at Sockburn (Durham),[16] his identity is, however, uncertain, and he may be meant to represent the god Odinn rather than a secular figure. At a much later date, hawks are used to identify the figures of Harold and Guy, Count of Ponthieu, in the opening sequence of the Bayeux Tapestry.[17] The figure of the aristocrat with hawk also appears in Anglo-Saxon poetry. The hawk is one of the hall-joys whose loss is mourned in the "lament of the last survivor" in *Beowulf*:

> Næs hearpan wyn,
> gomen gleobeames,   ne god hafoc
> geond sæl swinged,   ne se swifta mearh
> burhstede beated.[18]

The noble prince with a hawk on his glove signals the beginning of the battle in lines 5–10 of *The Battle of Maldon*:

> Þa ðæt Offan mæg   ærest onfunde,
> ðæt se eorl nolde   yrhðo gepolian,
> he let him þa of handon   leofne fleogan
> hafoc wið þæs holtes,   and to þære hilde stop;
> be þam man mihte oncnawan   þæt se cniht nolde
> wacnian æt þam wige,   þa he to wæpnum feng.[19]

The image is repeated in lines 16–18 of *Maxims II*, a poem which deals with the proper order of the world of nature and of man:

> Ellen sceal on eorle.   Ecg sceal wið hellme
> hilde gebidan.   Hafuc sceal on glofe
> wilde gewunian.[20]

This is not simply a literary *topos*, however. In the mid-eighth century, Æthelbert of Kent wrote to Boniface requesting him to send two falcons, for there were very few good birds to be found in Kent.[21] During this same period, Boniface sent Æthelbald of Mercia "as a sign of true love and devoted friendship," a hawk, two falcons, two shields, and two lances.[22]

Pl. 1.3. Elgin Cathedral slab. Photograph by T. E. Gray.

Secular figures with hawks can also be found in art contemporary with Bewcastle. They appear, for example, in eighth-century Pictish hunting scenes. Images of riders with birds of prey on their arms appear on the back of the Elgin cross-slab (pl. 1.3), as well as on the St. Andrews sarcophagus. Isabel Henderson has argued that the rider on the St. Andrews sarcophagus might refer to a line from Ps. 45.[23] She tentatively identifies the figure as David and, because he is also shown with a sword, suggests that the image refs to the line: "Accingere gladio tuo super femur tuum potentissime, specie tua et pulchritudine tua intende, prospere procede, et regna."[24] There is no mention of a bird in Ps. 45, however, the general theme of the psalm is kingship, and the bird of prey, as an attribute of kingship, would certainly be appropriate to the overall imagery of the text. While the rider with the bird could not, therefore, be interpreted as a portrait of a contemporary figure, it may be interpreted as an image of kingship readily identifiable to an eighth-century Insular audience.

In their discussion of the Bewcastle cross, Cramp and Bailey also note that on a religious monument secular figures would not be shown on the same scale as holy figures.[25] There is, however, no differentiation in scale between the figures in Pictish sculpture, or those depicted in the lower panel of the ninth-century Urswick cross-shaft. The identity of these latter figures is uncertain. Both are male and wear what is apparently secular dress, the "ruffs" at their necks being particularly close to the one worn by the Bewcastle figure. The figure on the left at Urswick carries a cross and reaches out to touch the shoulder of the figure on the right. It has been suggested that the scene may represent Christ welcoming the dead Torhtred into heaven, an episode from a saint's life, or a conversion scene.[26] The cross clearly identifies the man on the left as a biblical or ecclesiastical figure of some sort, yet his dress and height are identical to those of the secular figure towards whom he reaches. Secular and holy figures also appear on the same scale on the tenth-century cross of the scriptures at Clonmacnois in Ireland.[27] Admittedly these crosses are later than Bewcastle, and the Clonmacnois cross is Irish rather than Anglo-Saxon, however, they do suggest that there may be significant exceptions to the general principle of hierarchy of scale in early medieval art.

Much closer to the figure on the Bewcastle cross than the sculptural scenes are the images which appear on a series of *sceattas* generally dated to the first half of the eighth century (figs. 1.1 and 1.2). These, like the Pictish sculptures, are noted in the *Corpus* discussion of the Bewcastle cross, but there they are dismissed as having no direct relevance to the Bewcastle image.

The sheer number of the *sceattas*, and the variety of combinations of figure and bird that occur on them, make them worthy of closer examination. There are five series of coins, all iconographically interrelated, that are relevant to the Bewcastle image. Series B, the "bird-on-cross" type, is generally dated ca. 685–700/10, and displays a bust on the obverse, and a cross capped with a bird on the reverse. Series U, the "bird and branch" series, dated ca. 710–720, shows a figure with a cross or crosses on the obverse and a bird and branch on the reverse. One unique example from this series has an archer on the obverse and a bird and branch on the

Fig. 1.1. Sceat found at Walbury Camp, Berkshire (drawing not to scale). Courtesy of author.

Fig. 1.2. Whitby 12 (drawing not to scale). Courtesy of author.

reverse, a combination of images also found on the Ruthwell cross.[28] Series K, which succeeded Series U, is dated ca. 720–730, and includes a number of different types. The most relevant types show a bust or seated man on the obverse and bird and branch on the reverse. Type 20 has a bust with cup on the obverse, and a figure with cross and bird on the reverse. A Series K *sceat* found near Walbury Camp in 1974 shows on the obverse a draped and wreathed bust facing a falcon on a perch (fig. 1.1).[29] Series Q, ca. 725–735/45, is problematic, having variously a beast, bust, or bust with cross on the obverse and a bird or beast on the reverse.[30] The Series L *sceattas*, most recently dated ca. 730–40,[31] are iconographically closest to the Bewcastle cross. Moreover, while there may be little to connect the Bewcastle cross directly with Pictish sculpture, there are possible links between Bewcastle and the Series L *sceattas*. While the series has a relatively wide distribution over the south of England, it is generally associated with Æthelbald of Mercia (716–57), who dominated southern England during the second quarter of the eighth century. This is, of course, the same Æthelbald who received the gift of hawks and falcons from St. Boniface. The Mercian associations of the Bewcastle cross, with its possible references to Alcfrith and Cyniburgh, make the comparison of cross and coins particularly appealing. On these coins, as at Bewcastle, the man is generally shown facing left towards a hawk, or holding a cross in one hand, a hawk in the other. Whitby 12 is a particularly interesting example from this series (fig. 1.2).[32] The obverse of this coin is decorated with the bust of a figure holding a scepter, and the reverse with the figure of a man standing in a "boat" and holding a cross in his right hand, a hawk in his left. Below the figure's left hand is a T-shaped object very like the "perch" beneath the left arm of the Bewcastle figure. The inclusion of this detail is rare both on coins and in sculpture, and the similarity in shape of the perch on Whitby 12 and that of the Bewcastle cross is, therefore, particularly intriguing. The Bewcastle figure is usually described as holding a long rod or stick in his right hand, but the panel is very worn, and it is possible that he originally held a long cross, as do the figures on the *sceattas*.

The evidence for associating the Series L coins with Æthelbald of Mercia is as tenuous as that which connects the Bewcastle cross with Alcfrith. Nevertheless the coins do indicate that the iconography of the Bewcastle panel was current in eighth-century England in a secular context. It would also be impossible to call the images on the coins portraits of kings, however, as with the Pictish riders, they are easily recognizable as representations of kingship, with the hawk and the cross uniting symbols of the secular and religious worlds, or perhaps suggesting the idea of triumph or victory at both a secular and ecclesiastical level. This latter interpretation is, of course, particularly relevant to the function of the Bewcastle cross as a sign or "beacon" of victory.

In his discussion of the Bewcastle panel, É. Ó Carragáin stressed the significance of the stance of the figure, who is shown turning either toward or away from the hawk on his left. He states:

> The man's turning stance can reasonably be construed as inviting the onlooker to gaze at the bird he holds. . . . The way in which the stance of the human figure directs the onlooker's gaze to the bird seems theologically significant. Of the four evangelists, John was the great contemplative, who wrote of that "which we have seen with our eyes, which we have diligently looked upon and our hands have handled."[33]

He goes on to contrast the turning stance of the figure with the frontal presentation of Christ and John the Baptist in the upper two panels. However, on the majority of the *sceattas* the figures are also shown turning to the left. The busts on the obverse of the series U and K coins are shown with frontal torsos, their heads turning to face the cup or hawk to their left. The figures on the reverse of the series K and L coins are presented in a variety of poses. The most common image is that of the figure whose body is depicted frontally, while his head and feet turn to the left. The popularity of the turning figure on the coins suggests that there is unlikely to be any theological significance to the pose of the Bewcastle figure.

Another problem with the Bewcastle cross is its location. The cross stands within a Roman fort located along the important east-west highway formed by the Tyne-Solway gap. Bewcastle was clearly an important center, but it may have been an important secular rather than religious center, as there is no evidence of an early monastery on the site. Yet it is also clear that the cross was made by and for a literate, educated community—the presence of the inscriptions and the sundial indicate as much. One possibility is that the site was an *eigenkirche*, or "private church," an endowed site closely associated with a noble family.[34] As Ó Carragáin emphasizes, the commemorative inscription is in runes, and with the exception of the +*gessus kristtus* which appears below the panel of John and the Agnus Dei, there are no Latin inscriptions on the cross. This is in marked contrast to Ruthwell, and Ó Carragáin suggests that this may indicate that we are indeed dealing with an aristocratic establishment.[35] If this is the case, would the complex liturgical meaning and function he ascribes to the cross have been readily recognizable to such an audience? Possibly, the texts Ó Carragáin sites do all relate to the major feasts of the liturgical year. However, a combination of secular and sacred symbolism would be particularly appropriate to an aristocratic foundation, and there is a much more straightforward level at which the cross could be read.

The argument for interpreting the figure on the Bewcastle cross as that of John the Evangelist relies heavily on understanding the figure in the context of a coherent iconographic program. If the figure is to be interpreted as an image of a king or a symbol of kingship, it must also fit into the overall iconographic program of the cross, and it does. Beginning with the lowest panel on the west face, we have the figure of the king, with the hawk, a symbol of secular kingship. Above this is the inscription which identifies the cross as a commemorative monument; and such a monument could only have been commissioned by and for a member of the aristocracy. The inscription also effectively separates the figure with the bird from the two panels of sacred imagery at the top of the shaft. Above the inscription is the panel with Christ over the beasts, or Christ in his role as king of the world. This is emphasized by his position over the two beasts, and the presence above the panel of the inscription + *gessus kristtus*, Christ the Anointed One.[36] At the top of the shaft is the image of John the Baptist holding the Agnus Dei, symbolic of Christ as ruler of heaven and earth. The lamb is an image of the final triumph of Christ, as expressed in the Book of Revelation, in which Christ appears as "Lord of lords and King of kings" (Rev. 17:14). At a very basic level this face of the cross becomes a study in the hierarchy of kingship. The relevance of the program to an eighth-century aristocratic audience is obvious enough. Moreover, as Ó Carragáin notes, Christ recognized by the beasts refers to a line from the canticle of Habbakuk, "In medio duorum animalium innotesceris" ("In the midst of two animals you will be recognized"), the canticle sung at the moment commemorating Christ's death on Good Friday evening (as well as every friday morning at Lauds).[37] The death of Christ and the death of the individual commemorated by the cross are thus associated with each other on the monument; while the uppermost panel with John and the Agnus Dei holds out the promise of eternal life with Christ in heaven.

I do not wish to imply that this is the only way in which the cross may be read. Multivalency has long been recognized as a characteristic of Insular art, and the Bewcastle cross, like so many of the Insular monuments contains different levels of interrelated meanings. The iconographic progression on the west face from secular, earthly kingship to sacred and eternal kingship also provides an exegetical sequence which moves from literal kingship in the lowest panel to moral (or tropological kingship) in the middle panel to anogogical kingship in the uppermost level, a three-fold sequence employed by Bede (among others) in his exegetical writings.[38] The manner in which the three figures have been represented is particularly appropriate to this type of sequential, or typological reading. The Bewcastle figures are monumental, completely filling the panels in which they are confined. They are also iconic; all three presented alone with their respective symbolic animals, the hawk, the beasts, and the lamb. Each one also gazes straight out at the viewer. This is very different from the Ruthwell program in which a variety of figures of differing sizes are combined to form abbreviated narrative groups. The panels on the two broad faces of the Ruthwell cross, when read together, form a complex liturgical narrative whose meaning is made explicit by the accompanying Latin inscriptions. There are no such inscriptions on the Bewcastle cross, nor is there any sense of narrative. We focus instead on the hierarchy of forms and on the three separate but interrelated levels of meaning. Thus, while the cross can be read as a study in kingship at a very literal level, the juxtaposition of the three figures offers additional and more complex readings to an audience familiar with the exegetical tradition. Moreover, if the head of the Bewcastle cross originally contained the four evangelists and/or their symbols, and its similarities with Ruthwell suggest that this may have been the case, the liturgical meaning of the cross elucidated by Ó Carragáin would still be evident.

Finally, John the Baptist and the Agnus Dei, and Christ recognized by the beasts are also images which refer to the sacraments of Baptism and the Eucharist. The inhabited vine-scroll which decorates the east face of the cross is also a symbolic reference to the Eucharist,[39] and this meaning is further emphasized by the way in which the birds and beasts bite at the fruit which grows from the vine. The east face of the cross then becomes an image of the tree of life, and the cross as a whole a sign of both death, in its reference to the Crucifixion, and life, in its reference to the tree of life. The plant-scroll imagery is continued on the north and south faces of the cross, where stylized plants alternate with geometric and interlace ornament. The names of members of the Mercian and Northumbrian royal families, also appear in the borders between the panels. The individuals whose names are thus recorded may be described as inhabiting these last two faces of the cross, just as the birds and beasts inhabit the vine-scroll of the east side.[40] Moreover, both Cramp and Ó Carragáin point out that the sundial on the south face of the cross has been incorporated into the plant-scroll so that it forms a large leaf with a berry bunch growing from its top, turning the cross into a sort of "time-tree."[41] Whatever the liturgical meaning of the image,[42] the fact that the names of contemporary individuals are included on this face suggests that the sundial might also have had a more literal significance, providing an image of the passing of time within a dynastic or genealogical context. The cross then becomes itself a monumental tree of life and death, a Book of the Dead, on which a royal lineage has been recorded, and for which the figure of the man with the hawk, an image of temporal kingship, serves as an appropriate base.

NOTES

1. A full bibliography of scholarship on the subject can be found in R. Cramp and R. Bailey, *Corpus of Anglo-Saxon Stone Sculpture*, vol. II, *Cumberland, Westmorland and Lancashire North-of-the-Sands* (Oxford: Oxford University Press, 1988).

2. Close examination of this panel of the cross by the author and Dr. Jane Hawkes in July 1996 confirmed that the figure is indeed John the Baptist and not God the Father as some scholars have suggested. (See, for example, Paul Meyvaert, "Ecclesia and Vita Monastica," in Brendan Cassidy, ed., *The Ruthwell Cross*, Index of Christian Art Occasional Papers I [Princeton: Index of Christian Art, Dept. of Art & Archaeology 1992], 95–166, at p. 112.) The figure points with his right hand to the lamb, an iconography used exclusively for John the Baptist.

3. Quoted in A. S. Cook, *The Anglo-Saxon Cross* (Hamdon, Conn.: Archon Books, 1977), 134.

4. Cramp and Bailey, *Corpus*, vol. II, 70. Even though the editors find difficulties with this interpretation, they conclude that, "On the whole it seems more prudent to suppose that the figure is one of St. John the Evangelist with his eagle."

5. É. Ó Carragáin, "A Liturgical Interpretation of the Bewcastle Cross," in M. Stokes and T. L. Burton, eds., *Medieval Literature and Antiquities, Studies in Honour of Basil Cottle* (Woodbridge, Suffolk; Wolfeboro, N.H.: D. S. Brewer, 1987), 15–42, esp. 17–19; É. Ó Carragáin, "Christ over the Beasts and the Agnus Dei: Two Multivalent Panels on the Ruthwell and Bewcastle Crosses," in P. E. Szarmach and V. D. Oggins, eds., *Sources of Anglo-Saxon Culture* (Kalamazoo, Mich.: Medieval Institute Publications, 1986), 377–403.

6. ———, "Liturgical Innovations Associated with Pope Sergius and the Iconography of the Ruthwell and Bewcastle Crosses," in R. T. Farrell, ed., *Bede and Anglo-Saxon England*, B.A.R. Brit. ser. 46 (Oxford: British Archaeological Reports, 1978), 134–35; Ó Carragáin, "Bewcastle Cross," 25.

7. Ó Carragáin, "Bewcastle Cross," 19–24.

8. Evangelist symbols are not common in Anglo-Saxon sculpture. John and his eagle originally appeared in the upper arm of the west face of the Ruthwell cross, with an eagle, possibly the eagle of Christ, in the upper arm of the east face (the two are currently reversed). An eagle, again likely to be symbolic of the resurrected Christ, and figures who may represent the evangelists also appear on three eleventh-century cross-heads now in Durham Cathedral (R. Cramp, *Corpus of Anglo-Saxon Stone Sculpture*, vol. I, *County Durham and Northumberland* [Oxford: Oxford University Press, 1984], 68–71).

9. See J. Backhouse, D. H. Turner and L. Webster, eds., *The Golden Age of Anglo-Saxon Art* (Bloomington: Indiana University Press, 1984), catalog nos. 75, 118, 269.

10. An eighth- or ninth-century house-shaped memorial stone from Falstone now in the Museum of Antiquities, Newcastle upon Tyne (Nd. 1814.23), bears an inscription in both runes and Insular majuscule. The former reads, "+ [- aeftaer roe[- tae [*be*]cun ae[*f*]taer e[*o*- geb[*i*]daed þe[*r*] saule," and the latter "+EO[- TA AE[*FT*]AER HROETHBERHT[*Æ*] BECUN AEFTAER EOMAE GEBIDAEÐ ÐER SAULE" (See, R. Cramp and R. Miket, *Catalogue of the Anglo-Saxon and Viking Antiquities in the Museum of Antiquities Newcastle upon Tyne* [Newcastle: Museum of Antiquities of the University & Society of Antiquities of Newcastle upon Tyne, 1982], 24–25.). Similar runic commemorative formulae appear on Thornhill I, II, and III, all likely to date from the ninth century. The inscription on Thornhill III reads, "+gilsuiþ arærde æft{-} berhtsuiþe bekun on bergi gebiddaþ þær saule." The eighth- or ninth-century Great Urswick stone is inscribed, "+tunwini setæ æfter torogtredæ bekun æfter his bæurnæ gebidæs þer saulæ." (See, R. Page, *An Introduction to English Runes* [London: Methuen, 1973], 143–45.)

11. While the exact date of the Bewcastle cross and the names of all the indiviudals commemorated in its inscriptions are still very much a mystery, the generally accepted date of ca. 700, the presence of the name Cyniburgh and, probably, Alcfrith, and the memorial function of the monument encourage specu-lation. Bede tells us that Alcfrith was an active supporter of Wilfrid and the Roman rather than the Irish church, and that he was responsible for the conversion of his brother-in-law, the Mercian ruler Peada, to Christianity. It is tempting to connect

the classicizing style of the Bewcastle carving with Alcfrith's continental sympathies. (Alfred Smyth has made a similar suggestion, going on to surmise that the Bewcastle cross may have been raised as a monument to the victory of Wilfrid and the Roman church over the Celtic church after the 664 Synod of Whitby [A. P. Smyth, *Warlords and Holy Men Scotland A.D. 80–1000* (Edinburgh: Edinburgh University Press, 1984), 26–27]). Alcfrith's role as secular ruler and defender of the church might also be seen as lying behind the iconography of the cross with its juxtaposition of images of temporal and sacred kingship.

12. The iconography of the panel is discussed at greater length below.

13. Cramp, *Corpus*, vol. I, 150.

14. Cramp and Bailey, *Corpus*, vol. II, 70.

15. Ibid.

16. An unidentified figure in secular dress with birds perched on either shoulder also appears on a tenth-century cross-shaft at Kirklevington, Cleveland (R. Bailey, *Viking Age Sculpture* [London: Collins, 1980], pl. 57).

17. See D. Wilson, *The Bayeux Tapestry: the Complete Tapestry in Color* (London: Thames & Hudson, 1985).

18. 11.2262b–2265. By no means is their harp-joy, the pastime of the harp, nor does the good hawk fly through the hall, nor does the swift horse beat the castle-court.

19. When the kinsman of Offa first discovered that that earl would not endure slackness, he then let his dear hawk fly from his hands to the wood and advanced to the battle. By that, one could perceive that the knight did not wish to weaken at that battle when he took up arms.

20. Courage shall be in the earl. The sword-edge shall against the helmet experience battle. The hawk shall be on the glove, remain wild.

21. The gift is described in Boniface's accompanying letter dating from the period 732–51. See E. Kylie, *The English Correspondence of Saint Boniface* (New York: 1966), 157.

22. Ibid., 158.

23. Isabel Henderson, "Pictish Art and the Book of Kells," in D. Whitelock, R. McKitterick and D. Dumville, eds., *Ireland in Early Medieval Europe* (Cambridge: Cooper Square, 1982), 79–105.

24. Ibid., 102. Gird thy sword upon thy thigh, O thou most mighty. With thy comliness and thy beauty set out, proceed prosperously and reign.

25. Cramp and Bailey, *Corpus*, vol. II, 70. They are here citing an argument put forward by Saxl in his 1943 article on the Ruthwell cross (F. Saxl, "The Ruthwell Cross," *J.W.C.I.* 6 [1943]: 1–19.).

26. Cramp and Bailey, *Corpus*, vol. II, 150.

27. The panel on the base of the east face of the cross shows two figures, one generally identified as a layman, the other a cleric. The scene has been interpreted variously as depicting St. Ciaran and King Dermot founding the monastery, or as the Abbot Colman and King Flann Sinna erecting the cross. Most recently Roger Stalley has suggested that the figures may be those of Aaron and Moses with the brazen serpent (R. Stalley, "Irish High Crosses," *P.R.I.A.* 90C no. 6 [1990]: 135–58.). The similarity of the scene to that of the Urswick panel is interesting. Whatever the subject of the panel, the two figures are clearly on the same scale, as well as on the same scale as the holy figures depicted in the other panels of the cross. The secular figure, though bearded, has the same long hair and short tunic of the Bewcastle figure. The panel also appears at the base of the shaft, as at Bewcastle, though it is not in anyway separated from the rest of the panels on the east face.

28. The coin, found near Walbury Camp, Berkshire in 1975, is now in the Ashmolean Museum. It is illustrated, and its possible relation to the Ruthwell images discussed, in M. J. Morehart, "Anglo-Saxon Art and the 'Archer' Sceat," in D. Hill and D. M. Metcalf, eds., *Sceattas in England and on the Continent*, B.A.R. Brit. ser. 128 (Oxford: British Archaeological Reports, 1984), 181–92.

29. This coin, now in the Reading Museum, is illustrated in S. Rigold and D. Metcalf, "A Check-List of English Finds of Sceattas," *B.N.J.* 47 (1977): pl. 2.24. See also, D. M. Metcalf, "Sceattas Found at the Iron-Age Hill Fort of Walbury Camp, Berkshire," *B.N.J.* 44 (1974): 1–12 and plates.

30. S. Rigold, "The Principal Series of English Sceattas," *B.N.J.* 47 (1977): 24, 28.

31. P. Grierson and M. Blackburn, *Medieval European Coinage*, vol. 1 *The Early Middle Ages (5th–10th centuries)* (Cambridge: Cambridge University Press, 1986), 188. The exact dating of the various series has been disputed, though all are from the first half of the eighth century. See also, M. Blackburn, "A Chronology for the Sceattas," in Hill and Metcalf, *Sceattas in England*, 165–74.

32. The coin is illustrated in S. Rigold and D. Metcalf, "A Check-list of English Finds of Sceattas," *B.N.J.* 47 (1977): 31–52, pl. 2.28.

33. Ó Carragáin, "Bewcastle Cross," 20.

34. Ó Carragáin, "Bewcastle Cross," 42. Bede's descriptions of these foundations are somewhat contradictory. In V.23 of the *Historia ecclesiastica*, he writes:

> In these favorable times of peace and prosperity, many of the Northumbrian race, both noble and simple, have laid aside their weapons and taken the tonsure, preferring that they and their children should take monastic vows rather than train themselves in the art of war. What the result will be, a later generation will discover. (B. Colgrave and R. Mynors, *Bede's Ecclesiastical History of the English People*. [Oxford: Clarendon Press, 1969], 560–61)

While in the 734 letter to Ecgbert, soon to become Archbishop of York, he laments the practice:

> For—what indeed is disgraceful to tell—those who are totally ignorant of the monastic life have received under their control so many places in the name of monasteries, as you yourself know better than I, that there is a complete lack of places where the sons of nobles of veteran thegns can receive an estate. . . . But others, since they are laymen and not experienced in the usages of the Life according to the rule or possessed by love of it, give money to kings, and under the pretext of founding monasteries buy lands on which they may more freely devote themselves to lust, and in addition cause them to be ascribed to them by hereditary right by royal edicts, and even get those same documents of their privileges confirmed, as if in truth worthy of God, by the subscription of bishops, abbots and secular persons. (D. Whitelock, ed., *English Historical Documents, c.500–1042*, 2nd ed. [London and New York: Methuen and Oxford University Press, 1979], 741)

35. Ó Carragáin, "Bewcastle Cross," n. 42.

36. Ó Carragáin ("Bewcastle Cross," 29–30) stresses the baptismal significance of the inscription, citing a passage from Isidore of Seville:

> Chrisma Graece, Latine unctio nominatur; ex cuius nomine et Christus dicitur, et homo post lavacrum sanctificatur. Nam sicut in baptismo peccatorum remissio datur, ita per unctionem sanctificatio spiritus adhibetur; et hoc de pristina disciplina, qua ungui in sacerdotium et in regnum solebant, ex quo Aaron a Moyse unctus est. (*Isidori Hispalensis Episcopi. Etymologiarum sive Originum libri XX*, W. M. Lindsey, ed., 2 vols. [Oxford: Clarendon Press, 1911], I, VI.xix. 50–51)

The passage, however, specifically links the baptismal ceremony not only with the tradition of anointing into the priesthood, but also into kingship (et hoc de pristina disciplina, qua ungui in sacerdotium et in regnum solebant). Baptismal imagery is common on early medieval funerary and commemorative monuments throughout Britain and the continent, and the baptismal significance of the inscription would certainly have been recognized by a contemporary audience. Of equal importance, however, is the fact that the inscription also serves to unite the figures in the two panels as kings.

37. Ó Carragáin, "Christ over the Beasts," 385.

38. See George Hardin Brown, *Bede the Venerable* (Boston: Twayne, 1987), 42–61.

39. Bailey, *Viking Age Sculpture*, 148; I. Henderson, "Pictish Vine-Scroll Ornament," in A. O'Connor and D. Clarke, eds., *From the Stone Age to the "Forty-Five"* (Edinburgh: John Donald, 1983), 243–67; Ó Carragáin, "Bewcastle Cross," 30–33.

40. An interpretation also suggested by Ó Carragáin in "Bewcastle Cross," 30–33.

41. Cramp and Bailey, *Corpus*, vol. 2, 63; Ó Carragáin, "Bewcastle Cross," 35.

42. Ó Carragáin, ("Bewcastle Cross," 35–36), comments on the possible liturgical significance of the sundial. He connects the dial with the second Sunday in Advent and Luke 21:25–32:

> And there shall be signs in the sun and in the moon, and in the stars; and upon the earth distress of nations, by reason of the confusion of the roaring of the sea and of the waves. . . . And they shall see the Son of man coming in a cloud with great power and majesty. But when these things come to pass, look up, and lift up your heads, because your redemption is at hand. And he spoke to them a similitude. See the fig tree, and all the trees: When they now shoot forth their fruit, you know that summer is nigh; so you also, when you shall see these things come to pass, know that the kingdom of God is at hand. Amen, I say to you, this generation shall not pass away, till all things be fulfilled.

He also points out that the dial may connect with the imagery of the west side of the cross. The plant of which the sundial forms a part grows from the level of Christ's waist in the middle panel to just below the level of the Agnus Dei in the upper panel of the west side, and might function to unite the birth of Christ with that of John the Baptist, their births being linked in the liturgical year, "by means of the sun's course."

CHAPTER TWO

Jane Hawkes

SYMBOLS OF THE PASSION OR POWER?

The Iconography of the Rothbury Cross-Head

The broken cross-head which once topped the Northumbrian stone cross-shaft at Rothbury is carved with figural decoration on both its faces;[1] on one side are the remains of the Crucifixion of Christ,[2] and on the other, a figure is set within each of the three surviving cross-arms surrounding a much damaged central medallion (pl. 2.1). Generally these figures are identified as carrying the instruments of Christ's Passion, while the medallion is assumed to have contained a bust of Christ.[3]

Given its mutilated condition, this identification of Christ cannot be proved absolutely, but the outline of a bust can be discerned (in certain lighting),[4] and there is a small plaited fragment on the left of the medallion which is comparable with fringes of hair found elsewhere on the shaft.[5] This suggests that a long-haired figure was originally set at the center of the cross-head and, in Christian art of the early medieval period, the most likely candidate for such a figure in this context would be Christ who is depicted elsewhere on the cross-shaft with long hair.[6]

The real problem with the iconography of this face of the Rothbury cross-head lies with the identification of the objects held by the figures in the cross-arms. According to orthodox opinion (that these figures carry the instruments of the Passion), the mustachioed man in the upper cross-arm has been variously credited with holding a pair of pincers or a whip; the

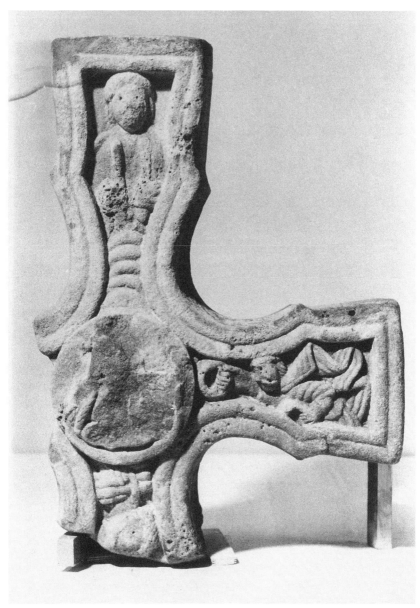

Pl. 2.1. The Rothbury Cross-head. Photograph courtesy of Museum of Antiquities, Newcastle upon Tyne.

figure in the right lateral arm is believed to bear two crowns of thorns, while that in the lower arm is described as carrying nails or a flail. One difficulty with this interpretation is that images of individual, non-angelic male figures holding the instruments of the Passion in this manner seem to be unparalleled; until the thirteenth century the only figures found in Christian art holding these particular tools were soldiers depicted at work on the Crucifixion,[7] a context which is not really comparable with the decoration of the Rothbury cross-head.

The instruments of the Passion are admittedly found in Christian art as isolated objects of reverence (without attendant figures), but even these are rare until the twelfth century and the portrayals are usually limited to the lance and sponge only.[8] Ninth-century illustrations of the Agnus Dei, for instance, include the lance and sponge with a chalice as attributes of the lamb, but never the nails or a crown of thorns.[9] The early ninth-century Utrecht Psalter, produced at Rheims,[10] does show all the instruments of the Passion draped over a cross (pl. 2.2), but this is a depiction of a specific iconographic image, the *Arma Christi*, which seems to be unique in this form prior to the twelfth century;[11] it illustrates the instruments displayed as the spoils of the victor after battle. However, neither this, nor the Agnus Dei images are really comparable iconographically with the Rothbury cross-head.

What these iconographic schemes do demonstrate is an interest in, and veneration of the symbols of the Crucifixion which was current on the continent during the Carolingian period.[12] In this respect, the conventional interpretation of the objects carved on the Rothbury cross-head is in keeping with Carolingian attitudes, and indeed, it must be admitted that the figures in the arms of the cross-head do seem to venerate the figure (of Christ) who once filled the central medallion. The right-hand and lower figures clearly present their attributes towards him in gestures of adoration, while the stance of the uppermost figure still expresses a certain authoritative power.

However, all this is not really comparing like with like. The fact that the figures may venerate Christ does not mean they hold symbols of his Passion,[13] and it must be emphasized that the iconography of the *Arma Christi* in the Utrecht Psalter is very different to that of the Rothbury cross-head. The cross in the manuscript is clearly draped with easily identifiable items; the Anglo-Saxon stone cross-head is carved with men holding objects which are not as easily identified, and do not really bear much resemblance to the standard whip, nails, or crown of thorns. Rather than seeing these attributes as the instruments of the Passion therefore, and given that the figure at the center of the cross-head was probably Christ, and that the figures in the cross-arms apparently present their attributes to

Pl. 2.2. The *Arma Christi* from the Utrecht Psalter. Photograph courtesy of Bibliotheek der Rijksuniversiteit, Utrecht.

him, it is possible that these symbolize Christ's divine authority and power, his kingship rather than his sacrifice and Passion.

According to this reading the upper figure would be interpreted as holding rods or scepters of power. It is clear that the two joined rods held firmly in front of this figure are similar to the double scepters of power and authority held by such figures as appear on the Alfred Jewel and at the center of the Fuller Brooch, both pieces of ninth-century southern Anglo-Saxon metalwork.[14] However, these latter symbols are foliated and pass over the shoulders of the figures holding them, while the rods on the Rothbury cross-head are plain and terminate below the figure's shoulders.

Another similar, and closely related motif is that of the separate rods or scepters held across the chest in the so-called Osiris pose, a motif found in Insular and Insular-related work of the eighth and ninth centuries. Examples include the eighth-century Lichfield Gospel portrait of Luke (pl. 2.3), which shows the Evangelist with two crossed rods, and the later Book of Kells image of Christ holding a floriated rod over each shoulder in the Osiris pose illustrated on the so-called Temptation page.[15] More relevant to Rothbury, however, may be the Tetramorph in the eighth-century Trier Gospel Book, probably from Echternach;[16] this creature is shown in the Osiris pose clasping a scepter and what has been described as a flabellum,[17] but here the attributes do *not* pass over the creature's shoulders. It is possible therefore, that the joined rods held by the uppermost figure at Rothbury represent a confusion between less ornate separate rods held in the Osiris pose (which could be relatively short), and the larger, joined floriated rods found in the ninth-century metalwork of southern England.

This hypothesis however, does not explain the plainness of the Rothbury scepters for which the best parallels probably lie with the short plain single scepters that are found, both as a recurrent motif in Christian and imperial art of the West, and as part of the regalia of Anglo-Saxon kingship. In Christian art the plain scepter, featured in scenes of Christ's life and miracles, such as those carved on the fifth-century doors of Santa Sabina in Rome,[18] was a symbol of Christ's divine authority inherited from imperial art where it featured in state portraits of the emperor and his consuls, on coinage and ivory diptychs, as a symbol of official power.[19] The diptychs, for example, produced to mark the inauguration of the emperor or consul, show the statesman enthroned with a single short scepter, sometimes topped by an ornamental boss (see pl. 2.4).[20] Such scepters were copied, not only in Christian art, but in the world of Germanic kingship where it seems that such Roman symbols of authority were simulated, from at least the fifth century onwards, as part of the royal insignia of local kings.[21] Although these Germanic scepters sometimes incorporated metal terminal ornaments, possibly under Celtic influence as has been argued for

Pl. 2.3. The Lichfield Gospel portrait of the evangelist Luke. Photograph by kind permission of the Dean and Chapter of Lichfield Cathedral.

the Sutton Hoo whetstone scepter,[22] they seem generally to have been short, relatively plain rods, not too dissimilar to those clasped by the figure in the upper arm of the Rothbury cross-head.

Pl. 2.4. The Diptych of Consul Anastasius, A.D. 517. Photograph courtesy of the Board of Trustees of Victoria and Albert Museum, London.

In other words, the short plain (joined) rods which are featured on the Rothbury cross-head may represent an amalgamation of the ornamented double or crossed scepters familiar (and more competently executed) in Insular manuscript and metalwork decoration of the eighth and ninth centuries, and the less ornate, single scepters held by state officials in late imperial art where the stance of the enthroned figure is very similar to that adopted by the Insular Osiris-pose figures and by that in the top arm of the Rothbury cross-head. This amalgam of artistic motifs many have held added significance and relevance in a world where relatively plain scepters were a recognized component of Anglo-Saxon regalia. Whatever their origin, the identity of the rods held by the uppermost figure at Rothbury does seem to be closer to the double scepters of power and authority than to a whip or pair of pincers.[23]

The mustachioed man in the right lateral arm of the Rothbury cross-head is generally identified as carrying two crowns of thorns, one held out towards the central roundel and the other half-hidden in the roll-moulding surrounding the cross-arm (pl. 2.1). However, there are no other depictions of this phenomenon in Christian art because the point of this particular instrument of torture was that it was unique, fashioned specifically to torment the "King of the Jews."[24] Because of its very uniqueness it is unlikely that the sculptor would have produced *two* crowns of thorns. And yet, despite this, and despite the severe spatial limitations of the cross-arm which even forced the sculptor to cut part of his figure, and so could have restricted the presentation to one crown, the sculptor has retained two circlets. It must therefore be assumed that he intended to depict the two, and given that they are unlikely to be crowns of thorns, their identity must be sought elsewhere.

In keeping with the reading of the double scepter held by the uppermost figure as deriving from iconographic traditions (whether Insular or imperial) evoking notions of regal authority, the two crowns held by the figure on the right might be compared with the crowns of victory and immortality depicted in imperial and Early Christian art. Late imperial coins, for instance, often show the emperor flanked by figures wearing windswept clothes who present him with a crown of eternal victory; here the wreath symbolizes the crown of life reserved for those whose virtues had won them the privilege of immortality.[25] On later coins, after the separation of the Empire into its Eastern and Western spheres of influence, the motif continued in use, but showed both emperors flanking a single figure holding two crowns symbolizing the unity between them.[26]

This iconography was adopted into religious art at an early date and is found in many contexts. One of the earliest is the decoration of the Roman *fondi d'oro* of the third and fourth centuries where portraits of Peter and

Paul flank the unifying figure who holds a crown over each of them (pl. 2.5).[27] Here the symbolism refers to the apostles as worthy recipients of the martyr's crown of immortality exalting them to heaven.[28]

In secular art of the Christian period, the wreath-bearing figure continued to be a popular motif, appearing commonly on the consular diptychs and coinage. The early sixth-century diptych of consul Anastasius (ca. A.D. 517) for instance, shows the consul with his short scepter of magisterial authority flanked by two diminutive cloaked figures holding up wreathed crowns containing his portrait (pl. 2.4). The nearly contemporary gold solidus of Theodoric (A.D. 493–553) shows the Ostrogothic emperor with a small wreath-bearing figure at his side, while the later coins of Justin II (A.D. 566) and Heraclius (A.D. 610–641) show the emperors flanked by crown-bearing victories.[29] The motif also found its way onto the coinage of later Germanic rulers; seventh-century Frankish coins and Anglo-Saxon coins of the fifth, seventh, and ninth centuries survive bearing the image of figures who present the king with a wreath.[30] The seventh-century Anglo-Saxon coin moreover, shows the survival, albeit heavily stylized, of double portraits flanking the crowning figure.

Within this context the figure holding two crowns on the Rothbury cross-head can easily be identified with a long and flourishing iconographic tradition of figures who wear wind-swept clothes and present wreaths in outstretched arms to those in authority whose virtues have exalted them to immortality. The appearance on the Northumbrian cross-head of the figure holding the two crowns with his clothing flying out behind him suggests at the very least, a familiarity with this iconographic tradition; the inspiration could have come from the coinage, which was reproduced in Anglo-Saxon England and sometimes showed a figure with two crowns, or from a model such as a consular diptych which featured the presentation of wreathed crowns to figures holding scepters as an attribute of their authority.

The fragmentary remains of the lower Rothbury cross-arm contain the third mustachioed figure who is usually identified as carrying in his upraised hand the nails used to transfix Christ to the cross (pl. 2.1). However, the object(s) held by this figure bear little resemblance to nails as we know them, or indeed, as they were known in Anglo-Saxon England; the remains of the seventh-century ship buried at Sutton Hoo, for instance, include a large number of iron rivets, bolts, and nails, all of which resemble their modern counterparts, having a straight length of iron terminating in a flat head.[31] Later Old English literary references further indicate, through their descriptions of iron nails, that similar metal implements were familiar throughout the period and were, moreover, thought of commonly in connection with the Crucifixion itself.[32] Compared with such implements, it is clear that the slightly tapering tubes held by the third Rothbury figure are

Pl. 2.5. Fifth-century Roman gold-glass portraits of Peter and Paul. Photograph courtesy of the Trustees of British Museum, London.

not easily identifiable as nails; indeed they bear more resemblance to the tubular folds of clothing worn by the majority of the figures on the cross-shaft.[33] They are, in fact, more easily explained as a piece of cloth clutched, and therefore slightly tapered in the hand of the lower figure.

The art of late imperial Rome seems to provide the most instructive parallels. The ivory consular diptychs of the fifth and sixth centuries, which show the crown and scepter motifs, depict the consul clasping the scepter in one hand and a *mappa circensis* (often upraised) in the other. This was a napkin lowered to signal the start of the games marking the inauguration of every consul and became one of the standard symbols of his official authority.[34] During the fifth and early years of the sixth century the *mappa* was depicted on the diptychs in a recognizable fashion, as a napkin, but after the first decades of the sixth century it tended to be represented as a small cushion-like object.[35] Thus, the *mappas* held by the consuls Anastasius (A.D. 517) (pl. 2.4), Philoxenus (A.D. 525) and Justinus (A.D. 540) are not well defined, but those held by Basilius (A.D. 430), Boethius (A.D. 487)[36] and Areobindus (A.D. 506) (pl. 2.6), with their clearly incised lines and rounded folds, could well have inspired the object held by the third figure in the lower arm of the Rothbury cross-head, especially given the tendency of the Rothbury sculptor to stylize drapery into regular tubular folds.

It might well seem that the iconography of fifth- and early sixth-century imperial artefacts would not be a likely source of inspiration for the Christian iconography of an Anglo-Saxon Northumbrian cross-shaft. There is, however, evidence that the consular diptychs were circulating in Europe during the seventh to ninth centuries, and that their iconography was widely influential in the decoration of other, non-imperial artefacts[37] The mid-eighth-century frescoes of San Clemente (Rome) for instance, included an image of the *Maria Regina* holding a *mappa* in her left hand as an attribute of her regal status;[38] images from a consular diptych were reproduced on a Visigothic stone column in the ninth century,[39] and similar scenes may have influenced the figural iconography of the West Cross at Monasterboice in Ireland where a figure is found enthroned at the base of the north face holding what may be a *mappa* in one hand and a large shield in the other.[40]

This widespread artistic influence is probably a reflex of the fact that from the seventh century imperial diptychs had begun to play a physical part in the liturgy of the Western mass; they were displayed on the altar and inscribed with the names of church members (living and dead) that were read out during the service. For instance, in the seventh century, the inner leaves of the fifth-century diptych of consul Boethius were painted with the list of names and with pictures of the Church Fathers and the Raising of Lazarus.[41] Similarly, the early sixth-century Clementinus diptych had a prayer written inside in the eighth century, while in the ninth century the *Kyrie Eleison* and *Gloria* were added to the inner leaves of the Philoxenus diptych.[42]

This liturgical re-use of diptychs is a practice thought to have begun with the early Irish and Anglo-Saxon missions of the seventh century which spread through the West during the eighth and ninth centuries.[43] Concurrent with this practice, and bearing in mind the iconography of the Rothbury cross-head, it is perhaps also worth noting that in the eighth century it became customary in the West for the celebrant to hold a ceremonial napkin (the *mappula*) in his right hand while officiating at the altar.[44] The iconography of the imperial diptychs was clearly a living part of Western ecclesiastical and liturgical life during the eighth century.

Pl. 2.6. The Diptych of Consul Areobindus, A.D. 506. Photograph courtesy of Schweizerisches Landesmuseum, Zurich.

There would thus seem to be ample evidence for familiarity with imperial iconography, such as appeared on consular diptychs, within a Christian context in western Europe (including Anglo-Saxon England) between the sixth and ninth centuries. The iconographic motifs of late imperial art were fairly standardized by the sixth century and typically featured the figure of authority holding a scepter and *mappa circensis* as symbols of his official power, flanked by figures holding crowns which referred to the virtues entitling him to immortality. The scepters and crowns were known in many contexts, but given the ecclesiastical use of the imperial diptychs, it seems not unlikely that the symbolism which associated the scepter, crowns and *mappa* with the panoply and authority of power was not only recognized in Anglo-Saxon England, but that it was these objects, rather than the instruments of the Passion, which were chosen for the Rothbury cross-head as symbols of Christ's kingship, adapted from a world of secular officialdom to one of religious majesty. On the cross-head they are thus presented to Christ in the central medallion as attributes of his divine authority and power, proper to the Son of God who overcame death on the cross and ascended into heaven to reign at the side of God the Father.[45]

The fact that the upper figure holds a double scepter, and the figure on the right holds two crowns, may have some reference to the double nature of Christ (as the Son of God and the Son of Man) and to his role as the Second Person of the Trinity. While the overall scheme can probably be seen in light of such phrases as appear in Alcuin's late-eighth-century poem on the Church of York:

> O sancti, populus fortis, gens diva . . . victrices
> aquilas caeli qui fertis in arcem aethereo regi
> regalia dona ferentes,[46]

the possible reference to the double nature of Christ and his status as the Second Person of the Trinity may have had some added interest in late-eighth- and early ninth-century Northumbria. The double nature of Christ had been declared at the Council of Chalcedon (A.D. 451), but in the late eighth century when members of the Spanish Church maintained that Jesus Incarnate was the Son of God only by adoption, Alcuin, at the Council of Frankfort (A.D. 794) was instrumental in passing the resolution against this "heresy" reaffirming that Jesus, the Son of God, was consubstantial with the Father.[47] It is possible that the iconography of the Rothbury cross-head should be viewed against such a background, although it must be remembered that the remains of this fragment form only part of a once impressive monument whose overall iconographic import cannot be completely reconstructed from the three surviving pieces.

NOTES

I am grateful to L. Allason-Jones, R. N. Bailey, C. Bourke, M. Ryan and S. Youngs for their comments and help during the production of this paper.

1. The Rothbury cross survives in three pieces, the cross-head, the top of the shaft and the base of the shaft (see J. Hawkes, "The Rothbury Cross: an Iconographic Bricolage," *Gesta* 35 (1996): 77–94; R. Cramp, *Corpus of Anglo-Saxon Stone Sculpture in England, vol. I, County Durham and Northumberland* [Oxford: Oxford University Press, 1984], I, 219–21 for find evidence). The piece from the top of the shaft has a round dowel hole in it; this and the slight variation in stone type used for the three pieces implies the cross was originally a composite monument.

2. The iconography of this Crucifixion has been fully discussed by E. Coatsworth, "The Iconography of the Crucifixion in Pre-Conquest Sculpture in England" (Ph.D. diss., University of Durham, 1979), 200–7, and more recently by A. J. Hawkes, "The Non-Crucifixion Iconography of Pre-Viking Sculpture in the North of England" (Ph.D. diss., University of Newcastle upon Tyne), 1989, 151–62 (see also Cramp, *Corpus*, 220–21).

3. T. D. *Kendrick, Anglo-Saxon Art to A.D. 900* (London: Metheun, 1938), 154–58; Cramp, *Corpus*, 219; Coatsworth, "Crucifixion Iconography," 200. C. C. Hodges, "The Ancient Cross of Rothbury." *Archaeologia Aeliana* 1 (1925): 159–68 provided an alternative explanation of the figures as adoring Christ and holding archaic musical instruments.

4. See Cramp, *Corpus*, 219; Hawkes, "Non-Crucifixion Iconography," 151.

5. E.g., the long hair of Christ in Majesty and the small fringe of hair under the woman's coif in the miracle scene, both at the top of the shaft (Cramp, *Corpus*, pls. 213.1213, 1215).

6. E.g. the *Majestas Christi* at the top of the shaft, originally under the Crucifixion (see Cramp, *Corpus*, pl. 213.1213). See Hawkes, "Non-Crucifixion Iconography," 185, n.106 for other possibilities.

7. G. Schiller, *Iconography of Christian Art, II*, trans. J. Seligman (Greenwich, Conn.: New York Graphic Society, 1972), 98, 244–46, pls. 298–300, 347. The sixth-century mosaics from the apse of San Michele in Affricisco, Ravenna (now in Berlin) do show two angels holding the lance and sponge (G. Schiller, *Ikonographie der Christlichen Kunst*, III, [Gutersloh: Gutersloher Verlagshaus Gerd Mohn, 1971], pl. 633), but these are not the instruments of the Passion claimed for Rothbury. It is possible that the angels on the small square grave slab at Newent (Gloucs.) dated to the eleventh century carry symbols of the Passion (Coatsworth, "Crucifixion Iconography," pl. 139).

8. Schiller, *Iconography* II, 189–90.

9. Alcuin Bible (ca. 834–843) f. 339v; Codex Aemilianensis (ca. 975); Cologne Gospels (ca. 1000) f. 190 in Schiller, *Iconography* II, pls. 397, 399, 401.

10. See G. Benson and D. Tselos, "New Light on the Origin of the *Utrecht Psalter*," *Art Bull.* 13 (1931): 13–79; D. Tselos, "A Greco-Italian School of Illuminators and Fresco Painters: Its Relation to the Principal Reims Manuscripts and to the Greek Frescos in Rome and Castleseprio," *Art Bull.* 38 (1956): 1–30; K. van der Horst, et al., *The Utrecht Psalter in Medieval Art. Picturing the Psalms of David* (London: Harvey Miller, and Netherlands: HES Publishers BV, 1996).

11. See Schiller, *Iconography*, II, 84ff.

12. For discussions see Schiller, *Iconography*, II, 189–90; G. Henderson, *Early Medieval* (Harmondsworth: Penguin, 1972), 237; Coatsworth, "Crucifixion Iconography," 203–5; S. McEntire, "The Devotional Context of the Cross Before A.D. 1000," in P. E. Szarmach and V. D. Oggins, eds., *Sources of Anglo-Saxon Culture* (Kalamazoo, Mich.: Medieval Institute 1986).

13. For instance, the arm of the ninth-century cross-head from Hoddom (Dumfries.) shows figures holding attributes which are not the instruments of the Passion; half-length figures of Peter and Paul in the left lateral cross-arm hold the keys and book (C. A. R. Radford, "Hoddom," *Trans. of the Dumfries. and Galloway Nat. Hist. and Ant. Society* 31 [1952–53]: pl. v).

14. For the Fuller Brooch and Alfred Jewel see David M. Wilson, *Anglo-Saxon Art: from the Seventh Century to the Norman Conquest* (London: Thames & Hudson, 1984), ills. 1, 121–22. For the transmission of this motif see C. A. Linder, "The 'Osiris Pose' in Early Medieval English and Irish Art" (Master's thesis, University of Texas at Austin, 1981). See also the Book of Kells, f. 7v (J. J. G. Alexander, *Insular Manuscripts: 6th to 9th Century* (London: Harvey Miller, 1978), ills. 233.

15. Alexander, *Insular Manuscripts*, ills. 255; for Lichfield Gospel, Ibid., no. 21.

16. Domschatz. Cod.61, f.5v (Alexander, *Insular Manuscripts*, no. 26, ills. 110). See also Netzer, *Cultural Interplay in the Eighth Century. The Trier Gospels and the Making of a Scriptorium at Echternach* (Cambridge: Cambridge University Press, 1994).

17. Alexander, *Insular Manuscripts*, 53.

18. Schiller, *Iconography of Christian Art* I, trans. J. Seligman (Greenwich, Conn.: New York Graphic Society, 1971), pl. 466.

19. Ibid., 163.

20. For coinage see R. Brilliant, *Gesture and Rank in Roman Art* (New Haven: Connecticut Academy of Arts and Sciences, 1963), figs 4.115–117; for diptychs see also W. F. Volbach, *Elfenbeinarbeiten der Spätantike und des Frühen Mittelalters* (Mainz am Rhein: Von Zabern, 1976), nrs. 2–3, 5, 12–13, 15, 23, 31–32.

21. See R. L. S. Bruce-Mitford, *The Sutton Hoo Ship-Burial* II (London: British Museum Publications, 1978), 311–17; V. Evison, "Pagan Saxon Whetstones," *Ant.J.* 55 (1975): 70–86.

22. M. J. Enright, "The Sutton Hoo Whetstone Scepter: A Study in Iconography and Cultural Milieu," *A.S.E.* 11 (1982): 119–34.

23. A twisted piece of cloth is the other identity suggested for these rod-like objects, an identification based on the five plain mouldings below the figure (e.g. Coatsworth, "Crucifixion Iconography," 200–7). The general parallel provided is that of the angels at the Crucifixion carrying a cloth or veil which cascades from outstretched hands in flowing folds; such drapery, however, does not fall in stacked folds (see e.g. a tenth-century Metz ivory, Schiller *Iconography* II, pl. 373). Moreover, the mouldings are not contiguous with the rods; rather the figure holding the rods emerges from *behind* these mouldings. I have argued elsewhere (Hawkes, "Non-Crucifixion Iconography," 168–84; Hawkes, "The Rothbury Cross," 81–85) that the Ascension scene at the base of the Rothbury cross-shaft (Cramp, *Corpus*, pl. 213.1218) is, in part, based on an apocalyptic scene of the Second Coming and it is probable that half-length figures emerging from clouds in such a scene provided the model for the uppermost figure of the cross-head. Early Anglo-Saxon Last Judgement scenes showing such a motif depict the clouds as solid, slightly curved mouldings (See e.g. J. Beckwith, *Ivory Carvings in Early Medieval England* [London: 1972], pl. 1), and half-length figures with attributes emerging from rather solid curved clouds also become a feature of Carolingian art, as in the Tours Gospels, early-ninth century, in J. Hubert et al., *Carolingian Art* (London: Harvey Miller and Medcalf, 1970), ill. 114. It is thus probable that with a carved model and the Rothbury sculptor's tendency to stylize his carving with repeated and regular shapes that the five plain mouldings were intended to represent clouds from which the figure emerges with the double rods of power and authority.

24. Matt.: 27, 29; Mark: 15, 18.

25. E. T. Goodenough, "The Crown of Victory in Judaism," *Art Bull.* 28 (1946): 139–59. For coins see Brilliant *Gesture and Rank*, figs. 4.122–123.

26. E. H. Kantorowicz, "The Quinity of Winchester," *Art Bull.* 29 (1947): 73–85; A. Grabar, *Christian Iconography: A Study of its Origins* (Princeton: Princeton University Press, 1961), fig. 165.

27. See J. Huskinson, *Concordia Apostolorum: Christian Propoaganda at Rome in the Fourth and Fifth Centuries*, B.A.R. 148 (1982); see also Kantorowicz, "Quinity," 77–78, figs. 26a, 26d.

28. Goodenough, "Crown of Victory," 145; Kantorowicz, "Quinity," 74.

29. D. T. Rice, ed., *The Dark Ages*: The Making of European Civilization (London: Thames & Hudson, 1965), 159, no. 1; 86, nos. 4, 7.

30. For Frankish coin see P. Le Gentilhomme, "Trouvaille de Monnaies d'Or des Mérovingiens et dans Wisigoths," *Revue de la Numismatiques* 39 (1936): 136,

pl. 3; for Anglo-Saxon coins see C. Oman, *The Coinage of England* (Oxford: Clarendon Press, 1931), pl. 1.5; M. Dolley, ed., *Anglo-Saxon Coins: Studies Presented to F. M. Stenton on the Occasion of his 80th Birthday, 17 May 1960* (London: Methuen, 1961), pl. 1.10; M. Dolley, Anglo-Saxon Pennies (London: Trustees of the British Museum, 1964), pl. XI.33. The fifth-century Anglo-Saxon coin is a close copy of the Eastern imperial coins showing the crowning motif.

31. R. L. S. Bruce-Mitford, *The Sutton Hoo Ship-Burial* I (London: British Museum Publications, 1975), 352, 362-64, figs. 277–79.

32. See e.g. the *wira gespon* nails of the Crucifixion in *Elene* (P. Gordon, ed., *Cynewulf's Elene* [Exeter: University of Exeter Press, 1977], ll. 1062, 1102, 1108, 1127, 1134.) See also *Dream of the Rood* (M. Swanton, ed., *The Dream of the Rood* [Manchester: Manchester University Press, 1970], l. 46.); Aelfric's *Saints' Lives* in B. Thorpe, ed., *The Homilies of the Anglo-Saxon Church*, 2 vols. (London: Printed for the Aelfric Society, 1844–46) I, 146, 216; II, 254, 306. Further, it would seem that the Crucifixion on the other face of the Rothbury cross-head shows Christ transfixed to the cross with a large-headed nail (Cramp, *Corpus*, pl. 211.1206).

33. See the *Majestas Christi* and the miracle scene at the top of the shaft and the Apostles of the Ascension at the base of the shaft (Cramp, *Corpus*, pls. 213.1213, 1215, 1218).

34. A. Maskell, *Ivories* (London: Methuen, 1905), 47ff.; E. Capps Jr., "The Style of the Consular Diptychs," *Art Bull.* 10 (1927): 62–63; M. Gough, *The Origins of Christian Art* (London: Thames & Hudson, 1973), 124–33. The *mappa* was not limited to diptychs—see e.g. the coins of Leo I, Phocus, and Justinian II (Rice, *Dark Ages*, 86, nrs. 2,6,9).

35. Maskell, *Ivories*, 47–81; Capps, "Consular Diptychs," 68–69. The difference may be due to the fact that the earlier diptychs were produced in Byzantium while the later ivories were made in Rome.

36. For the diptychs of Philoxenus and Justinius see Volbach, *Elfenbeinarbeiten*, nrs. 32–33; for those of Basilius and Boethius, ibid., nrs. 5–6.

37. It should also be noted that the form of the imperial diptych was adopted for Christian purposes and decorated with Christian religious subject matter from the fifth century onwards (Volbach, *Elfenbeinarbeiten*, nrs. 111–13, 119, 125, 137, 142, 145).

38. J. Osborne, "Early Medieval Painting in San Clemente, Rome: the Madonna and Child in the Niche," *Gesta* 20 (1981): 299–310; and "Early Medieval Wall-Painting in the Church of San Clemente Rome: The Libertinus Cycle and its Date," *J.W.C.I.* 45 (1982): 182–85.

39. P. De Palol, *Early Medieval Art in Spain*, trans. A. Jaffa (London: Thames & Hudson, 1987), fig. 33.

40. H. Roe, "The 'David Cycle' in Early Irish Art," *J.R.S.A.I.* 79 (1949): fig. 9; *Monasterboice and its Monuments* (County Louth: County Louth Archaeological Historical Society, 1981), pl. 1.

41. J. Hubert, et al., *Europe in the Dark Ages* (London: Thames & Hudson, 1969), fig. 148.

42. Maskell, *Ivories*, 47–81; Gough *Christian Art*, 133; Beckwith, *Early Christian*, 80–86; D. Gaborit-Chopin, *Ivoires du Moyen Age*, (Fribourg: Office du livre, 1978), 22–24. For the Clementinus diptych (A.D. 513) see Volbach, *Elfenbeinarbeiten*, nr. 15.

43. Maskell, *Ivories*, 47–81; G. B. Ladner, "The 'Portraits' of Emperors in Southern Italian Exultet Rolls and the Liturgical Commemoration of the Emperor," *Speculum* 17 (1942): 181–200; W. Levison, *England and the Continent in the Eighth Century* (London: Oxford University Press, 1946), 101; Beckwith, *Early Christian*, 80–86; R. McKitterick, *The Frankish Kingdoms Under the Carolingians: 751–987* (London: Longman, 1983), 210.

44. Maskell, *Ivories*, 47–81; T. Klauser, *A Short History of the Western Liturgy*, trans. J. Halliburton (London and New York: Oxford University Press, 1979), 61.

45. If, as seems likely, the iconography of imperial art was influential in the decoration of the Rothbury cross-head, this source may have inspired an object held by a figure in the (now missing) left lateral arm of the cross-head. Although such suggestions must remain highly speculative in the present absence of physical evidence, the attributes associated with the power of officialdom in imperial art included, not only the scepter, *mappa* and wreaths of immortality, but also garlands and orbs (see e.g. pl. 4; Volbach, *Elfenbeinarbeiten*, nrs. 16–21, 35), objects which could be presumed to have fitted within the confines of the cross-arm. They occur widely in Christian and secular art as part of the regalia of power and authority, as do the palm fronds found on imperial coinage (see Rice, *Dark Ages*, 159, no. 1).

46. "O saints, valiant host, divine race . . . who bear the standards of victory to the heights of heaven, carrying royal gifts to the heavenly king." P. Godman, ed., *Alcuin: The Bishops, Kings and Saints of York* (Oxford: Clarendon Press, 1982), 11. 9–11.

47. See M. Laistner, *Thought and Letters in Western Europe: a.d. 500–900* (London: Methuen, 1957), 286–92; D. Bullough, *The Age of Charlemagne* (London: Ferndule Editions, 1970), 112; C. R. Dodwell, *Painting in Europe 800–1200* (Harmondsworth: Penguin, 1971), 98–99; Schiller, *Iconography* I, 4–12; Coatsworth, "Crucifixion Iconography," 67; McKitterick, *Frankish Kingdoms*, 98.

CHAPTER THREE

Carol A. Farr

WORTHY WOMEN ON THE RUTHWELL CROSS

Woman as Sign in Early Anglo-Saxon Monasticism

Few of the surviving fragments of pre-Viking Anglo-Saxon sculpture present images of women at all.[1] On the Ruthwell cross, however, female figures are given prominence in the visual program, and one of its inscriptions refers to women. The lower part of the cross's shaft presents at least two large panels depicting the Virgin, in scenes of the Annunciation and Flight into (or out of) Egypt. Aside from the clearly identifiable Marian imagery, two other panels depict less frequently encountered scenes of women. One of the most prominent images on the entire cross presents Mary Magdalene washing and anointing the feet of Christ (pl. 3.1). The deeply carved relief presents formally striking qualities in its monumental, heavily draped figure of Christ and the expressiveness of the bending figure of Mary holding her curving mass of hair with an oversized hand. A small panel at the top of the cross-shaft presents the second unusual image: two women facing each other with arms extended in an embrace (pl. 3.2). Previous scholarship has interpreted the scene as either the Visitation or Martha and Mary, but the damaged inscription on the panel's frame retains the word *dominae*, usually taken to relate somehow to the two female figures.[2] These images of women belong to one of the most extensive and most studied of all surviving visual programs of the early Middle Ages. Scholarly discussion of this rich program, however,

45

Pl. 3.1. Ruthwell Cross, south side. Photograph by permission of Durham University, Department of Archaeology.

Pl. 3.2. Ruthwell Cross, south side: Martha and Mary, or the Visitation. Photograph by permission of Durham University, Department of Archaeology.

almost never considers, even in passing, the significance of these exceptional images of women.[3]

Meyer Schapiro, writing nearly fifty years ago, connected the image of Mary Magdalene anointing the feet of Christ with the prominence of women in early Anglo-Saxon monasticism, exemplified by Hild of Whitby. "The importance of female ascetics in England," Schapiro said, "perhaps inspired the elaboration of the legend of the Magdalene as an imposing prototype."[4] Nonetheless, even the perceptive and innovative Schapiro made this brief remark upon the importance of female monastics only following his discussion of the allegorical significance of Mary Magdalene and Martha, drawn from exegetical writings of John Cassian, Jerome, Gregory, and Bede. Moreover, he did not see fit to explore at any length his important observation on the conflation of the story of Mary of Egypt with Mary Magdalene, in Anglo-Saxon England. Thinking along the lines of traditional art historical methodology, Schapiro mentioned no sense of tension between the patriarchal viewpoint of his cited authors and the existence of powerful females in Anglo-Saxon monasticism. His short discussion of the Mary Magdalene/Mary of Egypt conflation focuses on the story's possible origin in Northumbria at an early date, the Ruthwell panel providing evidence for its formation in the seventh century and the impor- tance of Anglo-Saxon abbesses and double monasteries as an explanation for its first appearance in England.[5] Blind to the biases of art historical method and surviving monastic texts, Schapiro's discussion of the panel is typical of nearly all previous iconographic studies of the Ruthwell cross.

One may, however, reasonably question the relevance of feminist theory to the panels. One may search carefully, long, and fruitlessly for a patristic or an early medieval exegesis of Mary Magdalene or Martha and Mary that says anything about their meaning as specifically female figures or even as female monastics. Nearly all interpretations allegorize them as seemingly gender-neutral types of the church or monastic ideals. In fact, the Virgin and Mary Magdalene can exemplify perfectly the richness of medieval use of imagery in their universal appeal as intercessor and penitent.[6] Fur- thermore, the Ruthwell cross almost certainly addressed a broad audience. All large-scale stone crosses must have been, in some sense, public monu- ments. Recently scholars have argued cogently its dynamic and multivalent expression of meaning, designed to speak inclusively.[7] What then is the point of considering Ruthwell's program as an object of a masculine or a feminine gaze? Or even as having particularly anything to do with women at all? Why consider a gender-specific meaning or audience for a public monument like a great stone cross?

One reason is well known for at least considering some of the figures sculpted on the Ruthwell cross as images for or about women. The presence in monastery and court of educated and powerful aristocratic females can hardly have escaped the notice of anyone who has attentively read Bede's *History*. Moreover, Anglo-Saxon literature presents a range of female characters and types relating, as literary studies have shown, in definite ways to contemporary social constructs.[8] Such facts and connec- tions suggest that the recognized status and power of women in Anglo-

Saxon society may have found expression in prestigious and conspicuous monuments of eighth-century visual art.[9]

Feminist theory, such as that of Elizabeth Cowie recently discussed by Griselda Pollock, has brought to art historians' attention the importance of Levi-Strauss's "woman as sign," representations of women as signifiers of social order.[10] According to this view, cultural images of women are formed by and actively shape the nature of social practices and institutions, to which, in patriarchal societies, kinship is central. Cowie's ideas may apply to Anglo-Saxon sculpture of the eighth century. The patriarchy of the Church effected the give-and-take process of Christianization, a process requiring the transformation of native social structures. Thus, it may prove fruitful to consider a meaning of Ruthwell's images of women which resides not in the object itself but in interaction with the context of early Anglo-Saxon society.

A negotiation of the significance of women would seem especially important in early Anglo-Saxon England when the existing social and political powers of aristocratic women were not well-suited to the Christian culture gradually becoming dominant. On the Ruthwell cross, the remains of a runic Latin inscription carved around a panel bearing the figures of two embracing women may refer to aristocratic females. Most experts read the word *dominae* at the end of the surviving inscription: "*Martha et Maria merentes dominae*," translated "Martha and Mary worthy ladies."[11] The choice of the word *dominae* suggests women of high status. However, the identification of the panel's subject as the sisters Martha and Mary is often questioned because the image resembles depictions of the Visitation.[12] I suggest that it portrays Martha and Mary, but that the representation is modeled upon Visitation images, creating a resonance with the story in which the Virgin recites the canticle, the *Magnificat*.[13] Such a visual reference to the Visitation in conjunction with the *merentes dominae* title could have modified the significance of Martha and Mary to represent women of high status who are meritorious in a Christian sense, in a way that would be especially relevant to the ongoing process of Christianization in Anglo-Saxon society.

The panel of Martha and Mary matches up visually with other pairs of figures on the cross: Paul and Anthony, the Annunciation, and the miracle of the man born blind. Thematically, it is related to the image of the penitent woman in that this woman was believed to be Mary Magdalene, the sister of Martha.[14] While all the images on the cross work together to form many levels of meaning, I think the pairs of figures and the Mary Magdalene establish within the program a representation of monastic females that acknowledges their power and presence but simultaneously categorizes and subordinates them.

Bede's interpretation of Martha and Mary as types of the monastic ideal of the active and contemplative[15] suggests an equivalency of the sculpted panel on the other side of the shaft depicting Paul and Anthony, another pair considered to symbolize or signify the monastic ideal.[16] However, the position of the pair of women at the top of the shaft and the visual reference to the Visitation may serve to modulate the ideal, to fuse it with an image of humility: Martha and Mary attain worthiness through humility.[17] The Virgin's reference to herself in the Visitation story as the humble servant of the Lord[18] is commented upon in exegesis as signifying that she is the antitype of Eve. According to Bede, Eve brought "death into the world through (her) pride . . . , so the entrance of life was unfolded anew through the humility of Mary."[19] This inversion of Eve and Mary is paralleled in interpretations of the story of the penitent woman. Jerome[20] and Bede[21] describe her not only with Luke's word, *peccatrix* or female sinner, but also as *meretrix*, a feminine word meaning "prostitute." The word derives from the verb *mereo* or *mereor*, which can mean either "to be worthy of" or "to earn." In a Mediterranean, Christian patriarchal system in which the primary social relation is marriage and the concept of woman as erotic temptress is thoroughly established, a woman who earns money is a *meretrix*.[22] The stem of the verb in various inflections also provides the vocabulary used to describe martyrs, virgins and the humble, male and female, who are worthy of elevation to saintliness.[23] Bede interprets Mary Magdalene as a figure of the Church of the present and of the future, an allegory requiring careful explanation of her transformation from penitent *meretrix* at the feet of Christ into the woman worthy of anointing the head of Christ. Her transformation from sinner to worthy woman was accomplished with humility and tears, which "merited forgiveness of her sins."[24] The proud, lascivious Eve became the humble, chaste virgin, a transformation reaffirmed and elaborated in juxtaposition with the cross-shaft's Marian images of Annunciation and Flight.

While humility certainly finds no representation in exegesis as a virtue applying only to women, its emphasis in the images of women on the Ruthwell cross may have either served a polemical role or been formed by contemporary gender constructs in the context of early Anglo-Saxon monasticism. Stephanie Hollis has pointed out, in her recent study of Anglo-Saxon women and the Church, the polemical use of humility in the Whitby *Life of Gregory*.[25] Contrasting the *Life of Gregory* with the *Historia* and *Life of Cuthbert*, Hollis details Bede's promotion of a hierarchical church led by a spiritual elite of bishops and priests, the model which later succeeded and ultimately cut the double monastery out of the picture. The Whitby *Life of Gregory*, Hollis suggests, presents a counter-polemic to Bede's campaign for the sacerdotal office. The Whitby *Life* puts personal sanctity, especially humility, above miracles and exterior manifestations of holiness in its representation of the monastic ideal, in deliberate opposition to, Hollis says, the developing hierarchical concept based on the power and authority inherent in the priesthood.[26]

Hollis sees the polemics of the Whitby *Life* and Bede's *Life of Cuthbert* and *Historia* as part of a negotiation of the image of women ongoing in the eighth century. The promotion of the sacerdotal ideal was worked upon by and contributed to the larger agenda of christianization which included the transformation of the native gender construct, a construct based on the comitatus relationship but lacking a conception of the female as erotic tempter. Powerful royal monastic females fortified by their blood kinship ties as opposed to marriage bonds presented a double challenge to bishops who believed themselves to be the rightful controllers of monasteries and advisers of kings. The more egalitarian concept of sanctity prevailing in double monasteries was itself opposed to the sacerdotal model and could expose the hierarchical model's inherent paradox as an ideal for a Christian monastery.[27] In addition, eighth-century Anglo-Saxon abbesses, through kinship, participated in the royal system of control over monasteries. Hollis compares their power and overlordship with that of the queen, in Anglo-Saxon society a co-ruler.[28] Evidence also exists, for example, in Theodore's *Penitential* to suggest that abbesses had considerable pastoral responsibilities and that women in the early Anglo-Saxon church performed some sacerdotal duties in administering mass. On the other hand, the Church depended on the help of royal monastic women in the conversion of England and in its ministry.[29]

The competition aristocratic abbesses presented to bishops could be reduced without, however, losing the war against paganism. One method of doing this was by promotion of the sacerdotal ideal but modulating its authority with the image of Christ's humility. Moreover, in a process requiring centuries, the Anglo-Saxon gender construct would be transformed, heightening awareness of female sexuality, so that women became represented as profane temptresses. The Eve image, a polemical typology based on the aristocratic female ideal and inversions of the ideal, created a recognizable image that negotiated female roles and representations. The conception of female difference excluded women from any priestly functions, making them unfit advisers or co-rulers. Also, the promotion of the sacerdotal ideal was accompanied by an emphasis on miracles as the most important evidence of sanctity, as seen in portrayals of conversion, healing, and ministry in Bede's *Life of St. Cuthbert* and Felix's *Life of St. Guthlac*.[30]

This reordering of social structure was both a result and part of a gradual process of bringing the Anglo-Saxon church with its local variation into a homogenized church centralized on the continent. The process included much compromise and accommodation of existing social and ecclesiastical forms in the early period, such as the temporary, incomplete acceptance of the power of aristocratic females. Because the process focused on control of religious communities, the monastery became the site for the development of the cultural construct of women.[31]

Perhaps the Ruthwell sculpted images can be placed within this context. The visual parallel of the pairs of figures Martha and Mary and Paul and Anthony suggests that the two panels equally represent this monastic ideal in male and female. However, an egalitarian representation is difficult to support with the surviving fragments, because this depiction of Paul and Anthony also represents a sacerdotal image.[32] The pair are finishing off a contest of humility in which the two ascetics try to decide which is worthy to break a loaf of bread miraculously brought by a bird to their isolated habitation. They settle the matter by agreeing to break it between them. Ó Carragáin[33] and Meyvaert[34] have related the iconic presentation of the upright figures to the *cofractio panis* eucharistic rite of the Iona church. Whether or not this liturgy, restricted in use to Iona, helped shape Ruthwell's depiction of Paul and Anthony, the sculpted image probably presents the monastic ideal as sacerdotal, male, and based on humility and miracles. On the other hand, the female figures, although triumphant at the top of the shaft, suggest neither sacerdotal associations nor the miraculous.

A third pair of figures relates visually to the monastic pairs. The panel depicting Christ healing the man born blind presents a dramatic miracle, especially on a monument which teaches and inspires through sight and evokes a compelling devotional vision through its crucifixion poem. The relief scene probably nonetheless created many levels of meaning when contemplated in the context of the rest of the cross's imagery and its early medieval environment, but it states in relation to Ruthwell's monastic imagery a primacy of miracles in the ideal of sanctity. In Anglo-Saxon monastic hagiography, miracles are performed nearly always by male saints. Their assertion as a determinant of sanctity seems to have attended the promotion of the sacerdotal hierarchy.

The image of the penitent woman is one of the most striking of the cross's program and so may seem to represent a statement of the authority and prominence of women in Anglo-Saxon monasticism. But instead it may be seen as representing a modification of the monastic ideal to create a feminine category which coopts the values of personal sanctity and humility expressed in the Whitby *Gregory* while separating this feminine ideal from the sacerdotal. The image of Mary Magdalene touching the body of Christ potentially elevates her to the status of priest, who handles the Eucharist. However, in the Ruthwell image her massive hair obliterates any indication of actually touching the body, while pose, inscription, and iconic presentation of the figure of Christ emphasize humility and devotion on a personal level. Instead of representing a sacerdotal type, the figure of the penitent Magdalene on one level elaborates the ideal of humility by merging it with a familiar and concrete image of personal devotion.

Mary Magdalene, anointing Christ's feet presents the prototype of the figure of penitent sinner. Undoubtedly this type of image acted upon and was formed by a wide range of practices and participants in spirituality and personal devotion without regard to gender.[35] Nonetheless, Goscelin describes a specifically feminine, albeit later Anglo-Saxon, penitent image embroidered on an alb by St. Edith of Wilton. The saint depicted herself "in the role of the suppliant Mary kissing the feet of the Lord," as he sat in the midst of the twelve standing apostles.[36] Edith's self-identification with Mary, placing herself at the feet of Christ, parallels the depiction of tangible involvement of a patron or owner in the scene of supplication, showing a woman clinging to the bottom of the cross, in the frontispiece of the Weingarten Gospels.[37] The individual, mental self-involvement in the scene of penance, which this type of image based upon the suppliant encourages, may have been the main reason for its later use as a frontispiece image in privately owned manuscripts and perhaps in the eighth century on a public monument (Ruthwell) addressed to a broad audience, probably including monks, clergy, and laity[38] and likely also to have included females, among these nuns or abbesses holding high social status. Such an introductory image leads the viewer into a personal involvement with the object of study or devotion.[39] Suppliant images are known from at least three other fragments of Anglo-Saxon sculpture.[40] Two of the fragments, at Otley and Dewsbury, present damaged figures of tonsured monks as suppliants before standing figures. Possibly images of monks rather than Mary Magdalene were carved on these crosses because they were made for a masculine monastic audience or because they were produced under monastic male patronage. Perhaps the same reasoning may hold true for Ruthwell: the image may have encouraged the personal devotions of an audience which at least included females, whose devotions were further directed or amplified by the other sculpted figures and the inscriptions. The instigation of viewer self-identification with the monument's imagery is further reinforced by the first person "voice" of the cross heard in the Ruthwell crucifixion poem. However, even though monastic women clearly were powerful and important enough[41] to determine an important aspect of the imagery of a large-scale monument, a specific identification of patronage or audience as feminine remains speculation unless more can be learned of the eighth-century context at Ruthwell through archaeological excavation.

In the general context of Christianization during the eighth century, however, the Ruthwell figure of the penitent Magdalene can be understood as an image participating in the negotiation of the concept of women. The characterization of Mary Magdalene as *meretrix/merita* resembles the feminine types currently being drawn out of Anglo-Saxon literature, such as the typology set out by Jane Chance.[42] In Anglo-Saxon literature, women heroes or leaders are depicted along the lines of Germanic *comitatus* imagery, expressing the bond between lord and retainer in which the valiant and faithful are rewarded with treasure.[43] However, this image of the female hero can be either positive or negative because a Christian moral contrast, the "Eva/Ave,"[44] is applied to it in literature. In a positive sense, the female hero is the *miles*, the chaste warrior of God; in a negative sense, she is the "heathen, lascivious, [or] rebellious" woman. In these characterizations of women, chastity and piety are the keys to the exercise of political power (for example, the abbesses) and heroic action (Judith). Chance finds the explanation for this opposition of types in patristic and theological sources in which the chaste woman takes on the rationality ordinarily viewed as proper to males, while the lascivious woman fits the same chaotic mold as Eve and the devil, shaped by "female concupiscence."[45]

On the Ruthwell cross, however, visual representation of ideal and inversion differs from these literary examples. The cross's penitent Mary Magdalene, instead of simply inverting the roles, converts from one to the other, the *meretrix*/Eve becomes *merita*/Virgin. This dynamic inversion in which both positive and negative are represented in one figure, and moreover with positive reaffirmed in the image of the "worthy ladies," perhaps functions effectively in a visual presentation of the feminine ideal because it overcomes the temporal and narrative limitations of visual images. It makes a positive statement about the piety and power of female monastics, but at the same time it removes the indigenous power of the female aristocrat by spiritual subordination and subverts the native ideal with its implicit reference to *meretrix*/Eve. The power and strength imparted visually by the massive forms and swelling curves of the figure of Mary Magdalene on the Ruthwell cross depict a figure powerful in its dynamic qualities, and such a feminine ideal would make great sense in a monastic context in which women were not only present but high-ranking, but this is an ideal formed within the process of Christianization.

Mary Magdalene may indeed have had a special appropriateness for a feminine audience: the humble and pure may attain rationality and the highest reward. Perhaps it is this characterization of the feminine ideal which led, in the ninth century, to the success of the legend of Mary of Egypt, also known as Mary Magdalene, who attained perfect spiritual rationality on her own as a desert hermit. In a broader sense, the depiction of the penitent Mary Magdalene negotiates the feminine ideal: the powerful and triumphant are chaste and humble. It presents an ideal of sanctity based on personal devotion rather than sacerdotal office. The transformation of the *meretrix*, Eve-temptress into a Marian type is given positive typological reinforcement above and below on the shaft, with the triumphant *merentes dominae* above and the scene of the Annunciation below.

Furthermore, the visual and verbal imagery of Christian triumph, like the images and texts of the Visitation and suppliants, may have provided a basis for creation and audience reception of Ruthwell's depictions of the penitent Magdalene and Martha and Mary in connection with chastity, as well as humility. Aldhelm's *De Virginitate*, presents dozens of images of martyrs, especially virgin martyrs, who became *merentes*, bedecked with the crown and wreaths of martyrdom as they ascend under the standards, the vexilla, of Christ and sainthood, to the starry court of the heavens, ruled by the Thunderer. "By means of their chastity, they are worthy of the kingdom of Christ."[46]

Aldhelm's verses use the triumphal imagery occurring in visual form in late Roman imperial art and post-Constantinian Christian art. For example, the consular diptychs of Flavius Anastasius, dated first quarter of the sixth century, depict suppliant figures holding *vexilla*.[47] This Roman triumphal visual language appears sometimes on Germanic objects, as, for example, the helmet visor of Agilulf, the Lombard potentate, which may have served as a gift of reward from ruler to retainer.[48] In these visual images, the standard bearers face each other in profile or oblique view, creating a pattern resembling that of the pair of women carved on top of the shaft of the Ruthwell cross. The depiction of the *merentes domini* and the penitent woman may have, to the eighth-century viewer, resonated with texts and images of the triumph of humility and chastity, virtues prominent in the monastic ideal, but made on this stone cross especially relevant to female monastics and the concept of women in general.

While undoubtedly Ruthwell's complex program expresses many levels of meaning, within the richness of its significance women are presented in ways that play upon the indigenous construct but at the same time modify it to promote orthodox monastic ideals. However, many questions remain unanswered about the reasons for the existence of such a visual expression of the sacerdotal agenda at Ruthwell. If transformation of the cultural idea of women was essential to Christianization and monumental sculpture was a suitable site for the idea's negotiation, why are there so few images of women on pre-Viking Anglo-Saxon sculpted crosses? Several possible answers and speculations come to mind, such as the loss of most early sculpture and the possibility of substitution of public monuments for preachers and teachers in the frontier see of Whithorn during the brain drain of the eighth-century missions to the continent. Nonetheless, the images of women on the Ruthwell cross seem to acknowledge the presence and power of female aristocrats, to include them as a part of the monastic and Christian ideal, but their representation on the cross belongs to the early period of a long process of their subordination.

NOTES

I wish to thank the Humanities Center of the University of Alabama in Huntsville for funding travel to the 26th and 28th International Congress of Medieval Studies at which earlier versions of this paper were presented.

1. The tables in the first three volumes of the *Corpus of Anglo-Saxon Stone Sculpture* indicate only four possible examples which *may* predate the mid-ninth century: Auckland St. Andrew 1, Rothbury 1 (R. Cramp, *Corpus of Anglo-Saxon Stone Sculpture in England*, vol. I, *County Durham and Northumberland*, Part 1 [Oxford: Oxford University Press, 1984], 255, 286); Urswick 1C (R. Bailey and R. Cramp, *Corpus*, vol. II, *Cumberland, Westmoreland and Lancashire North of the Sands* [Oxford: Oxford University Press, 1988], 184); and Hovingham 5 (J. Lang, *Corpus*, vol. III, *York and Eastern Yorkshire* [Oxford: Oxford University Press, 1991], 240).

2. D. R. Howlett, "Two Panels on the Ruthwell Cross," *J.W.C.I.* 37 (1974): 334; D. R. Howlett, "Inscriptions and Design of the Ruthwell cross," in B. Cassidy, ed., *The Ruthwell Cross*, Index of Christian Art Occasional Papers I (Princeton: Index of Christian Art, Department of Art and Archaeology, 1992), 73; R. I. Page, *An Introduction to English Runes* (London: Methuen, 1973), 149–50.

3. J. B. Holloway, "Crosses and Boxes: Latin and Vernacular," in J. B. Holloway, C. S. Wright, and J. Bechtold, eds., *Equally in God's Image: Women in the Middle Ages* (New York: P. Lang, 1990), 68–69, gives a brief discussion within a broader study. See also M. Schapiro, "The Religious Meaning of the Ruthwell Cross," *The Art Bulletin* 26 (1944): 232–45, reprint in *Late Antique, Early Christian, and Medieval Art* (New York: Braziller, 1979), 151–76, 186–92.

4. Ibid., 164

5. Ibid., 163–64.

6. As shown, for example, for later medieval culture by C. Walker Bynum, *Holy Feast and Holy Fast: the Religious Significance of Food to Medieval Women* (Berkeley: University of California Press, 1987).

7. É. Ó Carragáin has written at length on this aspect in several articles, including "Christ Over the Beasts and the Angus Dei: Two Multivalent Panels on the Ruthwell and Bewcastle Crosses," in P. E. Szarmach and V. D. Oggins, eds., *Sources of Anglo-Saxon Culture*, Studies in Medieval Culture 20 (Kalamazoo, Mich.: Medieval Institute, 1986), 377–403; "Liturgical Innovations Associated with Pope Sergius and the Iconography of the Ruthwell and Bewcastle Crosses," in R. Farrell, ed., *Bede and Anglo-Saxon England*, B.A.R. 46 (Oxford: British Archaeological Reports, 1978), 131–47; "The Ruthwell Crucifixion Poem in Its Iconographic and

Liturgical Contexts," *Peritia* 6–7 (1987–88): 1–71; "Seeing, Reading, Singing the Ruthwell Cross: Vernacular Poetry, Old Roman Liturgy, Implied Audience," in *Art and Symbolism*, Medieval Europe 1992 Preprinted Papers (York: Unpublished, 1992), 91–96. See also K. E. Haney, "The Christ and the Beasts Panel on the Ruthwell Cross," *A.S.E.* 14 (1985): 215–31; S. McEntire, "The Devotional Context of the Cross Before A.D. 1000," in Szarmach and Oggins, *Sources of Anglo-Saxon Culture*, 345–56.

8. See H. Damico and A. Hennessey Olsen, eds., *New Readings on Women in Old English Literature* (Bloomington: Indiana University Press, 1990); C. Fell, *Women in Anglo-Saxon England and the Impact of 1066* (Bloomington: Indiana University Press, 1984); J. Chance, *Woman as Hero in Old English Literature* (Syracuse, N.Y.: Syracuse University Press, 1986); S. Hollis, *Anglo-Saxon Women and the Church: Sharing a Common Fate* (Woodbridge, Suffolk and Rochester, N.Y.: Boydell Press, 1992). Much of the following is based on these studies.

9. On the dating of Ruthwell see R. Cramp, "The Bewcastle Cross and its Context," in Bailey and Cramp, *Corpus* vol. 2, 20–22, and D. Mac Lean, "The Date of the Ruthwell Cross," in Cassidy, *Ruthwell Cross*, 49–70.

10. E. Cowie, "Woman as Sign," *M/F* 1 (1978), cited in G. Pollock, *Vision and Difference: Femininity, Feminism and the Histories of Art* (London: Routledge, 1988), 30–32. See also U. Eco, *A Theory of Semiotics* (Bloomington: Indiana University Press, 1979), 24–28.

11. Howlett, "Inscriptions," 73–74; Howlett, "Two Panels," 334; Page, *Introduction*, 149–50.

12. É. Ó Carragáin, "Ruthwell Crucifixion Poem," 39–40; É. Ó Carragáin, "Seeing, Reading, Singing," 92–94; Haney, "Christ and the Beasts Panel," 228; R. Farrell, "Reflections on the Iconography of the Ruthwell and Bewcastle Crosses," in Szarmach and Oggins, *Sources of Anglo-Saxon Culture*, 365–68.

13. Luke 1:46–55.

14. Bede, *In Lucae Evangelium Expositio* III, 28–42, C.C.S.L. 120, 166–67.

15. *In Lucae* X, 38, C.C.S.L. 120, 225, cited in Howlett, "Two Panels," 334, and Howlett, "Inscriptions," 80–81.

16. Haney, "Christ and the Beasts Panel," 222–26; É. Ó Carragáin, "Meeting of Saint Paul and Saint Anthony: Visual and Literary Uses of a Eucharistic Motif," in G. Mac Niocaill and P, Wallace, eds., *Keimelia: Studies in Medieval Archaeology and History in Memory of Tom Delaney* (Galway, Ireland: Galway University Press, 1988), 1–80 at 11–12, 41–44; P. Meyvaert, "A New Perspective on the Ruthwell Cross: Ecclesia and Vita Monastica," in Cassidy, *Ruthwell Cross*, 131–35. Also, their mention as monastic types as in the prayer *Ateoch frit*, attributed to Colgan Ua Duinechdha (end of the eighth century), cited by J. Hennig, "Die Chöre der Heiligen," *Archiv für Liturgiewissenschaft* 8 (1963), 454.

17. See also R. Deshman's discussion of Visitation iconography in papal images of the seventh to ninth century in "Servants of the Mother of God in

Byzantine and Medieval Art," *Word and Image* 5 (1989): 44–46. The Ruthwell depiction of Martha and Mary presents a general resemblance to the Visitation images in figures 3, 4, 5, 11 of Deshman's article.

18. Luke 1:46–48: Magnificat anima mea dominum: et exsultavit spiritus meus in deo salutari meo. Quia respexit humilitatem ancillae suae: ecce enim ex hoc beatam me dicent omnes generationes.

19. Bede, *In Lucae* I, 48, 720–23, C.C.S.L. 120, 37; "Decebat enim ut sicut per superbiam primae nostrae parentis mors in mundum intravit ita denuo per humilitatem Mariae vitae introitus panderetur." (Truly it was fitting that just as death entered the world through the pride of our first parent so the entrance of life was unfolded anew through the humility of Mary.)

20. Jerome, *Tractatus in Marci Evangelium* X, 92–95, C.C.S.L. 78, 498–99, on Mark 14:3: "Illa enim, quasi meretrix et peccatrix, adhuc pedes tenet: ista, quasi sancta, caput tenet. Illa, quasi meretrix, lacrimis suis pedes rigat salvatoris et crinibus tergit: videtur quidem pedes lavare lacrimis Salvatori, sed magis lavat peccata sua." (The first woman indeed, as if a prostitute and sinner, holds his feet: this woman, as if a holy woman, holds his head. The former, as if a prostitute, moistens the feet of the Savior with her tears and wipes them with her hair: she seems indeed to wash the feet of the Savior with her tears, but in a higher degree she washes her sins.)

21. Bede, *In Lucae* III, 24–28, C.C.S.L. 120, 166, on Luke 7:38: "Quidam dicunt hanc eandem non esse mulierem quae imminente dominica passione caput pedesque eius unguento perfudit quia haec lacrimis laverit et crine pedes terserit et manifeste peccatrix appellatur de illa autem nihil tale scriptum sit nec potuerit statim capite domini meretrix digna fieri." (Many say that this was not the same woman who on the sabbath before the Passion poured oil on his head and feet because this one washed his feet with her tears and dried them with her hair and clearly is called a sinner. However, no such thing has been written about that former one nor may a prostitute be considered worthy to stand at the head of the Lord.)

22. C. T. Lewis and C. Short, *A Latin Dictionary* (rev. ed.), s.v. meretrix.

23. See discussion below of Aldhelm's *De virginitate*.

24. Bede, *In Lucae*, III, 28–52, C.C.S.L. 120, 166–67, on Luke 7:38: "Verum qui diligentius investigant inveniunt eandem mulierem Mariam videlicet Magdalenam sororem Lazari sicut Iohannes narrat bis eodem functam fuisse obsequio semel quidem hoc loco cum primo accedens cum humilitate et lacrimis remissionem meruit peccatorum. . . . Secundo autem in Bethania, nam prius in Galilea factum est, non iam peccatrix sed casta sancta devotaque Christo mulier non solum pedes sed et caput eius unxisse repperitur. Quod et regulis allegoriae pulcherrime congruit quia et unaquaeque fidelis anima prius ad domini pedes humiliata peccatisque absoluenda curuatur dein augescentibus per tempora meritis laetae fidei flagrantia domini quasi caput odore perfundit aromatum et ipsa universalis ecclesia Christi in praesenti quidem incarnationis eius quae pedum nomine designatur mysteria

celebrando devota redemptori suo reddit obsequia in futuro autem et humanitatis gloriam et divinitatis eius aeternitatem quia caput Christi deus *simul intuendo perpetuis confessionum laudibus quasi pistica nardo glorificat.*" (Indeed, those who have looked into this carefully find that same woman to be Mary [who came to be known as Magdalen the sister of Lazarus, just as John tells of the woman who performed the same obedient act a single time] was indeed at that place when first approaching with humility and tears she merited forgiveness of her sins. . . . The second however was in Bethania, the first in Galilee, but now it is learned that not a sinner but a holy and devout chaste woman in Christ anointed not only his feet but also his head. Which agrees beautifully with the rules of allegory, for each individual faithful soul must first humbly prostrate itself at the feet of the Lord and obtain forgiveness of sins, then, as with time, [the soul's] merits increase, through the ardor of a joyful faith, [the soul] bathes the Lord's head with the fragrance of sweet spices. And the universal church of Christ, which here below celebrates the mystery of his incarnation, designated by his feet, hereafter will contemplate together both the glory of his humanity and the eternity of his divinity—for "the head of Christ is God" [1 Cor. 11.3]—glorifying him with genuine spikenard through the utterance of unending praise.) Parts of the above translation are given by D. Howlett, "Inscriptions," 80, and P. Meyvaert, "A New Perspective," 111.

25. *Anglo-Saxon Women and the Church,* 121–23, 125–30.

26. Ibid., 94–96, 104–5, 113, 125–57.

27. Ibid., passim, esp. 33–45, 50–53, 93–111, 126–27.

28. Ibid., 116–19, 156–63. The Benedictine rule, its influence particularly evident in Bede's representations of monastics and clergy, also sought an egalitarian ideal, but in terms different from those Hollis sees in the Whitby *Gregory* and accomplished through the negation of kinship ties. See H. Mayr-Harting, *The Venerable Bede, the Rule of St. Benedict, and Social Class* (Jarrow: Rector of Jarrow, 1976), especially 15–18; and R. N. Bailey, "The Cultural and Social Setting," in B. Ford, ed., *Prehistoric, Roman and Early Medieval,* vol I, *The Cambridge Guide to the Arts in Britain* (Cambridge: Cambridge University Press 1988), 111–13, as well as Hollis's discussion of egalitarian aspects residing alongside hierarchical ideals of Christianity, 113–14, 130.

29. Hollis, *Anglo-Saxon Women and the Church,* 67–74, 94–95, 135–37.

30. Ibid., 119–29, 156–58, 173–75.

31. Ibid., 46–74, 103–4.

32. See also É. Ó Carragáin, "The Meeting of Saint Paul and Saint Anthony," 40–42.

33. Ibid.

34. "A New Perspective," 131–35 and his discussion of the points brought out earlier by É. Ó Carragáin, "Meeting of Saint Paul and Saint Anthony."

35. For example, the figure of Dunstan depicted as a suppliant at the feet of Christ (Oxford, Bodl. Lib., MS Auct. F. iv, f. 32), illustrated in C. R. Dodwell, *Anglo-Saxon Art a New Perspective* (Manchester, England: Manchester University Press, 1982), pl. 8; and the figures appearing to represent monks on the more contemporary sculpted fragments from Otley and Dewsbury, discussed below.

36. Dodwell, *Anglo-Saxon Art*, pp. 57–58, who cites Goscelin, *La légende de Ste. Edith en prose et verse par le moine Goscelin*, ed. A. Wilmart, *Analecta Bollandiana* 56 (1938): 4–101, 265–307, and O. Lehmann-Brockhaus, *Lateinische Schriftquellen zur Kunst in England Wales und Schottland vom Jahre 901 bis zum Jahre 1307*, 5 vols., Munich 1955–60, 6448. See also William of Malmesbury, *De gestis pontificum anglorum* II, 87, ed. N. E. S. A. Hamilton (Wiesbaden: Kraus Reprint, 1964), reprint of London 1870, p. 189, on her exchange with Æthelwold over her luxurious clothing.

37. J. O'Reilly, "The Rough-Hewn Cross in Anglo-Saxon Art," in M. Ryan, ed., *Ireland and Insular Art A.D. 500–1200* (Dublin: Royal Irish Academy, 1987), 156–57.

38. T. Amos, "Monks and Pastoral Care in the Early Middle Ages," in T. Noble and J. Contreni, eds., *Religion, Culture, and Society in the Early Middle Ages: Studies in Honor of Richard E. Sullivan*, Studies in Medieval Culture 28 (Kalamazoo, Mich.: Medieval Institute, 1987), 165–80; H. Mayr-Harting, *The Coming of Christianity to Anglo-Saxon England* (University Park: Pennsylvania State University Press, 1991), 240–61.

39. An involvement played upon by Bede in his homily on John 11.55–12.11 (Mary Magdalene anointing Christ's feet), using a typological interpretation of the concrete image to vividly incite listeners to perform acts of charitable devotion, so that they will become suppliants anointing and wiping the head and feet of Christ (Hom. 2.4, C.C.S.L. 122, 210–11, lines 107–32, as pointed out by L. Martin, "The Two Worlds in Bede's Homilies: the Biblical Event and the Listener's Experience," in T. Amos, ed., *De Ore Domini: Preacher and Word in the Middle Ages*, Studies in Medieval Culture 27 (Kalamazoo, Mich.: Medieval Institute, 1989), 33. See also É. Ó Carragáin, "The Ruthwell Cross and Irish High Crosses: Some Points of Comparison and Contrast," in Ryan, *Ireland and Insular Art*, 122.

40. Cross 1, Otley—cross-arm (top) fragment; Dewsbury—fragment; Halton; see R. Cramp, "The Position of the Otley Crosses in English Sculpture of the Eighth to Ninth Centuries," in V. Milojcic, ed., *Kolloquium über spätantike und frühmittelalterliche Skulptur* 2 (Mainz am Rhein: P.v. Zabern, 1971), 58–59, Taf. 44,3; 46,4; 48,2.3.

41. See, for example, C. Fell's discussion of the "Letters of Lull," in "Some Implications of the Boniface Correspondence," in Damico and Olsen, *New Readings*, 29–43 at, 32–37.

42. Chance, *Woman as Hero*.

43. Ibid., xiv–xv, 1–10.

44. Hollis, *Anglo-Saxon Women and the Church*, 5–11, however, objects to Chance's projection of a particular type of Eva/Ave construction onto Anglo-Saxon literary types, because the full, conventional inversion came to fruition only in a later period.

45. Chance, *Woman as Hero*, pp. xiv–xv, and passim, pp. 10–64.

46. *De Virginitate Carmen*, lines 2814–2815, p. 467. In *Aldhelmi Opera*, ed. R. Ehwald, *Monumenta germaniae historica scriptores*, ser. 1, XV (Berlin: Weidmann, 1961, reprint of Berlin 1919), 350–471, translated by J. L. Rosier in *Aldhelm the Poetic Works*, trans. M. Lapidge and J. L. Rosier (Cambridge: Cambridge University Press, 1985), 165: "Integritate sua quae Christi regna merentur/Limpida stelligeri scandentes culmina caeli . . ." ("[the Lord's servants] who merit the kingdom of Christ by their chastity and ascend to the radiant heights of starry heaven").

47. W. Volbach, *Elfenbeinarbeiten der Spätantike und des frühen Mittelalters* (Mainz am Rhein, Von Zabern, 1976), 36–37, and Tafeln 8.18 (London: Victoria and Albert), 8.19 (St. Petersburg: Hermitage), 9.20 (Verona: Chapter Library), 9.21 (Paris: Bibliothèque nationale).

48. M. McCormick, *Eternal Victory: Triumphal Rulership in Late Antiquity, Byzantium, and the Early Medieval West* (Cambridge: Cambridge University Press 1986), 289–93, and figure 12.

CHAPTER FOUR

James Lang

SURVIVAL AND REVIVAL IN INSULAR ART

Some Principles

There is something of a pun in the term "Insular art." Taken literally, it is the native decorative art of the western fringe of early medieval Europe, and therefore the product of the islands which now comprise the nations of Ireland and greater Britain. But it is also "Insular" by nature, being turned in upon itself, blinkered against the artistic developments and inherited traditions of the wider Europe. This trait ran deep in the church which patronized the art which we in our generation have labelled Insular, and in Northumbria at least the conflict between the island and the continent was quick to surface. The language of the broader European view, as it is to some even in today's political context, was sometimes condescending in its sureness of an authority rooted historically and theologically in Rome. On the wild headland at Whitby in 664 the synod convened by King Oswy to determine the direction to be taken by the English church heard Wilfrid speak from high ground:

> . . . in these two remote islands of the world, and only in part even of them, (you) oppose all the rest of the universe.[1]

The triumph of the Roman faction over the Celtic tradition brought in its wake the art of the new authority with a Mediterranean hallmark,[2] with new

63

foci well away from the coastal monastic establishments of the Celtic
church. In the aftermath of that mighty shift to Europe, the defeated Colman
retreated westwards via Iona to Inishboffin, significantly turning to the
contemplation of the setting sun. Like him, Insular artists turned their backs
on a Europe rooted, like its very church, in classical antiquity. That pedigree
validated the church's authority throughout Christendom and it is no
surprise that in the establishment within Northumbria of a centralized
episcopal system, the art of the church's Roman roots should be employed
as its monumental expression.

When we recall that virtually all manuscript and sculptural art in the
Insular world, and a fair proportion of the metalwork, enjoyed ecclesiastical
patronage, it would seem reasonable to assume that the tune would be
called by the weightiest propagandist: in Wilfrid's case, blatantly so.

> . . . though your fathers were holy, do you think that their
> small number, in a corner of the remotest island, is to be
> preferred before the universal church of Christ through-
> out the world?[3]

This is the man who, consecrated in proper European manner in Gaul, was
to build the massive foreign churches at Hexham and Ripon.[4] The sub-
classical motifs found on stone carving at places like Otley,[5] such as vine-
scroll and three-dimensional portraiture, are a deliberate gear-change in
early Northumbria; it would be rash to argue for continuity or evolution of
style, since the momentum is against the Insular which only continues to
exist as mere survival. As survival it is unlikely to develop and more suscep-
tible to fossilize. For the sculptors of stone monuments in Northumbria
there was to be a constant dilemma as they shot the rapids of political and
ecclesiastical change over four hundred years: either to emulate Colman
turned in to the center of his island, where the center is always still, or to
reach eastwards to Europe for a different tradition, equally conservative but
more overtly eloquent. It was to be the choice of Stephen Dedalus centuries
later.

The evidence for survival of Insular motifs and methods of construction in the design is most thoroughly proven in the decorated wooden
objects retrieved from the excavations of Viking-age Dublin.[6] The chronology of many of the pieces bearing Insular ornament is determined very
precisely by their stratified contexts: that is to say, their dating is by objec-
tive archaeological method, including coin evidence, with deposition dates
(not necessarily dates of manufacture) in the mid- to late-tenth century.
What emerged from the study of this material was the perseverance of
Insular decoration throughout the tenth and early eleventh centuries, at

grass roots level, for these are ordinary artefacts rather than objets d'art. The survival is apparent either in a pure form preserving motifs current at a much earlier phase of Insular art, or as an amalgamation of elements from the native repertoire into imported Anglo-Scandinavian designs. However, what serves as a chronology for whittled sticks in downtown Dublin need not necessarily apply to high-status reliquaries in gold or to the work of a third scribe in the ornamentation of a gospel book. There is a difference of milieu, context, and even function.

An apposite image for the conservation of the Insular wood from Dublin would be the bagpipe drone accompanying the furtive melodies of changing imported styles which were fashionable for a day. That is one explanation of conservatism, or survival, working in terms of current taste. But there is another dimension to the insularity of Insular art. Survival may be stronger or weaker, not only depending upon location, social context, and ranking, but also due to the nature of the artefact which carries the decoration. A reliquary shrine, for example, will soon attract the status of the relic it contains by association, so that, while repair and addition in later styles occur, the original will be preserved and, what is more, remain visible. The "Soiscel Molaise" shrine displayed its eighth-, ninth- and eleventh-century features even when it was modified in the fifteenth.[7] The retention of the early decoration was in a sense part of the preservation of the relic itself. Hence, the criteria for assessing the chronology of styles for one kind of artefact may well be different from the next. Similarly, the rates of stylistic development, given that they might be evolutionary at all, may differ according to the class of object carrying the decoration. For example, the development of animal ornament in metalwork may not necessarily coincide with that of manuscript art.

Survival of Insular style may also be determined by the technique employed to create the object. Here, by way of exemplum, stone sculpture can serve as a model. The technique of cutting stone and shaping it into a monolithic or composite standing monument allows for little variation; indeed, the geology can often impose the tightest of restrictions. It is clear, for example, that on the Isle of Man it is far easier to cut a low relief slab from the laminated slates than a free-standing cross.[8] When the chronology of the styles of such a class of monument is being laid down, the caveat should remain admonitory. The same caution would apply to the late crosses at Kilfenora in Clare, where Insular features have become manifest in the twelfth century. Françoise Henry comments of one (pl. 4.1):

> . . . Kilfenora . . . remained slightly off the beaten track
> and the crosses which were fashioned out of a beautiful
> grey-golden limestone in these far-away monasteries

Pl. 4.1. Twelfth-century cross, Kilfenora, County Clare, Ireland. Photo by author.

retain an archaic and wild flavour which has no equivalent in other contemporary monasteries. The work of the sculptors was both fostered and conditioned by the existence of this excellent stone, which comes out in thin slabs. . . . It lends itself only to the fashioning of very thin monuments, generally decorated by engraved lines.[9]

A number of questions are implied here, despite the shrewd observation of the bedding of the local stone. Is the form and decoration of this cross at Kilfenora dictated by its location "off the beaten track" or by its geology? The first option begs the question of unity of style throughout a class of artefact in a particular country at a particular period. Regionalism or the idiosyncracies of local ateliers have not been taken into account. The geological determinant seems more acceptable, but what of the "archaic and wild flavour?" At this period does being in a backwater imply dragging one's heels in keeping abreast of Insular fashions, and what exactly is a backwater in the context of cultural centers like Iona and Lindisfarne? It is more prudent to doubt that formal interlace and frets on the Kilfenora cross are local fossils until an uninterrupted sequence of eighth- to eleventh-century examples can be established in County Clare.

The "engraved lines" noted by Françoise Henry are immaculately constructed. They lie upon an underlying grid in the manner of so many Insular patterns found in book decoration and stone sculpture throughout Britain and Ireland from the earliest period of the tradition. The frets and interlace have many parallels in eighth- and ninth-century pieces, such as the shaft from Penally in Pembrokeshire and the south cross at Castledermot in Kildare,[10] though their mode of construction first occurs in Hiberno-Saxon manuscripts such as the Lindisfarne and Durham Gospels. One could say that the Kilfenora formal patterns are "revival" while the grid method of laying them out is "survival." Gridding could easily have continued as a technique in a wide range of artistic expression, not necessarily confined to the stone sculpture of County Clare, but certainly in books and other portable artefacts. It has been demonstrated elsewhere that this design technique survived well into the Viking period across Ireland, the Isle of Man, and Northumbria.[11] However, an underlying grid does not impose the choice of archaic decorative motifs; any linear or angular pattern will be possible. The revival of "antique" ornament is for the most part conscious and deliberate rather than simple habit, and some motive or intention for such a choice must be sought.

The late high crosses of Ireland, it has been suggested, are very possibly royal and episcopal statements, as their inscriptions indicate.[12] The raising of a high cross in the twelfth century was most probably a considered act of archaism: an obsolete form of monument covered with an out-of-date formal ornament was a metaphor for its patron's title to political or ecclesiastical authority, symbolically rooted in the distant past. The crosses at Roscrea and Tuam are similar cases.[13] The great wheel-head, which adorns the Roscrea cross, and the symmetrically disposed ribbon animals with body extensions lapping their torsos each speak of a conscious reaching back to the geometry of earlier Insular habits. They are almost the stone equivalents of the later forged charters produced by monks anxious to assert their title to a distant estate. In the Church of Ireland cathedral in Tuam, a small fragment of such a late cross carries an inscription referring to Áed who was abbot from 1126, and archbishop in 1152. It goes on to describe him as "*comarba Jarlaithe*"—successor of St. Jarlath who actually founded the monastery at Tuam.[14] Revival can be the symptom of current politics.

Some caution should be exercised in placing reliance upon inscriptions. This is not to comment upon the difficulties of actually deciphering heavily worn script either from the stone itself or from plastic presses. Epitaphs or prayers could have been placed on the monuments within days of the decease, added at some later period, or even inscribed on a distant monument some miles from the grave. There is a distinction in funerary monuments between tombstones and cenotaphs. A case in point is the elaborate stone at Hackness, in North Yorkshire, a cell of Whitby.[15] It bears a puzzling array of inscriptions, some in runes and cryptic characters, though the most legible lines celebrate Oedilburga, identified as possibly one of two holy and well-loved women of the seventh century.[16] The ornament of the shaft, however, is characterized by its florid vine-scroll, affronted animals and portrait bust, which are diagnostic features of Yorkshire sculpture of about one hundred years later than the life that the stone commemorates (pl. 4.2). In both Ireland and England, the possibility should be entertained that the inscriptions may be retrospective; if so, then the firm attribution of a date to the style would be affected.

Sometimes the implications of dating a style can be too loose. The proposed date may refer to the time of manufacture of the artefact itself, the object which carries the stylistic or epigraphic clues. On the other hand, it may relate, more restrictedly, to the moment of the dedicatory inscription, and so merely date the epigraphy rather than the associated art. A provocative example of this predicament is Gautr's cross-slab at Kirk Michael in the Isle of Man (pl. 4.3). Its inscription *kaut + kirþi: þana:auk ala: imaun*— Gautr made this and all in Man[17]—contains a hanging demonstrative pronoun which as easily refers to the runes as the cross-slab itself. That not only begs the question of the contemporaneity of decoration and inscription, but also challenges the ethnic label one is tempted to apply to the ring-chain ornament: "Viking" or "Insular?"[18]

The dating of style is at its most circumspect when parameters of its currency are set. The decorated wood from Dublin, as we have seen, leads one to a healthy reluctance to pin too refined a date on a particular motif (witness DW 8 from a very late tenth-century deposition).[19] The result is that the time span of its currency can be so extensive as to be of little use as, say, a dating criterion for an isolated archaeological context in which it

Pl. 4.2. Anglo-Saxon shaft, Hackness, North Yorkshire, England. Photograph by permission of T. Middlemass and R. Cramp.

appeared. It is more profitable to look within those parameters for cultural reasons for the presence of Insular characteristics; that is, perhaps it is only half the story to attribute a date based on the recognition of a named abbot in an inscription at a known time in a known place. The politics and the

Pl. 4.3. Cross-slab, Kirk Michael, Isle of Man. Photograph courtesy of R. Trench-Jellicoe.

flavor of Christian thinking, which fed the mind of the patron, often may explain the survival or revival of the Insular repertoire. In a sense, this is art as propaganda, or it may simply be a need to establish continuity as a concept of the organization of the church at that time and in that place through the medium of monumental art. One has only to correlate the revival of Gothic architecture and the Oxford Movement in the nineteenth century in England, or the *floruit* of the Hibernian Revival in Dublin street decorations at the turn of the last century and Irish nationalist aspirations to appreciate the point.[20]

Returning to the model of Northumbrian sculpture in the pre-Conquest era, it is possible to distinguish a pendulum of taste swinging between a yearning for classically derived, European modes and motifs on one hand, and for the Insular tradition on the other. To regard this movement only in terms of changes of fashion is to apply twentieth-century perceptions, induced by the marketplace and arbiters of taste, to an early medieval mentality of quite a different mould. The Mediterranean contributions to the design of the carvings are most clearly discerned at two peaks in the pre-Viking period. The first is the Wilfridian age, when a forceful policy of implementing orthodoxy through European media was pursued. This is well documented in Bede and in Eddius' *Life of Wilfrid*[21] and must be viewed in the light of the Synod of Whitby and attempts to elevate York's bishopric to metropolitan status for the northern province of the English church. The second occurs at the end of the eighth century and the beginning of the ninth when southern Northumbria's links with the continent were enhanced by the presence of Alcuin, the York scholar, in the royal schools of Charlemagne in Aachen and Tours.[22] The latter period was one where centralism of secular government was in the air in Europe: Charlemagne in the Empire, Offa in Mercia, both issuing coins bearing their images in a manner reminiscent of Roman imperialism. Monuments like the Easby cross[23] were raised not to engender piety and compassion, but to make statements of ecclesiastical authority rooted in the Late Antique past. I have shown elsewhere that direct copying of late Roman funerary sculpture was undertaken at Otley with this end in view.[24]

Conversely, the initial conversion of Northumbria to Christianity by Paulinus having misfired at half-cock, and James the Deacon left with a faithful remnant at Catterick, the field was open to Insular artists in the late-seventh century. The Ionan success in establishing Lindisfarne and its related monasteries is reflected, albeit briefly, in sculpture which closely echoes the Hiberno-Saxon decoration of the books being produced by Insular artists, on their islands. The cross-fragment Lindisfarne 1 is dated by Rosemary Cramp to the end of the eighth or the beginning of the ninth century, though its manuscript sources are clearly much earlier.[25] Local copying at one level, such a reflex is probably an expression of the perpetuation of a tradition closely associated with their own saint, St. Cuthbert. Yet another hundred years on, in southern Northumbria and Cumbria, Hiberno-Norse settlement from the west became the vehicle for the reintroduction of the Insular repertoire into new stone monuments, erected by secular patrons for the most part. The settlers were already Christian, no doubt due to their colonial contacts in Ireland immediately before their incursion into Northern England. Their crosses carry the formal frets, symmetrical ribbon animals and on occasion iconography of the continuing Insular traditions of Ireland. The Allertonshire *atelier* in the northernmost part of Yorkshire is a telling example. A settler will metaphorically always try to preserve the umbilical cord, not immediately identifying with the culture into which he has recently arrived. There are many modern illustrations of this phenomenon in our own migration period. As a result, the "survival" of motifs in Ireland became the "revival" of Insular art in tenth-century Yorkshire. Our judgments concerning similar patterns which occur on either side of the Irish Sea should take this into account, for comparing like with like, a well proven art-historical method, need not necessarily imply "like date for like date," or even a common evolutionary development.

This argument works against the notion of continuity of development in Insular art in Northern England. The story may well be different for distinct parts of Ireland, the Isle of Man, or Cornwall. Uninterrupted evolution is too tidy an arrangement. Much more likely is a series of creative spurts followed by barren troughs. This is borne out by Anglo-Scandinavian sculpture in Northumbria where statistically the tenth century produced five times as many stone monuments as the pre-Viking period, and the absence of late Viking styles suggests a very short span for their production, perhaps as little as thirty years.[26] Such peaking of activity in the sculpture workshops raises problems, not least how the principles of cutting stone and laying out designs were maintained. Perhaps this expertise, as far as the Norse-Irish carvers of Northumbria were concerned, was preserved not locally in Yorkshire or Cumbria, but across the water which was so often the thoroughfare of the supremacy of the York-Dublin kingdom.

Such a view recommends a tightly regional approach to the topic of Northumbrian sculpture. The recent identification of *ateliers* in Allertonshire, Ryedale, and Lower Wensleydale[27] tends to group the carvings in areas only about fifteen miles across, each workshop displaying its own idiosyncrasies. It is more difficult after such grouping then to place the monuments in linear chronological series. That exercise can be done more convincingly in other tightly defined areas, like Wharfedale to the west of York in the pre-Viking period, where local eclecticism offers clues to the sources of obviously borrowed motifs.[28] But here the discussion concerns a local school rather than a workshop; the means of identifying the diagnostic features is looser.

Sometimes the designs are pronouncedly local, restricted to a single site with not even the next village was tempted to copy. The tenth-century group at Stonegrave in North Yorkshire is an example,[29] standing out with complete distinctiveness from the Ryedale school pieces which surround it. Its fret patterns and iconography certainly point westwards, not necessarily all the way to Ireland. This may well represent "estate sculpture" rather than anything approaching a local style, and it is consequently impossible to accommodate either stylistically or chronologically even in the Yorkshire series.

Sometimes the regionalism, with its associated conservatism, is accounted for by the local political climate or the entrenched patterns of thinking on the part of the local church. The early-eleventh-century carvings at Durham represent this complexity.[30] The community of St. Cuthbert, newly established at the site, was dedicated to preserving the relics and memory of their saint and during the first half of the tenth century had on the southern border of their estates, just across the River Tees, an Anglo-Scandinavian kingdom centered politically on York. It was by no means a confrontation of Christian and pagan, but it was one between old-established estate-holder and strange-tongued incoming land-taker. The Scandinavian colonial soon set about raising stone crosses bearing images of himself in warlike pose and embellishing the shafts with animal ornament. It is very likely that, a generation later, the community would react against those expressions and that style, reverting to the conventions of Insular interlace whose origins lay in the culture belonging to the saint whom they had recently translated from Chester-le-Street to Durham. It was in the interests of the fresh foundation at Durham to assert the notion of continuity.

It is interesting to observe that the Cuthbert community also seemed to reject the styles current in southern England at the very end of the tenth century. A church newly reformed by the Regularis Concordia, working cheek by jowl with a monarchy that claimed England in its entirety, seized upon the Winchester Style which also managed to show off its European awareness. The vestments in that style bestowed upon St. Cuthbert by Æþelstan were quietly placed in the coffin and ignored as stimuli for adopting new artistic fashions.

Æþelstan, between 927 and 939, was king of northern England; twelve years out of that short Viking supremacy at York which provided the political context for much of the Anglo-Scandinavian sculpture of the region. Throughout that period an archbishop continued to exert influence, for one side or the other if we remember Wulfstan, issuing coins on occasion or retreating to estates in Wharfedale.[31] The English, as against the Scandinavian, contribution to the tenth-century sculpture styles of York has been given less consideration than it deserves. An example of very local survival from the Anglian series in Wharfedale to the Anglo-Scandinavian workshops of York must here suffice.

A few tenth-century crosses from York retain as the principal panel of their decoration a frontally disposed haloed head, the nimbus being characteristically dished or concave. The shaft York Minster 4 with this feature must be Anglo-Scandinavian on account of its accompanying animal ornament.[32] It also occurs on the Newgate shaft[33] from York which relies heavily upon the Nunburnholme monument.[34] There is every probability that the latter was produced in York, as its geology might indicate. It is no accident that the haloed heads of this period in Yorkshire are confined to the city of York itself. The church, whose metropolitan status had been achieved centuries before by Wilfrid and whose continental connections had been confirmed by Alcuin, remained alive and influential: this is the message of these portrait carvings. The adjacent river valleys of the Ouse and the Wharfe contained a whole series of Anglian crosses beginning with the eighth-century shafts at Otley and moving along the dale to Ilkley and Collingham, eventually to York itself. All these monuments carry portrait heads. The presence of the haloes in the later York carvings is, to my mind, a deliberate revival to restate the claims of the York church to power, and perhaps land.

The haloes also occur on the great cross at Leeds (pl. 4.4) where, surviving by the skin of its teeth, the Insular tradition shows in the locking of the hair with the nimbus, as it does in the Irish portrait of St. Luke in London, B.L., Add. MS.40, f. 618.[35] The next step in the study of revival and survival must be in the direction of overlaps like this, for it cannot be explained by regarding Wharfedale as a backwater when it is so close to the ecclesiastical and political center of the region. Rather like the Dublin wood, the late pre-Conquest stone carvings of northern England seem to retain the old as well as embrace the new. If there was any conflict between Insular and classical models it was ultimately one of vision: how far was one prepared to look for inspiration without unsettling roots? The sculptors must have felt like the characters at the end of *Portrait of the Artist*:

> Mulrennan has just returned from the west of Ireland. European and Asiatic papers please copy. He told us he met an old man there in a mountain cabin. Old man had red eyes and short pipe. Old man spoke Irish. Mulrennan spoke Irish. Then old man and Mulrennan spoke English. Mulrennan spoke to him about the universe and stars. Old man sat, listened, smoked, spat. Then said: —Ah, there must be terrible queer creatures at the latter end of the world.[36]

Pl. 4.4. Anglo-Saxon cross, Leeds Parish Church, Yorkshire. Photograph by permission of A. Wiper and R. Cramp.

NOTES

1. Bede, *Historia Ecclesiastica Gentis Anglorum,* ed. C. Plummer (Oxford: Typographeo Clarendoniano, 1896), III, 25.

2. J. Lang, "The Anglian Sculpture of Deira: The Classical Tradition," *Jarrow Lecture 1990* (Jarrow: St. Paul's Church, 1991).

3. Bede, *Historia,* III, 25.

4. H. M. and J. Taylor, *Anglo-Saxon Architecture* (Cambridge: Cambridge University Press, 1965), vol. I, 297–312; vol. II, 516–18.

5. J. Lang, "Survival and Revival in Insular Art: Northumbrian Sculpture of the 8th to 10th Centuries," in R. M. Spearman and J. Higgitt, eds., *The Age of Migrating Ideas: Early Medieval Art in Northern Britain and Ireland* (Edinburgh: National Museums of Scotland, 1993), 261–67.

6. J. Lang, *Viking Age Decorated Wood: a Study of its Ornament and Style,* Medieval Dublin Excavations 1962–81, Ser. B, vol. 1 (Dublin: Royal Irish Academy, 1988), 4–7, 44, 49–52.

7. J. Raftery, *Christian Art in Ancient Ireland,* vol. II (Dublin: Stationery Office of Saorstat Eireann, 1941), 119–21; R. Ó Floinn, in M. Ryan, ed., *Treasures of Ireland* (Dublin: Royal Irish Academy, 1983), 161–63.

8. P. M. C. Kermode, *Manx Crosses* (London: Bemrose & Sons, 1907); A. M. Cubbon, *The Art of the Manx Crosses* (Douglas: Manx Museum, 1971).

9. F. Henry, *Irish Art in the Romanesque Period (1020–1170 A.D.)* (London: Methuen, 1970), 134.

10. V. E. Nash-Williams, *The Early Christian Monuments of Wales* (Cardiff, Wales: University of Wales Press, 1950), 200–2; F. Henry, *Irish Art During the Viking Invasions 800–1020 A.D.* (London: Methuen, 1967), pl. 67.

11. J. Lang, "The Compilation of Design in Colonial Viking Sculpture," *Universitetets Oldsaksamlings Skrifter* nr. 5 (Oslo: Universitetets oldsaksamling, 1985), 125–37.

12. Henry, *Irish Art in the Romanesque Period,* 123–27.

13. Ibid., 124, 128.

14. Ibid., 124.

15. J. Lang, *Corpus of Anglo-Saxon Stone Sculpture,* vol. III, *York and Eastern Yorkshire* (Oxford and New York: Oxford University Press, 1991), 135–41.

16. W. G. Collingwood, *Northumbrian Crosses of the Pre-Norman Age* (London: Faber & Gwyer, 1927), 116; P. Grosjean, "Un fragment d'obituaire anglo-saxon du VIIIe siècle, naguère conservé á Munich, Appendix I; l'inscription latine de Hackness," *Analecta Bollandiana,* 79 (1961): 340–43.

17. R. I. Page, "The Manx Rune Stones," in C. Fell, *et al.*, eds., *The Viking Age in the Isle of Man* (London: Viking Society for Northern Research, 1983), 136.

18. J. Lang, "Fine Measurement Analysis of Viking Age Ornament," in G. Fellows-Jensen and N. Lund, eds., *Beretning fra Tredie tværfaglige vikingesymposium* (Hojbjerg, Denmark: Forlaget hikuin og Afdeling for middelalderarkaeologi, 1984), 47–50.

19. Lang, *Viking Age Decorated Wood*, 44.

20. This, of course, is not an exclusively Insular phenomenon but an expression of late Romanticism across much of Europe.

21. Bede, *Ecclesiastical History*; Eddius Stephanus, *The Life of Bishop Wilfrid*, ed. B. Colgrave (Cambridge: Cambridge University Press, 1927).

22. Lang, *The Anglian Sculpture of Deira*, 11–15; Lang, "Survival and Revival in Insular Art."

23. M. Longhurst, "The Easby Cross," *Archaeologia* 81 (1931): 43–47.

24. Lang, "Survival and Revival in Insular Art."

25. R. Cramp, *Corpus of Anglo-Saxon Stone Sculpture*, vol. I, *County Durham and Northumberland* (Oxford: Oxford University Press, 1984), 194–95, pls. 188, 1039; 189, 1040–43.

26. R. Bailey, *Viking Age Sculpture in Northern England* (London: Collins, 1980), 80; J. Lang, "Recent Studies in the pre-Conquest Sculpture of Northumbria," in F. H. Thompson, ed., *Studies in Medieval Sculpture*, Society of Antiquaries Occasional Paper (new series) iii (London: Society of Antiquaries, 1983), 186.

27. Ibid., 185.

28. Lang, "Survival and Revival in Insular Art."

29. M. Firby and J. Lang, "The pre-Conquest Sculpture at Stonegrave," *Yorkshire Archaeol. J.* 53 (1981): 17–29.

30. Cramp, *Corpus*, I, no. 11, 73.

31. A. P. Smyth, "The Chronology of Northumbrian History in the Ninth and Tenth Centuries," in R. A. Hall, ed., *Viking Age York and the North*, C.B.A. Research Report no. 27 (London: Council for British Archaeology, 1978), 8–10.

32. Lang, *Corpus* III, 56–57, ills. 20–23.

33. Ibid., 105–07, ills. 342–46.

34. Ibid., 189–93, ills. 709–28.

35. F. Henry, *Irish Art in the Early Christian Period to A.D. 800* (London: Methuen, 1965), pl. K; A. McGuire and A. Clark, *The Leeds Crosses* (Leeds: Museum of Leeds, 1987).

36. J. Joyce, *Portrait of the Artist as a Young Man* (1916), ch. 5.

CHAPTER FIVE

Douglas Mac Lean

King Oswald's
Wooden Cross at
Heavenfield in Context

later medieval art historian once remarked to me, speaking of Cluny, that she was suspicious of an art history based on lost monuments, a positivist approach the early medieval art historian cannot always afford, whatever may be true of archaeologists. In the case of the lost wooden cross King Oswald of Northumbria erected at Heavenfield in 634, the mere fact of its former existence raises larger issues and has greater importance than any intrinsic resonance its presumably unprepossessing appearance might still offer, had it been preserved in amber.

In 633 Edwin, the first Christian king of Northumbria, was overthrown by the pagan Penda of Mercia and the Christian Cadwallon of Gwynedd, the last leader of the Celtic Britons to briefly reverse the tide of Anglo-Saxon expansion in Britain. Edwin's death ended Deiran kingship over Northumbria and the dispossessed house of Bernicia came home in the persons of the sons of Æthelfrith, of whom the apostate Eanfrith was killed by Cadwallon, while Oswald and Oswiu remained true to the Christian faith they had acquired in exile.[1]

It was Oswald who avenged the Angles of Northumbria through the death of Cadwallon at the battle of Deniseburn in 634. According to Bede, on the eve of the battle, at a place called Heavenfield, Oswald ordered a wooden cross made, then placed it in the ground himself, calling upon his army, whom Bede describes as "strengthened by their faith in Christ" (*fide Christi munito*), to kneel and pray for victory to the "almighty, everliving and true God."[2] But Christianity only began to take hold in Northumbria following Edwin's conversion a few years earlier,[3] and any Anglo-Saxon army at this early date would still have included substantially pagan elements. Bede tells us that there was "no symbol of the Christian faith, no church and no altar" anywhere in Bernicia before Oswald set up his cross at Heavenfield.[4] Had there been, the new king of Northumbria would not have had to call Aidan from Iona to Lindisfarne after the battle to, "build up and extend the church of Christ in his kingdom."[5] Bede's account poses two questions, which he leaves unanswered: Where did Oswald get the idea of erecting a wooden cross and why did his army kneel? Or, to recast the questions in art-historical terms: What prompted the patron to commission the object and why was the object well-received by its initial audience?

THE PATRON

Bede is characteristically vague about where the sons of Æthelfrith spent their exile during Edwin's reign, placing it, "among the Irish or the Picts, where they were instructed in the faith as the Irish taught it," and were baptized.[6] Eanfrith, at least, may have lived in Pictland, if he were indeed the father of the Pictish king Talorcan son of *Anfrith*, whose death in 657 is recorded in various Irish annals,[7] but Bede specifically attributes the baptisms of Oswald and Oswiu to the Irish.[8] Charles Plummer noted that Bede's geography imprecisely makes Iona part of *Scottia*, or Ireland, while Adomnán, who was better informed, always associated Iona with *Britannia*.[9] In order to establish the See of Lindisfarne, Oswald requested Aidan's services from the "elders of Irish birth" (*maiores natu Scottorum*) by whom the king had been baptized and Bede informs us in another passage that Aidan was sent from Iona.[10] Oswald's taste for freestanding wooden crosses may therefore have been acquired at Iona.

In his *Life of St. Columba*, Adomnán mentions three crosses at Iona which were associated with Columba. Two of them occupied the spots where Columba and his aged uncle Ernán stood when the latter suddenly fell dead, while at another site, where Columba rested by the roadside on the day of his death, a third cross was later (*postea*) set in a millstone.[11] Adomnán became ninth abbot of Iona in 679, when he was about fifty-two, and little is known of his earlier career. The earliest Iona abbot whom Adomnán seems to have met was his own predecessor Faílbe, who from 673 to 676 was in Ireland, where Adomnán could have met him.[12] Thus, Adomnán's knowledge of crosses at Iona cannot be shown to antedate his assumption of the abbacy in 679 and his chronology for the crosses is unclear, but he thought they had been there for some time and describes them as standing "to the present day" (*hodieque*), although even the two commemorating the death of Ernán might not have been erected before Columba's death in 597.[13] Despite Adomnán's vague dating of commemorative crosses at Iona, which in his time were presumably made of wood,[14] we should remember that the intended audience for his *Life of St. Columba* included the monks of his own monastery,[15] and it is quite unlikely that he would have tried to make the crosses seem older than they were, if senior members of the Iona community knew that they were not. Indeed, Adomnán's lack of chronological precision may owe as much to the primary audience of the *Life of St. Columba* as to its author; they knew better than he did how old the crosses were and, by respecting that knowledge, Adomnán inadvertently created unnecessary confusion for the modern scholar.

Adomnán does, however, provide a Columban context for Oswald's activities at Heavenfield. Oswald told Ségéne, the Iona abbot who sent Aidan to Lindisfarne, of a dream the king had the night before the battle of Deniseburn, in which a gigantic vision of Columba himself promised Oswald victory over Cadwallon. Ségéne repeated Oswald's story to the later abbot Faílbe, who in turn told Adomnán,[16] but the Iona account neglects Oswald's wooden cross, which we learn of instead from Bede. Had Bede told us of Oswald's dream, as well as his wooden cross at Heavenfield, we might suspect a deliberate literary imitation of Constantine's vision before the battle of the Milvian Bridge, but the vision is central to the latter story and only Adomnán describes Oswald's dream. Bede knew Rufinus's Latin translation of Eusebius's *Ecclesiastical History*, which includes the story of Constantine's vision, but Rufinus is not among the non-Biblical Latin sources identified in Adomnán's writings. Bede's description of the Heavenfield site near Hexham, his account of the erection of the cross and his discussion of miracles effected both by the moss that later grew upon it and slivers of wood taken from it, are so entirely circumstantial that we must accept the existence of the Heavenfield cross, which was still standing in Bede's lifetime.[17]

The crosses at Iona Adomnán mentions in his *Life of Columba* commemorated events involving saints, either Columba or his uncle, and we know from Adomnán's other book, *De Locis Sanctis*, that the author was also aware of an analogous contemporary wooden cross, then standing in the River Jordan to mark the site of Christ's baptism, as well as the most important commemorative cross then extant, the great silver cross on the site of the Crucifixion on Golgotha,[18] itself a replacement for the fifth-century jewelled cross removed by the Persians in 614. Nancy Edwards therefore suggests that the Insular development of both wooden and metal crosses may be attributable to an eastern impetus.[19] It must be emphasized, however, that Adomnán was not entirely dependent upon the wandering Frankish bishop Arculf, his informant for *De Locis Sanctis*, since he refers in it to additional written sources, which prompted his modern editor to argue that Iona already had access to pilgrim literature and geographical manuals.[20] Adomnán only met Arculf after becoming abbot of Iona and the three Iona crosses described in his *Life of St. Columba* apparently predated Adomnán's abbacy. The Insular practice of erecting freestanding crosses at sites associated with holy individuals therefore need not have depended upon the traveling Arculf, although the possibility remains that the emergence of Insular freestanding crosses may in part acknowledge textual sources for earlier developments in the Holy Land.

The Heavenfield cross, however, only became commemorative in retrospect; its original purpose was devotional. Other seventh-century Hiberno-Latin texts indicate various functions for crosses in a Gaelic context. The prescription for the punishment given monks who have "not approached the cross," listed among others in the Rule of Columbanus,[21] would have encouraged devotion. Monastic precincts were to be delimited by crosses, according to the seventh-century *Synodus Hibernensis* recorded in the *Collectio Canonum Hibernensis*, one of whose eighth-century compilers was the Iona *sapiens* Cú-chuimne, and the undecorated socket-stone of a cross base was found at Iona near a probable entrance through the *vallum*, the earthen rampart around the perimeter of the monastery.[22] Oswald's cross at Heavenfield may thus have had a territorial dimension as well, one through which he laid claim to Northumbria for God, with himself as God's viceroy. Oswald's conversion at Iona, where wooden crosses were apparently already in use, makes Iona the most likely location where Oswald first became acquainted with freestanding wooden crosses, of the type he later erected at Heavenfield.

THE AUDIENCE

The question remains, however: why did Oswald's Bernician army kneel before the symbol of an alien religion? Surely it could not have been just because the king asked them to do so, not when we recall the pagan reactions in Kent and Essex in the early seventh century, against the first tentative Christian missions sent out from Canterbury; or the dubious Rædwald of East Anglia hedging his bets by placing both a Christian and a pagan altar in the same temple; to say nothing of the apostasy of Oswald's own Bernician brother Eanfrith.[23] But offering respect to a freestanding wooden monument may not have been an alien act for Oswald's army, however Christian it had yet to become.

Bede refers to a number of seventh-century pagan idols in Anglo-Saxon England and has Gregory the Great suggest different responses to idols by bishops and kings, advising Augustine of Canterbury to destroy the idols in pagan temples, but to preserve the temples by converting them into churches, although the pope admonished Æthelberht of Kent to overthrow both the idols and their shrines in his kingdom. The apostasy of Kent following Æthelberht's death apparently revived idol worship and king Eorcenberht ordered their destruction anew ca. 640. Edwin of Northumbria, in contrast to the more careful East Anglian Rædwald, renounced idols at his conversion. A letter from Pope Boniface V instructed Edwin to hate idols and spurn their shrines and the king's own pagan *pontifex* Coifi resolutely burned the Anglian idols and shrine at *Godmunddingaham* in Deira.[24] Boniface's comparison between an idol and "a stone standing in one place" is potentially applicable to Yeavering's wooden equivalents and suggests some vague understanding of conditions in Britain; but the letter refers specifically to "those gods whom you yourselves have given the likeness of bodies,"[25] so the papal perception of the problem may owe more to Roman knowledge of classical statuary than true familiarity with the actual forms of Anglo-Saxon idols, which were apparently fashioned from at least two materials. In the mid-seventh century, Oswiu of Northumbria prevailed upon Sigeberht, king of the apostate East Saxons, to reintroduce Christianity in Essex, at the expense of pagan idols, since gods cannot be created out of "wood or stone."[26] But a plague outbreak in 664, shortly after the Synod of Whitby, led to a revival of idol worship in Essex and in greater Bernicia, where the disease carried away Prior Boisil of Melrose, leaving his successor, St. Cuthbert, to contend with a revival of idolatry in the neighborhood.[27]

No stone object has yet been unquestionably identified as an Anglo-Saxon idol, although the Sutton Hoo whetstone is perhaps imbued with idolatrous overtones.[28] The excavation of the Northumbrian royal site at Yeavering, however, provides archaeological evidence of a more pertinent kind. Bede tells us that Paulinus, the first archbishop of York, visited Edwin of Northumbria at his royal villa at Yeavering, where crowds of people were instructed in the faith and baptized,[29] but Edwin was of the royal house of Deira, while Yeavering is in Bernicia and its freestanding wooden monuments may be especially relevant to the reception by Oswald's Bernician army of his wooden cross at Heavenfield.

Yeavering's excavator, Brian Hope-Taylor, could only lament its paucity of precisely datable material, which has left open to question his chronological interpretation of the site, although the thoroughness of the excavation has been justly praised.[30] Disagreement has recently focused on Hope-Taylor's distinction between an indigenous Celtic British building type and early Anglo-Saxon architecture, in light of mounting evidence for the character of Anglian settlements in the region, of a type little known when Hope-Taylor addressed the problem.[31] But the excavator's interpretation of earlier activity at the site remains unchallenged. In Yeavering's prehistoric Phase IA, a ring-ditch with associated cremation burials at the western end of the site was provided with a central standing stone and encircled by stone uprights. At a later date (pl. 5.1), the standing stones were removed and a rectangular mortuary structure defined within the circular ring-ditch (WR-DC) by the insertion of wooden posts and a central wooden upright. Two of the inhumation burials associated with this Phase IB bring us to the "prehistoric or early historic" period, since they are exceptionally provided with iron knives, whose manufacture, as Hope-Taylor points out, is characteristic of both the Anglo-Saxon and the Celtic British worlds in the sixth and seventh centuries.[32] Meanwhile, a ditched Bronze Age round barrow (ER-DC) at the east end of the site received its own wooden post, which was to serve as an axial reference for successive structures at Yeavering. Hope-Taylor suggests a broad date range between

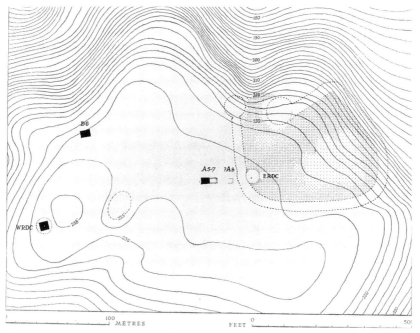

Pl. 5.1. Yeavering Phase IB. Plans by permission of Dr. Brian Hope-Taylor.

A.D. 300 and 500 for the erection of the post atop the eastern barrow and a date not later than 500 for the wooden rectangular replacement of the western prehistoric stone circle.[33] Freestanding wooden posts were to acquire particular significance at Yeavering, hinting to Hope-Taylor that "wood locally came to be regarded in the end as having some special ritual virtue of its own."[34]

Bede dates to 547 the beginning of Anglian rule over Northumbria under King Ida, the grandfather of the Bernician Æthelfrith, whom Rædwald of East Anglia overthrew to gain the Northumbrian throne for Edwin of Deira.[35] From Ida's reign through Edwin's, a period extending into the seventh century, freestanding wooden posts continued to receive respectful attention at Yeavering. Late in Hope-Taylor's Phase II (pl. 5.2), belonging roughly to the second half of the sixth century, a wooden outdoor theater (Building E) was built with just such a post behind the small dais that formed the apex of the structure.[36] Christopher Scull's recent argument, for dating Phase IB within the period of Anglo-Saxon settlement and combining it with buildings of Hope-Taylor's Phase II, suggests a slightly later possible dating framework for Building E, extending it into the early seventh century.[37] At about the same time, whether in the second half

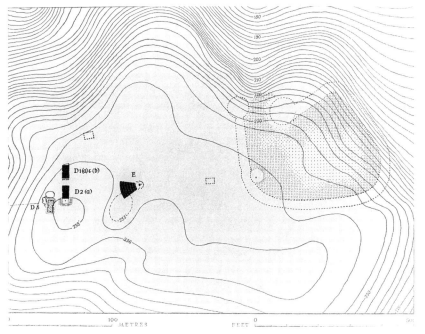

Pl. 5.2. Yeavering Phase II.

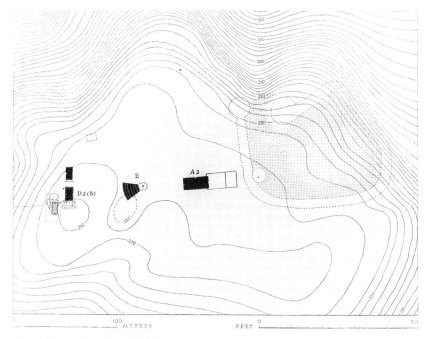

Pl. 5.3. Yeavering Phase IIIAB.

of the sixth century or not until the early seventh, a new building (D2) was constructed on a north-south axis to the west of the theater and was enclosed within a new exterior in Hope-Taylor's Phase IIIAB (pl. 5.3). This new double-shelled building is identified as a pagan temple, with central doors in its eastern and western walls, ox skulls gathered by its eastern door, and inhumation burials, with no associated grave goods, clustered around its southern end, but kept out of a burial-free enclosure featuring freestanding wooden posts. A massive, rectangular wooden upright was set outside the northwest corner of the temple, in a pit containing the teeth of sheep or goats.[38]

In Hope-Taylor's Phase IIIC (pl. 5.4), which he dates to the reign of King Edwin, the size of the theater was increased and another wooden post was placed in a pit with sheep or goat teeth, next to a grave containing a goat skull and a human skeleton with some sort of ceremonial staff. The post and grave were both aligned along an east-west axis with the wooden post atop the old Bronze Age barrow to the east and the grave situated at the eastern entrance of Yeavering's, and most likely, Edwin's great hall (Building A4). The wooden post by the grave at the doorway was removed before the building's destruction,[39] perhaps as a result of the conversion of part of the local population to Christianity, but the theater, the great hall, the

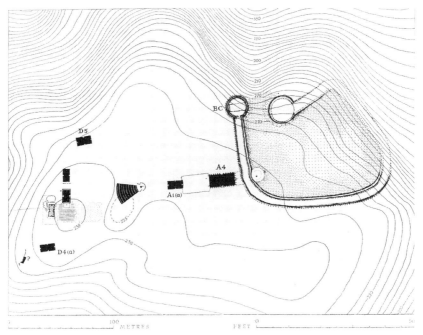

Pl. 5.4. Yeavering Phase IIIC.

temple, and its adjacent cemetery then continued in use until they were deliberately burned, an event Hope-Taylor links to the devastation wrought by Penda and Cadwallon after the death of Edwin ca. 632–33.[40]

At this point, one could simply conclude, on the basis of the Yeavering evidence, that Oswald's Bernician army was familiar with wooden monuments serving a variety of ceremonial, funerary, and pagan religious purposes and therefore accepted the wooden cross at Heavenfield without demur, but Yeavering's wooden uprights were not all Anglo-Saxon in origin. Wooden posts first appeared at Yeavering within the dismantled prehistoric standing stone circle at the west end of the site and atop the ditched Bronze Age round-barrow to the east. The Eastern Ring-Ditch was eventually surrounded by the "fort-like" Great Enclosure, but its round-barrow seems to have remained visible nonetheless, "since the siting of the enclosure and a series of free-standing posts involves continuing references to its existence;" although its visibility may have been enhanced by its wooden post.[41] Recent discussions of the dating of the western cemetery and the Great Enclosure ignore the early wooden uprights at opposite ends of the site,[42] but it remains highly probable that they were erected by the native Celtic Britons before Ida and his crew arrived on the Bernician coast. Bernicia continued to retain its Celtic name (Old Welsh "Berneich" became Anglo-Saxon "Beornice") while

Bede's name for Yeavering, "Gefrin," is also Brittonic and means "Hill of the Goats," a name which may link indigenous pagan beliefs with the goat remains associated with the wooden posts outside the temple and at the doorway and within the human grave at the eastern entrance of the great hall.[43] Hope-Taylor found nothing necessarily Anglo-Saxon about the grave, which he describes as "a ritual half-breed in its own curious limbo,"[44] a phrase that may also describe the Anglo-Saxon and British cultural confluence at Yeavering. The temple and great hall belong to a period of Anglian rule over Northumbrian Bernicia, but for Hope-Taylor, the contemporary unfurnished inhumation graves at Yeavering stand apart from normal Anglo-Saxon practice and indicate the continuation of local Celtic customs.[45] Given the entire Yeavering context, with its burials and posts, the acceptance of the Heavenfield cross by Oswald's army might then represent a transference of respect to the Christian monument from freestanding wooden posts whose pagan significance originated among the Celtic Britons, before their adoption by the incoming Angles.

It is notoriously difficult, however, to deduce ethnic identities and religious beliefs from grave-furnishings alone, or their absence; and, as Hope-Taylor has indicated, Bernicia poses special problems. Similarly, Professor Cramp points out that the "gradual cessation of the custom of burying the dead, richly clothed and with grave-goods" is paralleled elsewhere in England besides the North, concluding that the archaeological record in Bernicia is too meager to "speculate with any precision on the numbers and status of the invading English as well as the surviving Britons" in the area.[46] Roger Miket reaches much the same conclusion in his summary of the Bernician burial evidence. Even in the cases of cemeteries that have yielded metalwork objects at Howick Heugh, North and South Milfield and Great Tosson, "it is only the cumulative authority of the full assemblage" from these sites, "combined perhaps with features in the rite of interment, that prompt an Anglo-Saxon date at all." At North and South Milfield, as at Yeavering, the tentatively identified British element among the population, suggested by "unaccompanied extended inhumation," proved predominant, but the situation is too unclear to permit successful speculation on the nature of any synthesis which might have been achieved between British and Anglo-Saxon practices.[47]

The evidence for early building types at Yeavering is looking increasingly Anglo-Saxon,[48] while the burial evidence is inconclusive, but the names of Bernicia and Yeavering remained British and Yeavering's freestanding wooden posts still seem Brittonic in origin. But what sort of "Celtic" culture did Bernicia have at the time of the Anglian settlements? In the period prior to Bernicia's conversion, Hope-Taylor sees the region as culturally distinctive because of its apparent lack of the normal indicators of early Celtic Christianity found among its British neighbors to the north and west: long-cist cemeteries and inscribed memorial stones.[49] No memorial stones bearing inscriptions have yet been found in Bernicia. Cist burials may belong to the late-prehistoric period, but long-cist cemeteries characterized by stone-lined extended inhumation burials without grave-goods, especially those aligned on an east-west axis with the head placed at the west, are generally accepted as evidence of early Christianity in Celtic Britain and southern Pictland.[50] Long-cist inhumations were discovered in 1865 at Bamburgh, but Hope-Taylor notes that "the evidence is too slight and uncertain to preclude the possibility that these burials were prehistoric;" a point accepted by Miket, who sees the Bamburgh cemetery and two other Bernician examples, at Brierton and Cornforth in County Durham, as possible "antecedents . . . of later fifth to mid-seventh century Bernician burial traditions."[51] Two long-cist cemeteries in southern Scotland were also furnished with inscribed memorial stones: the Catstane from Kirkliston near Edinburgh and the Yarrow Stone in Selkirkshire.[52] Hope-Taylor effectively contrasts the juxtaposition of stone-lined graves and upright memorial stones among the Celtic Britons to the north with the sixth- and seventh-century situation at Yeavering, where the "orthostats were of wood and the graves were from the first unlined."[53]

Bede's description of the Heavenfield cross as the first Christian monument in Bernicia is potentially suspect, in view of his well-known antipathy to the Britons, but there is still no clear evidence to contradict his assertion.[54] Hope-Taylor therefore concludes that Bernicia was culturally different, within Celtic Britain, when the Anglian intruders arrived. The basic mass of the native population seems to have survived, remaining "relatively barbarous, backward, illiterate and pagan," only to have Christianity introduced under Anglian royal auspices. Edwin may well have taken Paulinus to address an essentially "Celtic folk-assembly" at Yeavering, where even a Christian Anglo-Saxon king from Deira could be expected to behave respectfully towards wooden posts with local pre-Christian religious associations.[55] But the behavior of Edwin at Yeavering and Oswald's army at Heavenfield need not have been entirely conditioned by an accommodation reached with the Celtic Britons of Bernicia.

Yeavering is not the only Anglo-Saxon royal site featuring a free-standing wooden upright. A massive posthole near the eastern entrance of the palace complex at Cheddar in Somerset provides us with another Anglo-Saxon example. Dating evidence is patchy for the earliest Anglo-Saxon occupation of the site. West Saxon overlordship of the area between Gloucester and Bath, to the north of Cheddar, probably began following the battle of Dyrham in 577 and extended to the south, past Cheddar, by the late-seventh century, when King Ine of Wessex established a church at

Glastonbury.[56] Cheddar is first attested in the documentary record in King Alfred's will, although the earliest datable find from the site is a coin of Æthelwulf of ca. 845, but Philip Rahtz, Cheddar's excavator, admits that Anglo-Saxon occupation might have begun as early as the late-seventh century.[57] Cheddar's wooden post, however, is no earlier than the ninth century.

Rahtz describes as a "flagstaff" the wooden upright that occupied the posthole by Cheddar's main entrance, where it would have been visible "on the skyline to anyone approaching the site from the west or south,"[58] a description which recalls the visibility of Yeavering's wooden post atop the Bronze Age round-barrow within the Great Enclosure. Cheddar's eastern boundary eventually comprised a pair of parallel ditches with two entrance gaps, of which the southern formed the principal entrance, marked to the west by three post holes on a north-south axis, perhaps indicating an "inner gate or barrier," with the freestanding wooden post, possibly "the earliest of these features," to the east of the entrance.[59] The entire eastern boundary complex seems to belong to Cheddar's Period 2 (post ca. 930 to the late-tenth or early eleventh century), although the "flagstaff" itself may already have been in place. Limestone boulders in the upper part of its posthole apparently supported, around the base of the upright, a layer of Roman brick, which is most likely to have still been available in Period 1 (before ca. 930). The posthole also yielded a ninth-century strap-end and a pottery sherd of fabric A, a type found elsewhere in England as late as the eleventh century, but one current at Cheddar late in Period 1.[60]

A late-ninth- or early tenth-century wooden post at an entrance to a palace site in Somerset may seem a bit removed in time and place from Yeavering, even if both sites were royal and Anglo-Saxon. But Rahtz draws a comparison between the Cheddar post and another at Epolding, Mühltal in southern Bavaria, which stood in a clearing amidst a group of rectangular Migration Period wooden buildings that antedates a later church and graves at the same site. Analogous posts elsewhere in Germany marked special graves or "the meeting place of the folk moot,"[61] recalling the wooden upright by the burial at the entrance of Yeavering's great hall and the post behind the dais in front of Yeavering's theater. Rahtz particularly relates the Cheddar post to royal assemblies, since the *witenagemot* was held at Cheddar in 941 under King Edmund, in 956 under Eadwig and in 968 under Edgar.[62]

Publication of the Yeavering and Cheddar excavations overlapped and it is obvious that neither Hope-Taylor nor Rahtz was able to take advantage of the other's discoveries. However Bernician-Celtic Yeavering's earliest wooden posts may have been, Cheddar now provides us with another royal site where a freestanding wooden post had distinctly Anglo-

Saxon royal associations, although there are significant differences between it and some of the Yeavering examples. Cheddar's wooden entrance post dates to a period when Christianity was one of the identifying characteristics Anglo-Saxons used to distinguish themselves from the Viking invaders. As such, it belongs to a different context than that of the freestanding posts by Yeavering's pagan temple, but the continental Migration Period antecedents proposed by Rahtz for the Cheddar upright are nearer in time and even more applicable to wooden posts erected at Yeavering during the first phase of Anglian rule in Bernicia, between the mid-sixth century and the burning of Yeavering, probably ca. 632–33. The Cheddar example is late enough for the full implications of its Germanic forebears to have been forgotten by its West Saxon audience, attributes which would still have been recognizable to the Angles of Bernicia when gazing upon freestanding wooden posts at Yeavering.

CONCLUSIONS

It is increasingly becoming a matter of general agreement that free-standing sculptured stone crosses first appeared in the Insular world in Northumbria, where they were predicated upon wooden precursors of the type first erected in Northumbria by King Oswald at Heavenfield.[63] The Heavenfield cross is therefore central to our comprehension of the development of Insular stone sculpture, but the full context of its creation must be understood in terms of the nature of its patronage and the ready acceptance of that patronage by the audience for whom it was originally intended. In his excavation report, Brian Hope-Taylor emphasizes the local Celtic origins of freestanding wooden posts at Yeavering and the uprights within the ring-ditches on opposite sides of the site were apparently still standing when Ida began establishing Anglian hegemony in Bernicia. The Cheddar "flagstaff," however, suggests that the Anglian intruders continued to erect wooden posts at Yeavering because they were already familiar with a variety of uses for such monuments in a royal setting. Indeed, their presence at Yeavering may have made the site additionally attractive to Bernicia's new rulers. Oswald, it seems, was already familiar with freestanding wooden posts at home in Bernicia, whether they were British or Anglian in origin, before he was converted to Christianity and became acquainted with freestanding wooden crosses at Iona. A similar familiarity enabled his army to accept the cross he offered them at Heavenfield, an acceptance further conditioned by their recognition of Oswald as their new king and the royal associations of the freestanding wooden uprights of the type detected at the Yeavering and later Cheddar palace sites. Had Oswald's army rejected the Heavenfield cross on the eve of battle with Cadwallon, the subsequent history of Anglo-Saxon England would have been radically altered and the names of Lindisfarne, Monkwearmouth and Jarrow would likely hold little meaning for us today. In choosing to kneel before Oswald's wooden cross, the Anglian army of Bernicia inadvertently paved the way for Oswald's foundation of Lindisfarne, the evangelization of much of England, the architectural patronage of St. Wilfrid and Benedict Biscop and the development of the Insular freestanding sculptured stone cross.

NOTES

I am most grateful to Professor Robert Farrell for inviting me to contribute an earlier version of this paper to the "Insular Tradition" sessions at the twenty-sixth International Congress on Medieval Studies at Kalamazoo, Michigan, in 1991; to Professor Rosemary Cramp for drawing my attention to Cheddar; and to Catherine Hills for additional discussion. I am especially indebted to Dr. Brian Hope-Taylor for his generous advice and for permission to reproduce his site plans at Yeavering.

1. B. Colgrave and R. Mynors, eds., *Bede's Ecclesiastical History of the English People* (Oxford: Clarendon Press, 1969), 212–15; additional notes and discussion in C. Plummer, ed., *Venerabilis Baedae Opera Historica*, 2 vols. (Oxford: Topographeo Clarendoniano, 1896), II, 119, 124; J. M. Wallace-Hadrill, *Bede's Ecclesiastical History of the English People: A Historical Commentary* (Oxford: Clarendon Press, 1988), 84, 87; C. Ireland, "Aldfirth of Northumbria and the Irish Genealogies," *Celtica* 22 (1991): 64–65, 75–76.

2. Colgrave and Mynors, *Bede*, 214–17: Deum omnipotentem uiuum ad uerum in commune deprecemur. Wallace-Hadrill, *Bede's Ecclesiastical History*, 89, notes Bede's belief that the site's name was already *Hefenfeld* and was therefore prophetic.

3. Ibid., 162–66, 182–86. For discussion of the different accounts of Edwin's conversion in Celtic British sources, see D. Mac Lean, "The Date of the Ruthwell Cross," in B. Cassidy, ed., *The Ruthwell Cross*, Index of Christian Art Occasional Papers I (Princeton: Index of Christian Art, Department of Art and Archaeology, 1992), 62–63. Wallace-Hadrill, *Bede's Ecclesiastical History*, 65, finds that "there may be something in" the British versions, but if they are to be "taken seriously then Bede's account must be wrong; and this seems broadly impossible, given the letters of Pope Honorius." The letter from Honorius to Edwin found in Colgrave and Mynors, *Bede*, 194–95, refers to Edwin's instruction by "orthodox teaching" (*orthodoxa praedicatio edocti*); but A.P. Smyth, *Warlords and Holy Men: Scotland A.D. 80–1000* (London: Arnold, 1984), 22–23, argues that Edwin may have undergone a second baptism by Paulinus, after first being baptized in exile at the British court of Rhun son of Urien of Rheged, a possibility which accommodates both Bede and the British sources.

4. Colgrave and Mynors, *Bede*, 216–17: Nec inmerito, quia nullum, ut conperimus, fidei Christianae signum, nulla ecclesia, nullum altare in tota Barniciorum gente erectum est.

5. Ibid., 220–21: ecclesiam Christi in regno suo multum diligenter aedificare ac dilatare curauit.

6. Ibid., 212–13: apud Scottos siue Pictos exulabant, ibique ad doctrinam Scottorum cathecizati et baptismati sunt gratia recreati.

7. The annal entries are collected in A. Anderson, ed., *Early Sources of Scottish History*, 2 vols. (Edinburgh: Oliver & Boyd, 1922), I, 176; see also M. Anderson, *Kings and Kingship in Early Scotland*, rev. ed. (Edinburgh; London: Scottish Academic Press; Chatto & Windus, 1980), 167, 171–72.

8. Colgrave and Mynors, *Bede*, 218–19, 296–97.

9. Plummer, *Baedae*, II, 186.

10. Colgrave and Mynors, *Bede*, 218–21.

11. A. Anderson and M. Anderson, eds., *Adomnán's Life of Columba*, rev. ed. (Oxford: Clarendon Press, 1991), 82, 220. I have revised my former understanding of the text, in D. Mac Lean, "The Origins and Development of the Celtic Cross," *Markers* 7 (1990): 232–75, esp. 236, and now believe that all three crosses still stood at Iona during Adomnán's abbacy.

12. M. Herbert, *Iona, Kells and Derry: The History and Hagiography of the Monastic Familia of Columba* (Oxford; New York: Clarendon Press; Oxford University Press, 1988), 47; A. Anderson, *Early Sources*, I, 183. Anderson and Anderson, *Adomnán*, xl, suggest that Adomnán may have been in charge at Iona during Faílbe's absence in Ireland.

13. Ibid., 82, 220. For the date of Columba's death, see A. Anderson, *Early Sources*, I, 103–6.

14. Royal Commission on the Ancient and Historical Monuments of Scotland (R.C.A.H.M.S.), *Argyll: An Inventory of the Monuments*, vol. 4, *Iona* (Edinburgh: H.M.S.O., 1982), 17.

15. See J.-M. Picard, "The Purpose of Adomnán's *Vitae Columbae*," *Peritia* 1 (1982): 160–77.

16. Anderson and Anderson, *Adomnán*, 14–16; discussed in Herbert, *Iona, Kells and Derry*, 41–42.

17. Colgrave and Mynors, *Bede*, 214–18. For Bede's knowledge of Rufinus, see J. Higgitt, "The Dedication Inscription at Jarrow and Its Context," *Ant.J.* 59 (1979): 343–74, esp. 364. The classic study of Adomnán's sources in the *Life of Columba* is still G. Brüning, "Adamnans Vita Columbae und ihre Ableitungen," *Z.C.P.* 17 (1917): 213–304; see also D. Meehan, ed., *Adamnan's De Locis Sanctis*, Scriptores Latini Hiberniae, III (Dublin: Dublin Institute for Advanced Studies, 1958), 13–18; Anderson and Anderson, *Adomnán*, lxvii, n. 206 lists other discussions of

Adomnán's sources. I am indebted to C. Neuman de Vegvar for suggesting this line of enquiry.

18. Meehan, *De Locis Sanctis*, 48, 86.

19. N. Edwards, "The Origins of the Free-standing Stone Cross in Ireland: Imitation or Innovation?," *B.B.C.S.* 32 (1985): 393–410, esp. 398–401; idem, *The Archaeology of Early Medieval Ireland* (Philadelphia: University of Pennsylvania Press, 1990), 163.

20. Meehan, *De Locis Sanctis*, 12, 90, 96, 98, 100, 102.

21. G. Walker, ed., *Sancti Columbani Opera*, Scriptores Latini Hiberniae, II (Dublin: Dublin Institute for Advanced Studies, 1957), 146–48: *crucem non adierit.*

22. H. Wasserschleben, ed., *Die Irische Kanonensammlung*, 2nd ed. (Leipzig, Germany: Bernard Tauchnitz, 1885), 175, note (c); J. Kenney, *The Sources for the Early History of Ireland: Ecclesiastical* (New York: Columbia University Press, 1929), 248–49; R.C.A.H.M.S., *Iona*, 17, 39, 215–16: No. 6 (103).

23. Colgrave and Mynors, *Bede*, 150–52, 190, 212.

24. Ibid., 112, 168, 182–86, 236.

25. Ibid., 170: . . . lapis in uno loco posita . . . eos deos, quibus uos ipsi imaginem corporis tradistis. Wallace-Hadrill, *Bede's Ecclesiastical History*, 69, notes that "the pope's view of the idols in human form he supposes Edwin to worship is, if naïve, at least direct and challenging."

26. Colgrave and Mynors, *Bede*, 280–82: dei creandi materiam lignum uel lapidum esse non posse.

27. Ibid., 310–12, 322, 432; B. Colgrave, ed., *Two Lives of Saint Cuthbert: A Life by an Anonymous Monk of Lindisfarne and Bede's Prose Life* (Cambridge: Cambridge University Press, 1940), 180–84.

28. R. Bruce-Mitford, *The Sutton Hoo Ship-Burial*, 3 vols. (London: British Museum Press, 1975–83), II, 357–77, esp. 373–77; for opposing viewpoints see also C. L. Neuman de Vegvar, *The Northumbrian Renaissance: A Study in the Transmission of Style* (Selinsgrove and London: Susquehanna University Press, 1987), 242–43, and M. Ryan, "The Sutton Hoo Ship Burial and Ireland: Some Celtic Perspectives," in R. Farrell and C. Neuman de Vegvar, eds., *Sutton Hoo: Fifty Years After*, A.E.M.S. 2 (Oxford, Ohio: American Early Medieval Studies, 1992), 85–90.

29. Colgrave and Mynors, *Bede*, 188.

30. B. Hope-Taylor, *Yeavering: An Anglo-British Centre of Early Northumbria*, Dept. of the Environment Archaeol. Reports, No. 7 (London: H.M.S.O., 1977). Hope-Taylor's dating framework is broadly accepted in E. Fernie, *The Architecture of the Anglo-Saxons* (New York: Holmes & Meier, 1983), 16–20; and in L. Alcock, "Bede, Eddius and the Forts of the North Britons," *Jarrow Lecture 1988* (Jarrow: St. Paul's Church, 1988), 7–9, 19–20, 24–27. R. Miket, "A Restatement of Evidence from Bernician Anglo–Saxon Burials," in P. Rahtz, T. Dickinson, and L. Watts, eds., *Anglo-Saxon Cemeteries 1979: The Fourth Anglo-Saxon Symposium at Oxford,*

B.A.R. Brit. ser. 82 (Oxford: British Archaeological Reports, 1980), 289–305, esp. 301, 303, accepts Hope-Taylor's chronology while disagreeing with his interpretation of the origins of several structures at Yeavering.

31. C. Scull, "Post-Roman Phase I at Yeavering: A Re-Consideration," *M.A.* 35 (1991): 51–63. I am indebted to Catherine Hills for this reference.

32. Hope-Taylor, *Yeavering*, 108–16, 157, 187, 199, 244, 256, 258–59, 282; Miket, "Restatement," 296–97. The discussion of possible dates for the inhumation burials in Scull, "Post-Roman Phase 1 at Yeavering," 60, leaves untouched the question of the dating of the wooden posts in the Western Ring-Ditch, which replaced the earlier standing stones.

33. Hope-Taylor, *Yeavering*, 73, 78, 83–85, 141, 157, 244, 67.

34. Ibid., 244, 256.

35. Colgrave and Mynors, *Bede*, 181, 562; genealogical table in Plummer, *Baedae*, II, 119. For archaeological evidence for possible late-fifth- or early-sixth-century Anglo-Saxon settlement in the area of Catterick, or *Catraeth* in Deira, see L. Alcock, "Gwŷr y Gogledd: An Archaeological Appraisal," *Archaeologia Cambrensis* 132 (1983): 14–17. For a possible reading of the textual sources for dating Anglian settlement in Bernicia to ca. 500, see D. Dumville, "The Origins of Northumbria: Some Aspects of the British Background," in S. Bassett, ed., *The Origins of the Anglo-Saxon Kingdoms* (Leicester: Leicester University Press, 1989), 218–19.

36. Hope-Taylor, *Yeavering*, 119–22, 124, 158, 161, 199, 245, 259, 270.

37. Scull, "Post-Roman Phase I at Yeavering," 60, dates the "first major buildings" at the site to the late-sixth or early-seventh century, without mentioning Building E, although it is included in his fig. 5.

38. Hope-Taylor, *Yeavering*, 97–102, 158, 199, 244–45, 259, 270, 282, 311–13. Scull, "Post-Roman Phase I at Yeavering," 60, suggests a late-sixth or early seventh-century date for the new western cemetery outside Building D2.

39. Hope-Taylor, *Yeavering*, 67, 69, 137, 141, 161–63, 200–3, 245–47, 251; for additional discussion of Anglo-Saxon and Welsh textual sources for doorkeepers and Hope-Taylor's suggestion that the staff might identify the burial as that of the hall's architect, see Neuman de Vegvar, *Northumbrian Renaissance*, 251–52, 313, n. 65.

40. Hope-Taylor, *Yeavering*, 43–45, 61, 97, 121, 151, 277–78. Scull, "Post-Roman Phase I at Yeavering," 57, 59–60 stresses that "the chronology suggested" by Hope-Taylor "for building phases I–III depends heavily on a dead-reckoning back from the fire horizon at the end of phase III, which is attributed to destruction by Penda and Cadwallon," an association Scull leaves otherwise undisputed while placing D2 (the temple) and A4 (the great hall) "within the same date-range." Alcock, *Bede, Eddius*, 8, notes that Bede makes no mention of an attack on Yeavering.

41. Hope-Taylor, *Yeavering*, 157, dates the insertion of the wooden post after the construction of the earliest version of the Great Enclosure.

42. Scull, "Post-Roman Phase I at Yeavering," 54, 57–58; Alcock, *Bede, Eddius,* 7–9, 19–20; idem., "The Activities of Potentates in Celtic Britain, A.D. 500–800: A Positivist Approach," in S. Driscoll and M. Nieke, eds., *Power and Politics in Early Medieval Britain and Ireland* (Edinburgh: Edinburgh University Press, 1988), 34, accepts as British the western "cemetery which occupied the site of the dismantled stone circle."

43. Hope-Taylor, *Yeavering,* 15, 260. For the name of Bernicia, see K. Jackson, *Language and History in Early Britain* (Edinburgh: Edinburgh University Press, 1953), 701–5.

44. Hope-Taylor, *Yeavering,* 246–47.

45. Ibid., 248–50, 264–65, 277–78.

46. R. Cramp, "Anglo-Saxon Settlement," in J. Chapman and H. Mytum, eds., *Settlement in North Britain 1000 B.C.–A.D. 1000: Papers Presented to George Jobey, Newcastle Upon Tyne, December 1982,* B.A.R. Brit. ser. 118 (Oxford: British Archaeological Reports, 1983), 263–97, esp. 269–70.

47. Miket, "Restatement," 294–96, 298–99, includes discussion of "two bronze rings" or "annular brooches," lost since 1938, found at Galewood Farm, which he places among those sites "where dating cannot be refined further than to say they lie within the early Anglo-Saxon period"; but Scull, "Post-Roman Phase I at Yeavering," 60–61, 62, n. 53, dates the Galewood "brooches" more specifically between the late-fifth and late-sixth centuries. See also G. S. Keeney, "Anglo-Saxon Burials at Galewood, within Ewart, near Milfield," *Proc. Soc. Antiq. Newcastle-upon-Tyne,* 4th ser., 7 (1935–36): 15–17. For the Bernician locations of Galewood, Great Tosson, Howick Heugh, and North and South Milfield, see Miket, "Restatement," fig. 17.1 and Scull, "Post-Roman Phase I at Yeavering," fig. 2.

48. For a possibly analogous late-sixth- or early seventh-century *urbs regis,* see I. Smith, "Sprouston, Roxburghshire: An Early Anglian Centre of the Eastern Tweed Basin," *P.S.A.S.* 121 (1991): 261–94.

49. Hope-Taylor, *Yeavering,* 256–58, 282.

50. A. C. Thomas, "The Evidence from North Britain," in N. Barley and R. Hanson, eds., *Christianity in Britain 300–700* (Leicester: Leicester University Press, 1968), 107–8; G. Ritchie and A. Ritchie, *Scotland: Archaeology and Early History* (London: Thames & Hudson, 1981), 147–48, 174–75.

51. Hope-Taylor, *Yeavering,* 254; Miket, "Restatement," 300.

52. J. R. Allen and J. Anderson, *The Early Christian Monuments of Scotland,* with an introduction by Isabel Henderson, 2 vols. (Balgavies: Pinkfoot Press, 1993), III, 426, 432; Thomas, "Evidence," 105, 107. Dumville, "The Origins of Northumbria," 219, wishfully admits that "Sub-Roman north-British history and pagan Anglo-Saxon settlement history are matters which we shall have to leave largely to the archaeologists; it would of course help if in the course of their activities they could present us with another Yarrowkirk-style inscription or two!"

53. Hope-Taylor, *Yeavering*, 256.

54. Wallace-Hadrill, *Bede's Ecclesiastical History*, 89, argues that "Bede has already provided evidence that this was very unlikely to be true," without identifying the evidence in question; perhaps he was mindful of Colgrave and Mynors, *Bede*, 217, n. 5: "Yet Edwin had a seat at Yeavering and Paulinus baptized a large number in the river Glen near by." R. Cramp, *Corpus of Anglo-Saxon Stone Sculpture*, vol. I, *County Durham and Northumberland*, part 1 (Oxford: Oxford University Press, 1984), 1, dates to Edwin's reign Building B at Yeavering, which Hope-Taylor, *Yeavering*, 73–74, 164–66, 168, 278–79, 309, 312, identifies as a church but attributes instead to Oswald, after the abandonment of the Great Enclosure in Phase IV. For Bede's views on the Britons see T. Charles-Edwards, "Bede, the Irish and the Britons," *Celtica* 15 (1983): 42–52.

55. Hope-Taylor, *Yeavering*, 289, 320.

56. P. Rahtz, *The Saxon and Medieval Palaces at Cheddar: Excavations 1960–2*, B.A.R. Brit. ser. 65 (Oxford: British Archaeological Reports, 1979), 3–5; F. Stenton, *Anglo-Saxon England*, 3rd ed. (Oxford: Oxford University Press, 1971), 29.

57. Rahtz, *Cheddar*, 5, 13–14, 373.

58. Ibid., 168.

59. Ibid., 55 and fig. 12.

60. Ibid., 52, 55, 166–70, 314–15.

61. Ibid., 166–67.

62. Ibid., xv, 6, 14–16, 167.

63. See, for example, W. Collingwood, *Northumbrian Crosses of the Pre-Norman Age* (London: Faber & Gwyer, 1927), 5; R. Cramp, *Corpus*, vol. I, part 1, n. 5; Edwards, "Origins," 399; J. Lang, *Anglo-Saxon Sculpture* (Aylesbury, Bucks: Shire Publications, 1988), 9; Mac Lean, "Origins," 237–38.

CHAPTER SIX

Shirley Alexander

Daniel Themes on the Irish High Crosses

The narrative themes from the Book of Daniel, such as the Three Young Men in the Fiery Furnace, Daniel in the Lion Pit, Susanna and the Elders, were popular in Early Christian art and liturgy. By the ninth and tenth centuries, the period to which most of the developed Irish crosses are assigned, biblical teaching was conveyed in Western European art far less frequently through these subjects, although many continued in use in several groups of Irish crosses. Thus, Daniel in the Lion Pit occurs sixteen or so times in most parts of Ireland where crosses survive.[1] The subject seems to be lacking only in the early north-western group of Donegal and in the fully developed monuments of Clonmacnois, Monasterboice, and Durrow, but it reappears later at Drumcliff and Dysart O'Dea.

The Daniel iconography on the crosses is diversified to the point that most examples are unique in Ireland. All that the Irish panels have in common are the frontal pose of the centrally placed figure and the fact that he is clothed. The diversity appears in Daniel's pose (whether standing with arms at his sides, or in the orant position, or in the crucifixion pose; or with hands on the lions' heads; or a seated Daniel); in the number of lions (seven, four, or two); and the position of the lions (standing normally, or placed vertically with respect to the figure, or seated facing Daniel, or turning away from him, or rampant).

The Daniel panels are further diversified by their position on the crosses and by their position with respect to other subjects. Thus, Daniel is on the base of the cross at Moone, Ahenny south, Oldcourt, and Dysart O'Dea; on the base of the shaft at Castledermot south; within the shaft on the first Clones fragment, Galloon west, Arboe (pl. 6.1); on the lower arm of the cross-head at Castledermot north, Kells south, Kilree, Drumcliff; and in the center of the cross-head on the second Clones fragment, and on the Kells Market cross.

The Daniel panel, regardless of its position on the cross, is most frequently associated with the themes of the Fall, and Abraham about to sacrifice Isaac (Moone [pl. 6.2], Castledermot north [pl. 6.3], Arboe, Clones shaft [pl. 6.4], Kells Market cross [pl. 6.5]). Less commonly juxtaposed to the Daniel subject are the Three Young Men (Moone, Arboe, Kells south) and the man between masked figures (Castledermot south, Kells Market, possibly the Clones cross-head, and Galloon west).

The numerous variations in iconography and the position of the subject on the cross do not connect the Irish work with early sculpture in Italy or Gaul, with contemporary or earlier west European sculpture, or with Byzantine art.[2] The closest and most consistent parallels are with the third- and fourth-century catacomb paintings of Rome. Like the catacomb paintings, the Irish examples are concerned with the meaning of the subject rather than with the apocryphal additions to the story (for example, the lions kissing the prophet's feet), or with the details of eastern dress. The catacomb paintings have many of the more important features which characterize the Irish representations of Daniel, namely, the orant and possibly crucifixion poses, and Daniel in the central position of a composition, the place normally reserved for Christ. The variety in number and placement of lions in the Irish work is not found in the catacombs.

This paper is concerned with the meaning of the Daniel theme on the Irish crosses, and the clues the sculptors have provided for the interpretation of the subject. Every biblical subject has more than one meaning, as noted several times by Augustine in his writings. For example, in the early Christian literature Daniel is variously associated with patience, humility, obedience, fortitude in suffering, and power of prayer. He is the model of faith and fasting; he is a type of Christ and the prophet of the coming of Christ, both the Incarnation and the Second Coming. He is also the prophet of the Resurrection.

In the Old Testament Book of Daniel there are two accounts of Daniel in the Lion Pit. The first, Dan. 6.1–28, does not specify the number of lions, but records that the angel of God protected the prophet by closing the mouths of the animals. The intended meaning of the episode is given in

Pl. 6.1. Arboe (County Tyrone): east side of shaft. Photograph by author.

Pl. 6.2. Moone (County Kildare): east side of base. Photograph by author.

Dan. 6.17 "Your God whom you serve so constantly will come to rescue you," and Dan. 6.27 "He is the living God, enduring forever; his kingdom is never destroyed, and his dominion is without end (28). He is a savior and deliverer, performing wondrous miracles in heaven and on earth . . . ."[3] In

Pl. 6.3. Castledermot North (County Kildare): west side. Photograph by author.

the second account, Dan. 14.21–42, Daniel was put into the pit with seven lions for seven days. On the sixth day Habacuc was transported by an angel from Judea to Babylon in order to offer food to Daniel. The story is given

Pl. 6.4. Clones (County Monaghan): head and shaft of two spearate crosses. Photograph by author.

meaning by the prophet's words in Dan. 14.25 "The Lord my God . . . is a living God" and Dan. 14.38 "You have remembered me, God, you have not deserted those who love you."[4] These two versions of the Daniel story in the Old Testament convey the same message: that the one true God, whose kingdom is everlasting, brings salvation to those who remain faithful to him.

Pl. 6.5. Kells Market cross (County Meath): east side. Photograph by author.

The narrative sections of the Book of Daniel are but one part of the Book, forming the canonical chapters 1–6 and the deuterocanonical chapters 13 and 14. A second part includes the canonical chapters 7–12, which comprise four visions or apocalypses related by Daniel for the

purpose of strengthening the faith of the Jews during the period of tribula-
tion. In the New Testament, which contains the Christian meaning and
application of passages from the Hebrew Scriptures (the Old Testament),
the only direct reference to Daniel concerns these visions of the end of
time, which are his prophecies (Matt. 24.15). But the New Testament frequently alludes to the imagery of the visions in the Book of Daniel to an
extent which clearly indicates that these visions were the most significant
parts of the Book in Christian interpretation.

The most numerous references are to Dan. 7.13, in the vision of the
Four Beasts:

> In my night vision I then saw with the clouds of the
> heavens there came one in human likeness. . . . (14) To
> him was given dominion—glory and kingship. Every
> nation, tribe and tongue must serve him; his dominion is
> to be everlasting, never passing away; his kingship never
> to be destroyed.

Christians interpreted this as a prophecy of the beginning of the new age at
the Second Coming of Christ, the Son of man (Matt. 24.30) when he would
judge the nations and establish his kingdom of the elect. The "Son of man"
is a phrase which Christ applied to himself (Mark 14.62).

An important passage which makes Daniel the prophet of the
Resurrection is Dan. 12.2:

> Many of those who sleep in the dust of the earth shall
> awake, some to everlasting life and some to shame and
> everlasting contempt.

This is referred to in Matt. 25.31 where Jesus says that the Son of Man will
come in glory to judge the world. Those who neglected virtue will go to
eternal punishment and the righteous will gain eternal life, a sentiment
echoed in John 5.27–29.

By contrast there are few references in the New Testament to Daniel
in the Lion Pit. The most obvious is 2 Tim. 4.17 where Paul, the author of
the letter, describes how he was deserted by his supporters:

> But the Lord stood by me and gave me strength. . . . So I
> was rescued from the lion's mouth. (18) The Lord will
> rescue me from every evil and save me for his heavenly
> kingdom.

The theme is divine help in the hour of need and final salvation at the end of time.

From these references it may be concluded that for Christians the most significant aspects of Daniel were:

1. as the chief prophet of the Second Coming of Christ when he would judge the nations and establish his Kingdom;
2. as the prophet of the Resurrection of the elect to eternal life;
3. as the prefiguration of Christ, the savior of the faithful.

The Byzantine *Hermeneia*, or Guide for Painters, an eighteenth-century compilation from different sources and periods with details of materials, methods and iconography for the use of Byzantine painters, indicates two important meanings for Daniel.[5] For a painting of Daniel in the Lion Pit, the treatise directs that the prophet be represented as standing with upraised face and arms and in a dark pit, surrounded by seven lions. The Archangel Michael holds Habacuc by the hair above Daniel while he offers cooked food and a basket of bread. One meaning for this scene may be a person saved from death by divine help because of his faith and prayer. For a painting of the Second Coming, the treatise says that Daniel should be shown with other prophets, holding a scroll with the words of Dan. 12.2:

> Many of them that sleep in the dust of the earth shall awake, some to everlasting life, and some to shame and everlasting contempt.

Thus, the two most obvious interpretations in this Byzantine handbook are Daniel as a prophet of the resurrection of the faithful, and Daniel as a pre-figuration of Christ as the savior of the faithful.[6] Each had its own icono-graphical composition according to the *Hermeneia*, making the meaning unambiguous. On the Irish crosses every depiction of Daniel shows him among the lions, but several clues to the meaning should be taken into consideration before the assumption is made that the interpretation must be the same in each case.

In visual art, when a subject has been selected, composed and appropriately placed on the cross, the meaning assigned to it, the message gained from it, are entirely up to the viewer. Origen stated this most clearly when he said that the Bible could be interpreted on different levels according to the biblical sophistication of the person making the inter-pretation. The most important requirement for any image was that it be recognizable. Thus, the most easily identifiable episode from a biblical narrative was selected, such as Abraham sacrificing Isaac, David composing the Psalms or killing the lion, Noah's Ark, and Daniel in the Lion Pit. Once the subject was recognized, the viewer could endow it with whatever depth of meaning his biblical knowledge was capable of. Thus, the scene of Daniel among the lions served the purpose of calling to mind the significant Christian meanings applied to the various parts of the Book of Daniel, and, as has been shown, the episode in the lion pit was not necessarily the most important.

If the designer of a cross had a specific meaning in mind for the Daniel motif, how could this meaning be conveyed to the onlooker if Daniel was always shown among the lions? The interpretation of a panel could be varied both by the iconography and by the position of the panel on the cross. Thus, Daniel among the lions with no other attribute, and placed in a non-emphatic position on the cross may well have the meaning of the Christian delivered from death; or the power of prayer. Daniel standing in the crucifixion pose suggests the prophet as the prefiguration of the Incarnation, the Passion, the triumph of Christ, of the Resurrection. On a more subtle level, Daniel in the crucifixion pose dominating the lions by his stance may be identified with Adam, who was given power over the animals in paradise, and with the second Adam who had power over the animals in a Second Temptation (Mark 1.13).[7] The presence of seven lions may refer to the Habacuc episode (Dan. 14.33–39) where life-sustaining bread is a type of the Eucharist, a meaning clearly indicated on the cross-marked loaves of Early Christian sarcophagi in Gaul.[8] Or Daniel's six days without food may be a prefiguration of Christ's fast in the desert.

On the Irish crosses, the position of the Daniel panel was as decisive for the meaning as were the iconographical details. Thus, Daniel on the lower arm of the cross-head is brought into close relationship with such themes as the Fall in the center of the head on the west side of Castledermot north (pl. 6.3), balancing the Crucifixion and the Twelve Apostles on the east side. This brings together the ideas of sin, redemption, and resurrection, where the first Adam and the second Adam are contrasted as in Rom. 5.12–21 and 1 Cor. 15.21,22. Daniel in this case may be a type of Christ and a prefiguration of the Resurrection. On the more advanced south cross at Kells, Daniel is also placed on the lower arm of the cross-head with a symbolic rendering of the seven gifts of the Holy Spirit in the center. Daniel here may represent the prophet of the Resurrection to balance the central themes of the Judgment and Crucifixion on the west side. The gifts of the Holy Spirit are necessary for salvation.

Even more explicit is Daniel in the center of the cross-head at Clones (pl. 6.4) and on the Market cross at Kells (pl. 6.5). In both cases, Daniel seems to be surrounded by representations of David and the sacrifice of Isaac, and the man between masked figures. At Kells, the central theme of the cross-head on the west side is the Crucifixion, so that Daniel on the east side may be interpreted as the prefiguration of the Crucifixion, or as the prophet of the Second Coming, or of the Resurrection. However, the panel showing the guards at the Tomb of Christ on the lower part of the east side of the shaft is usually interpreted as the Resurrection (note the comparable position of Daniel on Castledermot south), so that an alternative meaning for Daniel would be appropriate. The presence of a small Virgin and Child in the central scene[9] may be the clue that the Daniel figure should be interpreted as the prophet of the Incarnation in accordance with the prophecy of the seventy weeks of Dan. 9.24–27.

It might be asked why the New Testament scenes are not used directly on the crosses instead of their Old Testament prefigurations. The answer lies in the nature of the formation of the Christian religion. The desire to demonstrate continuity between the Old and New Testaments led to a Christian interpretation which saw the Old Testament as prophecy and the New Testament as fulfillment of the prophecy. The use of an Old Testament prefiguration for a passage of New Testament doctrine emphasized the New Testament teaching concerning the continuity of God's plan of salvation from Creation to the Second Coming.

The division of the Book of Daniel into narratives and apocalyptic visions presented certain problems for the visual artist, especially as the most significant Christian meanings derived from the Book are interpretations of the visions. The designers of most of the Irish crosses, to judge from the above descriptions, chose the narrative subject of Daniel in the Lion Pit even when the intended meaning of the panel was based on the more abstract ideas contained in the visions. These were difficult to illustrate in scenes that enabled the viewer to recognize the subject easily. For example, how could an artist adequately represent Dan. 12.2 ("Many of those who sleep in the dust . . .") as a figured panel that readily conveyed not only the idea of resurrection, but resurrection that was an essential part of God's plan of salvation, prefigured in the Old Testament?

An illustration of Dan. 7.13, the vision of the Son of Man, had greater possibilities:

> In my night vision I then saw with the clouds of the
> heavens there came one in human likeness . . .

By illustrating this specific passage rather than representing the usual Daniel in the Lion Pit, the designer considerably limited the possible interpretations, but at the same time he assumed that the viewer would be able both to identify the subject through his knowledge of the Bible, and make the appropriate Christian connections of meaning. Interpretations inherent in the scene of Daniel among the lions (the power of prayer, salvation through faith, Daniel as a model of fortitude, patience, wisdom, or as a prefiguration of different aspects of Christ) are hardly possible with this limited image.

This method of direct illustration of Daniel themes was used on some of the later Irish crosses. On the west cross at Monasterboice, the Crucifixion is represented at the center of the cross-head on the west side, surrounded by scenes from the Passion of Christ.[10] The balancing scene on the east side shows a frontally standing Christ armed with a shield and sword, and holding in his right hand a scepter with an ornamental terminal. His garment reaches to his feet, which are planted on three horizontal banks of clouds. Five people holding shields and swords are placed on each side of Christ, and a small figure appears close to Christ's head on his left side. The scene was identified by Macalister as the Ascension: "Christ crowned and armed, as a victor, holding a flowering scepter. Around Him the eleven apostles, likewise armed (an allusion to the 'Church Militant')."[11] Henry followed Helen Roe in associating the scene with Ps. 23 (24): "Lift up your gates, O ye princes . . . the King of Glory shall enter. Who is the King of Glory? The Lord of Hosts. He is the King of Glory." However, she added that a further interpretation of the scene might be possible.[12] Helen Roe saw the scene as Christ Militant, the Second Coming of Christ to Judgment. He is

> shown as the King of Glory and the Lord of Hosts . . . standing on a "floor" of tightly packed clouds. Clad in a long robe He holds a sword and round shield in one hand and a long spear in the other. He is accompanied by ten armed men, five on either side—the apostles?— while close to the left side of His head a small angel hovers.[13]

Helen Roe noted that a simpler version of the subject appears on the Market cross at Kells. None of the authors associated the scene with the Book of Daniel.

The clues on the cross which connect the subject with the Book of Daniel are the clouds on which the figure is standing and the angel placed close to the left side of Christ's head. In Dan. 7, the Vision of the Four Beasts, God (the Ancient of Days) presides over the court of heaven to judge the nations of the ancient world. The nations are cast down and "one in human likeness" comes with the clouds of heaven and is given glory and kingship (Dan. 7.13). "Every nation, tribe and tongue must serve him; his dominion is to be everlasting, never passing away; his kingship shall never be destroyed." The "one in human likeness" or the Son of Man was identified with the Messiah, and was a title which Christ applied to himself (Matt. 9.6, John 5.27).[14] The Christian interpretation is the establishment of the Kingdom of Heaven by Christ, appointed by God. Thus, Christ is shown holding a scepter as the eternal king, armed with the sword of the Spirit which is the word of God, and with the shield of faith which renders harmless the flaming arrows of the devil (Eph. 6.16,17). In the vision, Daniel asks one of the angels in God's entourage to explain the dream (Dan. 7.17). The angel says that the Four Beasts were the four great earthly kingdoms (all of which were destroyed and passed away). "But then the holy ones of the Most High will receive the kingdom and possess it forever . . ." (Dan. 7.18). The figures surrounding Christ on the cross may be the holy ones of God, holding the shield of faith and the sword which is the word of God, who will inherit the kingdom of God for ever.

The Market cross at Kells (pl. 6.5) was discussed earlier with reference to the presence of Daniel in the Lion Pit in the center of the cross-head on the east side of the cross. The inclusion of the Virgin and Child above the central scene suggested an interpretation of the Incarnation based on Dan. 9.24–27, with the Soldiers asleep at the Tomb representing the Resurrection. If the panel above the Resurrection is now seen as an illustration of Dan. 7.13, with the same meaning and iconography as on the west cross at Monasterboice, the sequence of panels presents the Fall, the Incarnation, the Resurrection, and the Establishment of the Kingdom of the Elect, shown mostly in Old Testament scenes to emphasize the continuity through history of the divine plan of salvation. The west side of the cross depicts the Crucifixion and significant miracles of Christ.

A less extensive but similar cluster of subjects occurs on the east side of the cross at Drumcliff (pl. 6.6). Daniel in the Lion Pit on the lower arm of the cross-head may be interpreted as the prefiguration of the Resurrection. The center panel shows a frontally standing figure holding a cross-staff in his right hand. On either side of the figure, and in the three remaining cross-arms are human heads. These could be the Elect in the Inauguration of the Kingdom of Dan. 7.13. Adam and Eve are represented near the base of the shaft on this side of the cross, while the Crucifixion and New Testament scenes occur on the west side, as at Kells. Thus, both the Drumcliff and the Market cross at Kells include two panels from the Book of Daniel, the prophet among the lions, and the Son of Man appearing among the clouds.

It will be seen from the foregoing that while there are basic Christian meanings to be derived from several sections of the Book of Daniel, there is a flexibility and variety in the interpretations in any subject which allows the interpreter to adjust the meaning to given circumstances, such as the seasons of the liturgical year. In the case of the Irish crosses and comparable

Pl. 6.6. Drumcliff (County Sligo): east side. Photograph by author.

monuments of art, the changing circumstances are represented by the several panels whose arrangement and juxtapositions may alter the significance of a subject and allow the viewer to choose one meaning in preference to another, from several which appear in the Bible itself or from the meanings given in patristic literature. Thus, there is not one meaning per subject, but so wide a selection that each interpretation is personal to the individual who makes it.

Notes

1. Crosses with surviving subjects from the Book of Daniel:

(a) *Daniel in the Lion Pit.* 1. Clare, Dysart O'Dea base; 2. Fermanagh, Galloon west; 3. Kildare, Castledermot north; (pl. 6.3); 4. Kildare, Castledermot south; 5. Kildare, Moone base (pl. 6.2); 6. Kilkenny, Kilree; 7. Louth, Monasterboice west (?); 8. Meath, Kells market (pl. 6.5); 9. Meath, Kells south; 10. Meath, Killary (?); 11. Monaghan, Clones shaft fragment (pl. 6.4); 12. Monaghan, Clones cross-head (pl. 6.4); 13. Sligo, Drumcliff (pl. 6.6); 14. Tipperary, Ahenny south base; 15. Tyrone, Arboe (pl. 6.1); 16. Tyrone, Donaghmore; 17. Wicklow, Oldcourt base (?).

(b) *Daniel's Vision.* 1. Louth, Monasterboice west; 2. Meath, Kells market; 3. Sligo, Drumcliff(?).

Helen Roe ("An Interpretation of Certain Symbolic Sculptures of Early Christian Ireland," *J.R.S.A.I.* 75 [1945]: 1–23) does not consider the panel on the east side of the Arboe cross (pl. 6.1) to represent the Daniel motif. She classes it with her Group 2 (central human figure flanked by human figures with marked animal attributes). She states (p. 6) that in early continental and Coptic sources there is no example of the Daniel motif depicting rampant animals pushing their muzzles against Daniel's head. My reasons for grouping the Arboe panel with the Daniel subjects are: the central figure stands in the "crucifixion pose" on the important east side of the cross; the two animals represent actual felines rather than disguised human beings; the animals resemble lions more than they resemble the bird or goat/ram-headed representations of Helen Roe's Group 2; the lions lick Daniel's face with long tongues on the Clones cross-head fragment and on the Market cross at Kells; the panel at Arboe is associated with the Three Young Men as on the Moone base, Kells south and Monasterboice west (panel of the Establishment of the Kingdom discussed below). Large rampant lions on either side of a central figure occur in Byzantine and Persian art, for example the Shroud of Saint Victor (illustrated in A. T. Lucas, "'In the Middle of Two Living Things': Daniel or Christ?" *Figures From the Past*, edited by E. Rynne [Dun Laoghaire: Glandale Press for the Royal Irish Academy, 1987], fig. 5.3, p. 95). A second example in Irish work may be that on the east side of the cross base at Oldcourt, discussed and illustrated in P. Ó hÉailidhe, "The Cross Base at Oldcourt, near Bray, Co. Wicklow," in Rynne, *Figures From the Past*, 98–110.

The panel of a man between two animals on the west cross at Monasterboice (illustrated in Lucas, "Daniel or Christ?" 93) is more difficult to accept as a representation of Daniel. It is placed on the north side of the cross, unusual for such an important prophet as Daniel, and is thus removed from the subjects usually associated with Daniel panels.

2. H. Roe, "An Interpretation of Certain Symbolic Sculptures in Early Christian Ireland," *J.R.S.A.I.* 75 (1945): 1–23.

3. Biblical quotations are from the (non-denominational) Anchor Bible: L. F. Hartman and A. A. Di Lella, *The Book of Daniel* (Garden City, N.Y.: Doubleday, 1978), except for Dan. 12.2 which is the translation of *The Oxford Annotated Bible*, Revised Standard Version.

4. C. A. Moore, *Daniel, Esther and Jeremiah, The Additions* (Garden City, N.Y.: Doubleday, 1977).

5. *The "Painter's Manual" of Dionysius of Fourna*, trans. P. Hetherington (London: Sagittarius Press, 1974).

6. Both F. Henry and H. Roe applied these meanings to certain representations of Daniel on the crosses.

7. J. Daniélou, *Sacramentum Futuri. Études sur les Origines de la Typologie biblique* (Paris: Beauchesne, 1950), 5–9.

8. E. Le Blant, *Les Sarcophages chrétiens de la Gaule* (Paris: Impr. nationale, 1886); and *Étude sur les Sarcophages chrétiens antiques de la Ville d'Arles* (Paris: Beauchesne, 1878).

9. H. Roe, *The High Crosses of Kells* (Meath: Meath Archaeological and Historical Society, 1959).

10. H. Roe, *Monasterboice and its Monuments* (Louth: County Louth Archaeological and Historical Society, 1981), 50.

11. R. A. S. Macalister, *Guide to Monasterboice* (Dundalk: Dundalgan Press, 1944), 14.

12. F. Henry, *Irish Art During the Viking Invasions 800–1020* (Ithaca, N.Y.: Cornell University Press, 1967), 174.

13. Roe, *Monasterboice*, 57.

14. Further discussion of the Son of Man theme in M. McNamara, "Daniel," *A New Catholic Commentary on Holy Scripture* (London: Nelson, 1969, reprint 1984), 650–75.

CHAPTER SEVEN

Roger Stalley

THE TOWER CROSS
AT KELLS

The stone crosses which survive at the ancient monastic site of Kells (Meath) are difficult and frustrating monuments to study.[1] The Market cross, with its extensive cycle of Christian iconography, stands at a busy road junction, where trucks and vans pass within inches of its thousand-year-old carvings. Inevitably the surfaces are badly corroded and the sharpness of the original sculpture has been lost. Some distance up the hill to the west, in the relative solitude of the Protestant churchyard, lies the so-called Broken cross, once an impressively tall monument, but now shorn of its cross-head. Here the carvings are better preserved, though many of the scenes are hard to decipher. The cross stands in front of the west door of the nineteenth-century church, a building which almost certainly lies on the site of the major church of the old monastery. To the southeast is the "Unfinished" cross, where only a few areas of carving were completed before the project was abandoned. Nobody is too sure when this cross was begun and the reason for its abandonment remains a matter for speculation. Southwest of the church lies the "Tower" cross, taking its name from the adjacent round tower. This cross is relatively well-preserved and the subjects depicted on it are, for the most part, easy to identify (pls. 7.1, and 7.2). The decay of its sandstone surfaces, however, has deprived the sculpture of much of its visual quality. Some distance away beside the late-medieval bell tower is a base of rounded form, all that is left of a fifth cross.

Both in scale and design, the crosses at Kells are very different from each other, differences which raise a number of questions about the

Pl. 7.1. The Tower cross at Kells, from the west, with the Crucifixion prominent on the shaft. All photographs by the author unless otherwise indicated.

Pl. 7.2. The Tower cross at Kells, from the east; the Three Hebrews in the furnace are depicted above the Fall.

purpose of high crosses, about why they were erected and about the historical circumstances in which they were carved. The existence of a group of crosses also raises questions about the way archaeologists and historians have in the past approached the study of these monuments.

Some Assumptions and Preconceptions

Fifteen years ago the study of the crosses seemed a relatively straightforward business. By turning to the work of Françoise Henry or Helen Roe, one could find an apparently secure framework and few people dared to question the opinions of these undoubted authorities. But in recent years much has changed. The debate has been widened and several of the old "orthodoxies" have been challenged.[2] The issues are now seen to be more complicated, and more intriguing, than had hitherto been imagined. While these are exciting times in high cross studies, scholarship still tends to be dominated, and distorted, by at least one preconception inherited from the past. A high proportion of writers cling to the notion of development or typological progression as a means of explaining differences of design, suggesting a Darwinian-like faith in the process of evolution. When confronted with contrasts in style or technique, whether in stone crosses or penannular brooches, for example, the first instinct is to explain the differences by reference to date. It is as if one of the key objectives in any research is to discover the sequence or "genetical chain" which somehow links the objects together. While it is perfectly legitimate to search for patterns of development, the problem is that such modes of thought tend to be restrictive and prevent us from looking at material in other ways. Works which do not fit the preconceived pattern are ignored or squeezed into categories to which they do not comfortably belong, and works that share features with different chronological groups are branded as "transitional," a favorite word among those geared to the evolutionary approach.[3] Art historians, brought up on critical appraisals of Vasari's _Lives of the Artists_, have for long been alerted to the dangers of this organic method, but it is still followed, often without question, in much archaeological writing.[4] This is understandable, particularly among authors dealing with prehistoric or poorly documented eras, where alternative methods of bringing a sense of coherence are hard to find. Moreover, a search for evolutionary patterns is valid enough for simple artefacts, especially those with a functional or utilitarian purpose—ring pins or rowel spurs, for example. But the method is of limited value when dealing with artefacts as complex as the Irish high crosses.[5]

There are several factors, other than date, which must be borne in mind when comparing one cross with another. First there is the type of stone employed. This obviously depended on what was locally available and the nature of the blocks it was possible to extract from the quarry.[6] Then there was the range of artistic models that the particular monastery could offer its sculptors. Local traditions were clearly important and in some cases previous (and perhaps now destroyed) crosses had a bearing on design. But most important was the purpose of individual crosses and the historical circumstances which accompanied their manufacture. It has been recognized for many years that the Ahenny crosses belong to a distinctive local "school," perhaps inspired by a revered prototype in one of the neighboring monasteries.[7] Yet because the cross-shafts are covered by abstract ornament, apparently of eighth-century character, there is a tendency to assume that ornamental crosses invariably precede those with panels of figure sculpture.[8] Such differences are likely to be a product of place as much as of time. Similarly, comments on the Iona crosses need to be treated with caution. Their unusual structure, with extensive use of mortices and relatively thin blocks, is as much a reflection of the local geology and the scarcity of suitable stone as it is of date.[9]

Although scholars have been aware of these factors, they have not always been given the emphasis they deserve. Françoise Henry, who defined the regional "schools" of Irish carving very effectively, attempted to place them in chronological order, almost regardless of history and geography.[10] The result was that the earliest crosses appeared in such unlikely places as Carndonagh and Ahenny.[11] The desire to plot a "developmental" pattern proved irresistible. Yet the notion of regional schools, operating concurrently, has for long been accepted as part of the framework for studying Romanesque sculpture. Another consequence of the "developmental" approach is the temptation to spread out the crosses at roughly even intervals over the assumed period of their manufacture, that is, from ca. 750 to ca. 950. Yet there is no a priori reason to suggest that this is what happened.

Underlying these problems of method is the fact that we do not know for sure why the crosses were made. A certain amount is known about how they functioned and their role in the religious life of the communities,[12] but this does not explain what patrons, be they kings or abbots, hoped to gain from them. The construction of crosses as large as those at Kells or Monasterboice involved a considerable investment and it is hard to believe they were undertaken for purely altruistic or religious motives. The fact that surviving inscriptions mention the names of abbots and kings indicates the extent to which they were regarded as objects of status.

DESCRIPTION OF THE TOWER CROSS

Bearing in mind these reservations about method, it is time to return to the high crosses at Kells, in particular to the Tower cross. Its total height is 3.26 meters (excluding the projecting tenon), which makes it the shortest of the four crosses. The shaft and cross-head are cut from one block of stone and decorated with a mixture of Christian iconography and abstract patterns. The east face contains four Old Testament subjects: Adam and Eve, placed together with Cain and Abel; the Three Hebrews in the furnace; Daniel in the Lions' den, and the Sacrifice of Isaac (pl. 7.2). The scene in the upper arm depicts the Miracle of the Loaves and Fishes, combined rather curiously with David and his harp.[13] The right arm shows St. Paul and St. Anthony fed by the raven in the desert. The opposite (west) face has only two major Christian scenes: the Crucifixion located on the shaft and the *Majestas Domini* in the cross-head (pls. 7.1 and, 7.3). Immediately above the head of Christ in the latter scene, the symbolic figure of St. Matthew raises aloft a medallion containing the Agnus Dei. The ends of the south and north arms contain subjects usually identified as David killing the lion and bear respectively (pl. 7.5). Among the "decorative" motifs are panels of fret designs, interlocked men, animals, inhabited vine scrolls, interlace, and spiral bosses. At the top of the north face of the shaft are two ecclesiastical figures, seated side by side and holding books.[14] These have been interpreted as St. Peter and St. Paul, but in view of the inscription on the cross, one wonders whether they might not have been intended as St. Patrick and St. Columba.

The pyramidal base is decorated on the two main faces with enigmatic figure carvings. The western side shows a figure with a motley collection of animals, usually taken as Noah driving the animals into the ark or alternatively a hunting scene;[15] the eastern side depicts a procession which includes two horsemen and a chariot (pl. 7.1).[16] The remaining faces are filled with interlace. A Latin inscription, which reads PATRICII ET COLUMBE CR[UX] is carved on the east side of the base, on the upper step.[17]

The selection of Christian subjects at first sight represents a rather disparate choice, particularly the arrangement on the east face. While three of the Old Testament subjects (the Three Hebrews, Daniel in the Lions' den, and the Sacrifice of Isaac) can be read as deliverance scenes, it is the theme of the Eucharist which best explains the choice further up. The Sacrifice of Isaac was a standard Old Testament "type" for the sacrifice of Christ on the cross, while the Feeding of the Five Thousand, as well as saints Paul and Anthony with the raven, allude to the eucharistic bread. These three scenes are arranged around the center of the cross (pl. 7.2). The lack of figure sculpture in the center itself might seem odd, but as É. Ó Carragáin has pointed out, the seven bossed motif was quite capable of allegorical interpretation.[18] The motif reads like a metal plaque and, among many examples of bosses and discs in this position, there is a good parallel at Kinnitty (846–62).[19]

The location of the Crucifixion on the shaft, rather than within the cross-head, has occasioned much comment (pls. 7.1, and 7.3). The same arrangement is found at Clonmacnois (south cross) and at Killamery, and one recent commentator has gone so far as to conclude that "its position on the shaft indicates that these crosses belong to a period before it was customary to place it on the cross-head."[20] It is hard to follow this reasoning, which is a good example of "developmental" thinking. One glance at the Tower cross suggests that it was a way of devoting more space to the Crucifixion and giving it greater prominence. The location of the subject can thus be explained in terms of design. The particular iconography employed, which is closely related to a series of metalwork plaques,[21] could not have been fitted into the cross-head without considerable distortion. One other curiosity of the Tower cross is the lack of moulded borders between the various figural scenes, a technique which has been compared with that on the crosses at Iona and Kildalton.[22] Again, this feature has been interpreted in "developmental" terms, with suggestions that it marks "a transition towards" the paneled organization of the scripture crosses.[23] The elimination of the borders, however, allowed more space for figure carving and it is safer to regard it as an alternative, rather than necessarily an earlier way of doing things.

THE IMPORTANCE OF THE TOWER CROSS IN IRISH ART

Modern writers have had little doubt about the importance of the Tower cross, several describing it as "crucial" to our understanding of the crosses as a whole.[24] This emphasis is based on a number of considerations: First, there is the almost unanimous chorus of opinion that it is the earliest of the crosses at Kells, many writers being convinced that it was carved no more than a decade or two after the monastery was founded in 804/807,[25] others placing it somewhat later between 830 and 850.[26] Moreover, the fact that Kells was a daughter house of Iona means the Tower Cross is assumed to represent a link between the Irish crosses and those in western Scotland. Those scholars who believe the ringed cross was first evolved in Iona lay particular stress on this point.[27] The fact that Kells became the head of the Columban federation, certainly by the tenth century, if not before, adds to the importance of the sculpture. The crosses almost certainly acquired a status and influence beyond that of similar monuments elsewhere. Finally, the decoration of the cross is thought to reflect the influence of the Book of Kells.[28] This assumption, however, depends on the question of where and when the Book of Kells was painted. If it was produced at Kells, or brought there soon after the Viking onslaught on Iona in 806, there is no problem. If the Book did not reach Kells until 878, as several modern scholars have argued,[29] the cross must postdate 878, assuming the sculptors were indeed influenced by the decoration of the manuscript.

THE TRADITIONAL DATE OF THE TOWER CROSS

Assessments of the Tower cross and its importance are thus inextricably bound up with assumptions about its supposed date. Before proceeding further, it is worth examining the arguments used to support these assumptions.

First, several writers, including Françoise Henry, have stressed the parallels that exist with the south cross at Clonmacnois, in particular the iconography of the Crucifixion and its location on the shaft of the cross.[30] There are also similarities in the choice of decorative motifs, notably the presence of vine scrolls (rare in Ireland), miniature bosses, and fret patterns.[31] The Clonmacnois cross has traditionally been dated to about 800, but there is no compelling evidence for this. The opinion appears to be based on the view that its design was influenced by the Ahenny crosses, themselves traditionally ascribed to the eighth century. Dr. Edwards, the author of the most recent study of the Clonmacnois cross, was forced to admit that its dating was "difficult."[32] While the parallels with the Tower cross at Kells are unquestionable, they provide little help in providing a date for either cross.

Second, some scholars feel the design and arrangement of scenes on the Tower cross represent an "early" stage of development. The lack of a systematic scheme of panels and the placing of the Crucifixion on the shaft have both been cited in this context.[33] As we have already seen, this argument is difficult to sustain.

Third, the inscription recording the names of St. Patrick and St. Columba has been taken as the sign of an "early" date. It is the only inscription in Latin on one of the Irish high crosses and Dr. Higgitt, who has made a special study of Insular inscriptions, suggests that it may represent an early fashion which soon became outmoded.[34] Françoise Henry and Liam de Paor have both argued that the inscription specifically refers to the unusual circumstances of the founding of Kells in 804/807. While a dedication to St. Columba is only to be expected in a Columban house, the joint dedication including St. Patrick is more surprising. As the founding saint of Armagh, Patrick was the champion of a rival *paruchia* which was seeking to extend its influence throughout Ireland. Françoise Henry was ready to see the foundation of Kells in more philanthropic terms, as an act of benevolence, with Armagh providing a place of refuge for the Columban monks as they tried to escape the Vikings. The inscription "would then appear as commemorating this gift."[35] Liam de Paor has interpreted the situation in a more prosaic fashion, regarding the inscription as a "document of compromise," in which Armagh's primacy was formally acknowledged in return for recognition of the new Columban house.[36] Under the year 803, *recte* 804, the annals of Ulster explain that Kells was given "without battle," which tends to suggest a negotiated agreement.[37] While both interpretations are plausible, both are hypothetical. Neither version of events finds favor with Dr. Máire Herbert, the most recent historian of Iona and Kells.[38] The monastery of Kells lay within the lands of the southern Uí Néill, apparently in a border area of several small Brega kingdoms. It is possible that the Clann Cholmain may have supported the transfer of the old royal fort at Kells to the Columban community as a way of weakening the influence of their rivals the Síl nÁedo Sláne.[39] Equally, the king of Tara, Áed mac Neill of Ailech, known as Áed Oirdnide (Aed the anointed) may have been involved. The official granting of the site in 804 coincides with the date of the assembly at Dún Cuair,[40] attended by both the abbot of Armagh and king Áed Oirdnide, and it is possible that the negotiations for the new foundation took place on this occasion. However, given our fragmentary picture of events, it is difficult to know exactly what the political implications were.

Fourth, for many centuries the Book of Kells was kept within a few yards of the Tower cross and there are some undoubted analogies between the painting and the sculpture. William O'Sullivan felt the cross "reflects the spirit of the incomparable book, combining illustration with the older elements of Irish decoration,"[41] and Helen Roe described the cross as a "manuscript one," on account of its profusion of surface decoration.[42] Françoise Henry was impressed by the sculptured *Majestas* surrounded by the four Evangelist symbols: "It is striking that the Cross of the Tower at Kells, which probably belongs to the early ninth century, is the only one of the Irish high crosses to have the symbols of the four Evangelists. . . . In any case, the symbols are there and they link the Cross and the Book."[43] The link, however, is fragile. The Book of Kells was not the only set of Gospels to illustrate the four Evangelists and those depicted on the cross bear little resemblance to those in the manuscript. Even if the sculptors were influenced by the book—and this is by no means certain—it still provides no

Pl. 7.3. The Tower cross at Kells: detail of the Crucifixion on the west face.

Pl. 7.4. The Tower cross at Kells: detail of the *Majestas Domini* on the west face.

Pl. 7.5. The Tower cross at Kells from the south, showing David and the lion on the end of the arm.

Pl. 7.6. The Market cross at Kells from the west, showing David and the lion on the end of the arm.

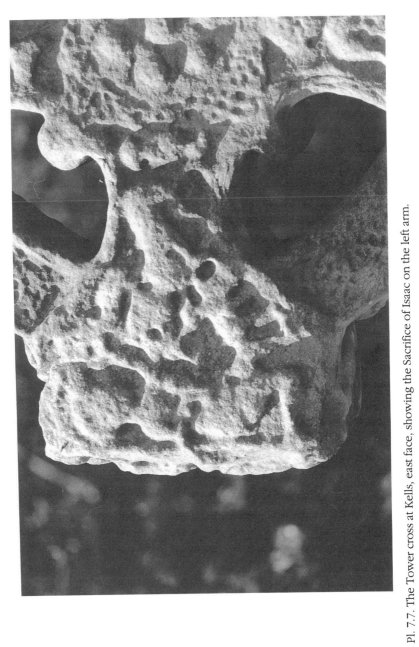

Pl. 7.7. The Tower cross at Kells, east face, showing the Sacrifice of Isaac on the left arm.

Pl. 7.8. The Market cross at Kells, south face, showing the Sacrifice of Isaac on the left arm.

Pl. 7.9. The Broken cross at Kells, panel from the east face, showing the Baptism of Christ.

Pl. 7.10. Muiredach's cross at Monasterboice, east face: detail of the Last Judgment.

evidence for the date of the cross, merely a *terminus post quem.* This is either 804/807, for those who believe the manuscript was made at Kells or was brought there after the attack on Iona, or after 878 for those who believe it was brought to Ireland along with the other relics of St. Columba in that year. One comparison with the Book of Kells, which has not previously been made, lies in the area of figure style. The profiled head of Cain, with an acutely pointed chin, recalls many a figure in the manuscript (pl. 7.2).

THE HISTORY OF KELLS IN THE NINTH AND TENTH CENTURIES

It should now be apparent that none of the arguments used to date the Tower cross are conclusive. Before advancing some alternative propositions, it is worth considering the history of the monastery of Kells. The crosses were not carved in an historical vacuum, and it is important to consider their social and political context. Five events, or series of events, stand out in the early history of the monastery.[44]

First, the foundation and construction of the new house between 804/807 and 814. The Annals of Ulster provide a terse record, with the words: "Constructio nove civitatis Columbae Cille hi Ceninnus" (806 *recte* 807) and "Cellach, abbas Iae, finita constructione templi Cenindra, reliquit principatum" (813 *recte* 814). Historians are divided on the question of whether Kells was intended at the outset to replace Iona as the head of the Columban federation.[45] While it was obviously intended as far more than a temporary refuge, it did not immediately supplant Iona as head of the *paruchia.* Indeed religious life continued on the island and the major relics of Columba stayed there until 878.[46] The Irish annals are silent about Kells between 814 and 878, which suggests it did not immediately acquire the importance it attained in the tenth century.

Second, the transfer of the shrine of Columba and his *minna* (reliquaries) to Kells in 878 "to escape the Foreigners."[47] Although Viking pressure brought about the transfer, Iona had become increasingly isolated after 843, when the Scottish and Pictish kingdoms were united under Kenneth Mac Alpin. The choice of Dunkeld in central Scotland as the chief ecclesiastical center of the kingdom meant that Iona was now far more peripheral than it had been before. There is no reason to suppose that the transfer of the relics was intended to be permanent, but after a few years at Kells it probably became obvious that they would never return. The importance of the "relics" should not be underestimated. They provided the most forceful and tangible link with the founder of the *paruchia* and buttressed the authority of the abbot of Kells. Among the "relics" may have been the Book of Kells, described by the Annals of Ulster as "the chief relic of the western world" and "the great gospel book of Colum Cille."[48] Together these precious items must have transformed the status of Kells within the Columban federation.

Third, the reign of Abbot Máel Brigte mac Tornáin (891–927).[49] The rule of Máel Brigte coincided with a decisive period in the history of Kells. He was already Abbot of Armagh when appointed to Kells and his obit in the Annals of Ulster describes him as "*comarb Patraic ocus Coluim Cille.*"[50] The fact that he was abbot of both Kells and Armagh[51] is remarkable and it is not easy to explain how it came about. Dr. Herbert has suggested that a prime factor may have been his family background, since he was of Cenél Conaill descent, the family to which Columba himself belonged.[52] Whatever the reasons, the political union of Armagh and Kells, albeit temporary, was a startling development. Máel Brigte was styled *comarba* of Colum Cille, the title previously held by the abbots of Iona. The title confirms the impression that Kells was now recognized as the de facto head of the *paruchia*.

Fourth, the attack on Kells in 904 by King Flann Máel Sechnaill, the high king of Ireland. This is recorded in the Annals of Ulster in the following terms: "the profanation of Cenannes by Flann, son of Máelsechnaill, against Donnchad, i.e. his own son; and a great many people were beheaded around the oratory."[53]

Fifth, the Viking raids of the tenth century. After the bloodthirsty events of 904, the monastery increasingly became a target of attack, which implies that it had acquired a degree of prosperity and wealth. In 920 "the '*doimliac*' (stone church) of Cenannas was broken by Gentiles, and great numbers were martyred there."[54] In 951, Gothfrith, son of Sitric, with the Vikings of Dublin plundered Kells and a number of neighboring churches, "on which occasion three thousand men, or more, were captured, together with a great booty of cows and horses, of gold and silver."[55] Further raids took place in 970 and 997, establishing a pattern which lasted throughout the eleventh century.[56]

THE STYLE AND ICONOGRAPHY OF THE CROSS

Despite this record of events, our knowledge of Kells, particularly the internal life of the monastery, remains sparse. The historical facts alone do not provide any conclusive evidence about when and why the crosses were made, though they provide a few hints. Clearly the foundation of the house is one potential time for cross carving and so, too, are the years after

878, when the status of the monastery was enhanced. The arrival of the shrine of Columba could have prompted a desire to embellish the monastic *termon* to provide a more fitting and honorable setting for the relics. During the subsequent abbacy of Máel Brigte, there is little doubt that the monastery had the resources necessary to carry out major programs of sculpture. In fact, one cross, the Market cross, was almost certainly erected during his period of office. The style and iconography of this imposing monument are associated with the scripture crosses at Monasterboice, Clonmacnois, and Durrow, now generally accepted as belonging to the years around 900.[57] Personal and political contacts may explain the relationships, for the south cross at Monasterboice was probably erected by the Muiredach who was vice abbot of Armagh and Máel Brigte's deputy. Muiredach was a man of considerable influence to judge from his obit in the Annals of Ulster, where he is described as high-steward of the southern Uí Néill and "head of counsel of all the men of Bregh, lay and clerical."[58] Together with Máel Brigte, he appears to have been closely associated with a policy of cross construction.

Where does the Tower cross fit into this scheme? Most commentators have tended to stress the differences between the Tower cross and the Market cross, while saying little about the similarities. Some of the iconographical arrangements are almost identical: the awkward squeezing of the Sacrifice of Isaac into an arm (pls. 7.7, and 7.8), for example, the placing of David and the lion on one end (pls. 7.5, and 7.6), the twinning of Adam and Eve with Cain and Abel, and the prominence given to Daniel (pl. 7.2). The similarities extend even to iconographical details. If the picture is widened to include the whole group of the "Midland" scripture crosses (Monasterboice, Clonmacnois west, and Durrow), the iconographical context of the Tower cross becomes more obvious. The scene with the Three Hebrews in the furnace, including soldiers stoking the fire with faggots, resembles the equivalent scene on the west cross at Monasterboice, where the striped robes on the crucified Christ are also repeated.[59] Durrow reproduces the Agnus Dei. Moreover, the figure of Christ, armed with a cross and a flowering rod, is found at all four sites (Monasterboice south, Durrow, Clonmacnoise west, as well as the Tower cross).[60]

A similar pattern is revealed when we turn to the carvings on the base. The chariot and horsemen appear at Monasterboice (south) and Clonmacnois (west), and the latter also includes the enigmatic animal scene. Some of the same decorative patterns reappear, notably the inhabited vine scroll and the panel of entangled men.[61]

The style of the carvings on the Tower cross appears to be flatter than that on the scripture crosses, but this is partly because the surfaces are badly abraded.[62] In the few places where the sculpture is well preserved, as in the face of Christ in Majesty (pl. 7.4) or the legs of Stephaton and Longinus, the rounded technique of the scripture crosses is clearly evident. Indeed the circular-shaped face of Christ, adorned with curly (?) hair, immediately recalls the cheerful chubby faces of Muiredach's cross (pl. 7.10). A brief glance at the neighboring Broken cross brings out the distinctive features of this approach. Here the figures, with their oversized heads and small bodies, seem rather uncouth in comparison (pl. 7.9). In addition to the rounded faces seen on the scripture crosses, the Tower cross includes a different form, in which the head is seen in profile. This is the so-called Kells profile where the faces are given a pointed jaw and the hair falls in a curl at the nape of the neck. It is best seen in the figure of Cain (pl. 7.2) and there are innumerable examples in the Book of Kells.

Some of the technical aspects of the carving are equally revealing. The relief of the sculpture attains a maximum depth of 2.5 cm. (on the Crucifixion), and, while that is not as deep as some of the carving on Muiredach's cross, it is substantial in an Irish context. Moreover the panels of figure sculpture project forward of the angle mouldings, rather than being set in the same plane. This is an accomplished technique, which does not imply an early or experimental approach. Finally, the general form of the cross, not least the slight taper to the upper shaft above the ring, is not out of place in the context of the scripture crosses.

CONCLUSION

The combined evidence of iconography, style, technique, and form underlines the association between the Tower cross and the scripture crosses of ca. 900. There can be little doubt that the Tower cross belongs to a similar era. The sculpture may well have coincided with the rule of Máel Brigte, *comarb* of Patrick and Columba. Can it be coincidence that the words of Máel Brigte's obit echo those of the inscription, PATRICII ET COLUMBE CR[UX], an appropriate dedication at a time when Armagh and Kells were united under the authority of the same abbot? It is unlikely that the Tower cross is a record of Armagh's benevolence in 804 or a "document of compromise." Rather it seems to be a testimony to the expanding status of Kells, after the monastery acquired the main relics of Columba in 878. It may also reflect the authority of an unusually powerful abbot.

NOTES

1. In 1996 the Market cross was moved to a less exposed site nearby. This paper was prepared before the publication of Peter Harbison's monumental study

of the Irish crosses, *The High Crosses of Ireland*, 3 vols. (Bonn: R. Habelt, 1992). The most comprehensive account of the crosses at Kells is to be found in Helen Roe, *The High Crosses of Kells*, 2nd. ed. (Meath: Meath Archaeological and Historical Association, 1966). See also H. S. Crawford, "The Early Crosses of East and West Meath," *J.R.S.A.I.* 56 (1926): 72–78; H. S. Crawford, *Handbook of Carved Ornament from Irish Monuments of the Christian Period* (Dublin: Royal Society of Antiquaries of Ireland, 1926); E. H. L. Sexton, *Irish Figure Sculpture* (Portland, Maine: Southworth-Anthoensen Press, 1946), the latter containing a good bibliography of the earlier literature.

2. Peter Harbison is foremost among the scholars who have questioned earlier views, for example his article of 1979 ("The Inscriptions on the Cross of the Scriptures at Clonmacnois, County Offaly," *P.R.I.A.* 79C: 177–88), which produced a swift retort from Henry ("Around an Inscription: the Cross of the Scriptures at Clonmacnois," *J.R.S.A.I.* 110 [1980]: 36–51). Important contributions to recent debates have also come from: Carola Hicks, "A Clonmacnois Workshop in Stone," *J.R.S.A.I.* 110 (1980): 5–35; Nancy Edwards, "An Early Group of Crosses from the Kingdom of Ossory," *J.R.S.A.I.* 113 (1983): 5–46; "The South Cross, Clonmacnois," in J. Higgitt, ed., *Early Medieval Sculpture in Britain and Ireland*, B.A.R. Brit. ser. 152 (Oxford: British Archaeological Reports, 1986): 23–36; Susanne McNab, "Styles Used in Twelfth Century Irish Figure Sculpture," *Peritia* 6–7 (1987–88): 265–97; "Classical and Celtic Influences in the Figure Styles of Early Irish Sculpture," *Irish Arts Review Yearbook, 1990–91* (Dublin): 164–71; Dorothy Kelly, "Irish High Crosses: Some Evidence from the Plainer Examples," *J.R.S.A.I.* 116 (1986): 51–67; "Crucifixion Plaques in Stone at Clonmacnois and Kells," *Irish Arts Review Yearbook 1990–91* (Dublin): 204–9; Liam de Paor, "The High Crosses of Tech Theille (Tihilly), Kinnitty and Related Sculpture," in Etienne Rynne, ed., *Figures from the Past* (Dun Laoghaire: Glendale Press for the Royal Society of Antiquaries of Ireland, 1987), 131–58; Michael Herity, "The Context and Date of the High Cross at Disert Diarmada (Castledermot), County Kildare," in Rynne, *Figures from the Past*, 111–30; Ann Hamlin, "'Dignatio diei dominici': an Element in the Iconography of Irish Crosses?" in D. Whitelock, R. McKitterick and D. Dumville, eds., *Ireland in Early Medieval Europe* (Cambridge: Cambridge University Press, 1982), 69–75; "Crosses in Early Ireland: the Evidence from the Written Sources," in M. Ryan, ed., *Ireland and Insular Art A.D. 500–1200* (Dublin: Royal Irish Academy, 1987), 138–40; and Éamonn Ó Carragáin, "The Ruthwell Cross and Irish High Crosses: Some Points of Comparison and Contrast," in Ryan, *Ireland and Insular Art*, 118–28; "The Meeting of Saint Paul and Saint Anthony: Visual and Literary uses of a Eucharistic Motif," in G. Mac Niocaill and P. Wallace, eds., *Keimelia: Studies in Medieval Archaeology and History in Memory of Tom Delany* (Galway, Ireland: Galway University Press, 1989), 1–58.

3. See for example the discussion of the south cross at Clonmacnois in H. Richardson and J. Scarry, *An Introduction to Irish High Crosses* (Cork, Ireland: Mercier, 1990), 17.

4. For the concept of artistic progress see E. H. Gombrich, "The Renaissance Conception of Artistic Progress and its Consequences," in *Norm and Form: Studies in the Art of the Renaissance* (London: Phaidon, 1966), 1–10.

5. de Paor ("The High Crosses of Tech Theille," 143–44), has some judicious comments about methods: ". . . the normal documenting methods of art history are not available. We must fall back on the methods of archaeology—not wholly suited to this purpose. There is a temptation to resort to dubious, pseudo-art historical methods; to invent a documentation, largely by rash, even random analogies and comparisons between different cultures whose actual relationships with one another may remain very obscure even to the most diligent historical researcher. The temptation is all the more dangerous if we indulge the illusion that Dark Age Christian culture was in church matters at least, one and indivisible like the seamless garment of Christ. On the contrary every local church had its own culture—even in church matters—and could turn the small common stock of Christian ideas and images to its own purposes and its own meaning."

6. There are some brief but excellent comments on this by Françoise Henry, *Irish High Crosses* (Dublin: Three Candles, 1964), 15–16.

7. Françoise Henry, *Irish Art in the Early Christian Period (to A.D. 800)* (London: Methuen, 1965), 140; Helen Roe, *The High Crosses of Western Ossory* (Kilkenny, Ireland: Kilkenny Archaeological Society, 1969), 8; Peter Harbison, "On Some Possible Sources of Irish High Cross Decoration," in O–H. Frey, ed., *Festschrift zum 50 jahrigen Bestehen des Vorgeschichtlichen Seminars Marburg*, Marburger Studien zur Vor und Frühgeschichte Seminars Marburg (Gladenbach: Kempkes, 1977), 283–87. The Ahenny crosses are discussed at length by Henry, *Irish High Crosses*, 21–24; by Judith Calvert, *The Early Development of Irish High Crosses and their Relationship to Scottish Sculpture in the Ninth and Tenth Centuries* (Ph.D. diss., University of California, Berkeley; Berkeley: University of California Press, 1978), 71–83, and by Edwards, "An Early Group of Crosses," 5–46.

8. The Ahenny crosses, along with others in the Ossory group, have usually been dated through their analogies with eighth-century metalwork. Thus, Henry felt that they belonged "at the latest to a period around 750" (*Irish Art in the Early Christian Period*, 139). Henry's views have generally been followed since, as, for example, by Calvert (*The Early Development of Irish High Crosses*, 71). Richardson, while regarding the group as the earliest, cautiously states that the crosses "probably date from the eighth to ninth centuries" (Richardson and Scarry, *Introduction to Irish High Crosses*, 17). Edwards ("An Early Group of Crosses," 31–32), is well aware of the precarious basis of the traditional dating, concluding that the crosses "may be ascribed to any time during the eighth or early ninth centuries," though finally coming down in favor of ca. 800. Crawford (*Irish Carved Ornament*, 4), opted for a date in the middle of the ninth century, although he nonetheless felt the Ahenny crosses were the earliest group in Ireland. The problem is that the dating of Irish metalwork is notoriously uncertain and that it provides only a *terminus post quem* for the stone sculpture. If metalwork objects were deliberately being copied, it is possible they had already acquired a degree of venerability by the time they were used as models.

9. R.C.A.H.M., *Royal Commission on the Ancient and Historic Monuments of Scotland* (Edinburgh: H.M.S.O., 1982) 17–19, 192–211. The authors of this volume believe the Iona crosses belong to the middle or later part of the eighth century,

and assume that the Viking attacks on Iona in 802 and 806 provide a *terminus post quem*. They also suggest (18) that the "Iona crosses are an early and experimental group," giving Iona a crucial role in the formation of the ringed cross. This echoes the views of R. B. K. Stevenson ("The Chronology and Relationships of some Irish and Scottish Crosses," *J.R.S.A.I.* 86 [1956]: 85–89), and Calvert (*Early Development of Irish High Crosses*, 107), who concluded that "The forms of the Irish cross were derived from experiments on the Iona crosses, but the Irish added their own inventions to the final design." M. Werner ("On the Origin of the Form of the Irish High Cross," *Gesta* XXIX/1 [1990]: 98–110) also regards Iona as crucial.

10. Henry, *Irish Art in the Early Christian Period*, 117–58.

11. Ibid., 128. According to Henry, the Carndonagh cross "marks the final victory in the attempt to free the cross from the slab." The seventh- or early eighth-century date accorded to Carndonagh by Henry has been rejected by Stevenson ("Chronology and Relationships," 93–96), and Peter Harbison ("A Group of Early Christian Carved Stone Monuments in County Donegal," in Higgitt, *Early Medieval Sculpture in Britain and Ireland*, 51–52).

12. What is known about the functions of the crosses is summarized by Hamlin in "Crosses in Early Ireland," 138–40. See also pertinent comments by John Higgitt, "Words and Crosses: the Inscribed Stone Cross in Early Medieval Britain and Ireland," in Higgitt, *Early Medieval Sculpture in Britain and Ireland*, 125–52.

13. The only explanation for this curious mixing of Old and New Testament so far given is that suggested by Françoise Henry (*Irish Art During the Viking Invasions, 800–1020 A.D.* [London: Methuen, 1967], 150–51), who writes that the source of inspiration may have come from "illuminations of Greek or Oriental manuscripts such as the Rossano Gospels or the Sinope Fragment, where prophets holding scrolls accompany each Gospel scene." Isolated carvings of David playing his harp are not uncommon on the Irish crosses, however, and an example appears amidst the Blessed in the Last Judgment on Muiredach's cross at Monasterboice (Helen Roe, *Monasterboice and its Monuments* [Louth: County Louth Archaeological Historical Society, 1981], 42).

14. Roe, *High Crosses of Kells*, 25.

15. Ibid., 13; Sexton, *Irish Figure Sculpture*, 184. A recent discussion of these scenes can be found in P. Ó hÉailidhe, "The Cross-Base at Oldcourt, near Bray, Co. Wicklow," in Rynne, *Figures from the Past*, 102–4.

16. The chariot scenes on the bases of the high crosses have proved difficult to interpret. They appear at Ahenny (north), Clonmacnois (west), Killamery, Monasterboice (south) as well as on the Tower cross at Kells. Roe (*High Crosses of Western Ossory*, 16–17, 45), argued that the Ahenny example represented a translation of relics, though as Edwards ("An Early Group of Crosses," 24–25), has pointed out, no shrine is visible in the carving. Henry (*Irish Art in the Early Christian Period*, 151–52), regarded the Ahenny scene as "an allegorical image of the spread of Christianity."

17. R. A. S. Macalister, *Corpus Inscriptionum Insularum Celticarum* (Dublin: H.M.S.O., 1945–1949), no. 587; Roe, *High Crosses of Kells*, 10; Higgitt, "Words and Crosses," 127–29.

18. Ó Carragáin, "Meeting of St. Paul and St. Anthony," 16–20.

19. de Paor, "High Crosses of Tech Theille," 136–43.

20. Edwards, "South Cross," 25.

21. Kelly, "Crucifixion Plaques in Stone," 204–9.

22. Calvert, *Early Development of Irish High Crosses*, 131–34.

23. Richardson and Scarry, *Introduction to Irish High Crosses*, 17.

24. Calvert, *Early Development of Irish High Crosses*, 102, 165–66; Edwards, "South Cross," 31.

25. Henry, *Irish High Crosses*, 60; Henry, *Irish Art During the Viking Invasions*, 151; Kelly, "Crucifixion Plaques in Stone," 207–8; de Paor, "High Crosses of Tech Theille," 147–48; Richardson and Scarry, *Introduction to Irish High Crosses*, 18, 39–40; Helen Roe believed that it predated the recorded foundation of the monastery and that it was "at least as early as the second half of the 8th century." Roe, *High Crosses of Kells*, 8.

26. Edwards, "South Cross," 31; Calvert, *Early Development of Irish High Crosses*, 295–96; Stevenson ascribes the small boss decoration on the cross to the mid-ninth century, comparing it with examples at Meigle and Dunfallandy. See "Chronology and Relationships," 92.

27. Calvert, *Early Development of Irish High Crosses*, 303: "The principal models were found on Iona and the crosses of Monasterboice and Kells were copied from them . . ."; Stevenson, "Chronology and Relationships," 93.

28. W. O'Sullivan, "The Book of Kells," in *Great Books of Ireland*, Thomas Davis Lectures (Dublin: Clonmore & Reynolds; Burns & Oates, 1967), 18; Roe, *High Crosses of Kells*, 10; Richardson and Scarry, *Introduction to Irish High Crosses*, 18; Henry, *Irish Art During the Viking Invasions*, 70, 164; Françoise Henry, *The Book of Kells* (London: Thames & Hudson, 1974), 218.

29. George Henderson, *From Durrow to Kells. The Insular Gospel-books 650–800* (London: Thames & Hudson, 1987), 194.

30. Henry, *Irish Art during the Viking Invasions*, 151; Roe, *High Crosses of Kells*, 11; Edwards, "South Cross," 25.

31. Ibid., 31–33. The vine scroll patterns have been described at length by Edwards.

32. Edwards, "South Cross," 31. Fragments of an inscription have been recovered on the south cross at Clonmacnois by Domhnall Ó Murchadha and Giollamuire Ó Murchú but the fragmentary letters do not provide any direct evidence for the date of the cross. Ó Murchadha and Ó Murchú, "Fragmentary Inscriptions from the West Cross at Durrow, the South Cross at Clonamcnois, and the Cross at Kinnitty," *J.R.S.A.I.* 118 (1988): 53–66, at 61–66.

33. Henry, *Irish Art during the Viking Invasions*, 151; Edwards, "South Cross," 25; Richardson and Scarry, *Introduction to Irish High Crosses*, 17.

34. Higgitt, "Words and Crosses," 128.

35. Henry, *Irish Art during the Viking Invasions*, 18–20, 138.

36. de Paor, "High Crosses of Tech Theille," 146–47.

37. See W. M. Hennessy and B. MacCarthy, eds., *The Annals of Ulster* (Dublin: H.M.S.O., 1887–1901), hereafter AU.

38. Máire Herbert, *Iona, Kells and Derry, The History and Hagiography of the Monastic Familia of Columba* (Oxford: Clarendon, 1988), 68–70.

39. Ibid., 68–69.

40. AU 803 (*recte* 804).

41. O'Sullivan, "Book of Kells," 18.

42. Roe, *High Crosses of Kells*, 10.

43. Henry, *Book of Kells*, 218.

44. For the history of Kells at this time see Philip O'Connell, "Kells—Early and Medieval," *Ríocht na Midhe* 2.1 (1959): 18–36; Herbert, *Iona, Kells and Derry*, 68–87.

45. Calvert (*Early Development of Irish High Crosses*, 22–25), claims there is no evidence that Kells was of major importance before the mid-ninth century and Herbert (*Iona, Kells and Derry*, 68), points out that "it does not appear that the entire transfer of the island community to the new foundation was contemplated." Herbert also shows (72) that Iona continued to function as the head of the Columban community. G. MacNiocaill ("The Background to the Book of Kells," in P. Fox, ed., *The Book of Kells. MS 58, Trinity College Library Dublin, Commentary* [Luzern: Faksimile Verlag Luzern, 1990], 31), comes to a similar conclusion: "The overall silence of the ninth-century annals on Kells suggests that it retained its status as a kind of secondary Iona for most of that century." He goes on to argue that it only came into prominence after 878, when the relics and shrine of Columba were brought to Ireland.

46. Herbert, *Iona, Kells and Derry*, 70–71.

47. AU 877 (*recte* 878).

48. AU 1006 (*recte* 1007).

49. Herbert, *Iona, Kells and Derry*, 74–77.

50. AU 926 (*recte* 927).

51. Later in the century, Armagh and Kells were again linked together under a single abbot during the rule of Dub-dá-leithe (Herbert, *Iona, Kells and Derry*, 84).

52. Ibid., 74–75.

53. AU 903 (*recte* 904).

54. AU 919 (*recte* 920).

55. AU 950 (*recte* 951).

56. AU 969 (*recte* 970), AU 996 (*recte* 997).

57. Henry, "Around an Inscription," 36–51. Despite the obvious connections between the Market cross and the scripture crosses at Monasterboice, Durrow, and Clonmacnois, few writers have placed much emphasis on the associations.

58. AU 923 (*recte* 924).

59. The curious arrangement of the robes, with interlacing strips of drapery, has a long history in Hiberno-Saxon art. It first appears in a tentative form in the Crucifixion miniature of the Durham Gospels (Durham, Cathedral Library, MS A.II.17) (J. J. G. Alexander, *Insular Manuscripts 6th to the 9th Century* [London: Harvey Miller, 1978], pl. 202). Kelly has used its presence in eighth-century Gospel books as a support for the dating of the Tower cross to the first decade of the ninth century (Kelly, "Crucifixion Plaques in Stone," 207–8). However, it not only reappears in the Crucifixion on the west cross at Monasterboice (usually ascribed to the early-tenth century), but also in the Book of Mac Durnan. This Mac Durnan is the same Máel Brigte Mac Tornáin, abbot of Kells and Armagh between 888 and 927 (Alexander, *Insular Manuscripts*, pls. 326, 328, 354).

60. These attributes of Christ are discussed by Henry, *Irish Art during the Viking Invasions*, 164–66; *Book of Kells*, 190–92. A related Christ figure appears on the cross at Termonfechin.

61. Versions of the interlaced design, involving four men set diagonally, their limbs entwined, appear at Monasterboice (south and west), Clonmacnois (west) and Ahenny (north). The version on the Tower cross shows some slight differences from the others.

62. The present flatness of the outer plane of the sculpture is deceptive and has persuaded some observers that the cross was cut in relatively thin relief; compare, for example, Calvert, *Early Development of Irish High Crosses*, 135.

CHAPTER EIGHT

Isabel Henderson

VARIATIONS ON AN OLD THEME

Panelled Zoomorphic Ornament on Pictish Sculpture at Nigg, Easter Ross, and St. Andrews, Fife, and in the Book of Kells

O
f late the cross-slab at Nigg, Easter Ross has not lacked study.[1] But apart from references by Wilson in the St. Ninian's Isle Treasure publication, the zoomorphic ornament on the cross-head has attracted little attention. Even J. R. Allen's description of this part of the monument is uncharacteristically perfunctory and inaccurate.[2] The principal aim of this study is to describe the ornament in order to make it possible to assess its position within the repertoire of zoomorphic ornament in Pictish art, and within Insular zoomorphic ornament in general. Elsewhere I have argued that features of the snake-boss ornament, which flanks the central portion of the shaft of the cross and aspects of the Paul and Anthony panel placed immediately above it, can be related to the art of the Book of Kells.[3] In making this study, I was therefore particularly interested to see how the ornament on the cross-head related to Kells. In January 1989, I was allowed to examine a number of pages in the manuscript in order to look closely at some of the panels of zoomorphic ornament. This was a salutary experience, for it revealed just how little detailed work has been published on these panels. The violent color contrasts and splendid grotesquerie of the initial and interlinear animals make them infinitely more striking to the eye, but the panelled animal ornament contains a whole world of creativity of the most delicate sort. Much of it is drawn freehand, and so when examining

143

it in detail one feels very close to the mind and hand of the artist as one observes the solutions he finds to the filling of his borders and panels. It was with these observations in mind that I approached the ornament on the Nigg cross-head. The analytical drawings of the ornament on Nigg and St. Andrews reproduced here, are by Ian G. Scott formerly of the Royal Commission on the Ancient and Historical Monuments of Scotland. They are a vast improvement on my own on-site sketches, which I used to illustrate my lecture at the conference. He, too, worked in front of the monuments so his drawings provide a valuable check on my interpretations.[4]

THE NIGG SLAB CROSS-ARMS

The type of zoomorphic ornament being discussed here is used for the cross-head only (pl. 8.1; fig. 8.1). The shaft is decorated with a diagonal key-pattern and the background decoration consists of the well-known high relief bosses and snake-bosses, and the equally remarkable, plastically rendered, spiral panels below them. In the manner of individual cross-carpet pages in a manuscript, the design on the reverse of the slab has its own decorative repertoire. It consists of an arch-topped frame filled with panels of a variety of different interlace and key-patterns executed in shallow relief or incision.[5]

THE RIGHT ARM

This arm is decorated with a quatrefoil composition made out of four animals. The crossed necks of pairs of the animals meet at the center to form a diamond-shaped space. The design appears to be symmetrical, with four heads in the center and four sets of hindquarters at the corners. In fact, the necks, which are crossed belong to animals with differently arranged bodies. Figure 8.1 shows all four in their relative positions but disengaged from each other. The animals on the right of the panel have coiled hindquarters, whereas those on the left have elongated S-shaped bodies. All are quadrupeds with spindly forelegs held forward in a lizard-like pose, as though seen from above. The legs emerge from thickened foreshoulders. The tails hook round the thinner stick-like legs to create an interlace-filled background. The heads are reptilian, with high foreheads, slightly open mouths, and drilled eyes. Some, but not all, of the heads are shown in profile. The crossed necks of two similar animals, but on a smaller scale, filled the constricted part of the arm, but most of this ornament has flaked off. The crossed necks of these smaller animals can be seen within the bodies of the animals on the left of the arm.[6]

Pl. 8.1. Cross-slab, Nigg, Ross and Cromarty. Photograph courtesy of Royal Commission on the Ancient and Historic Monuments of Scotland.

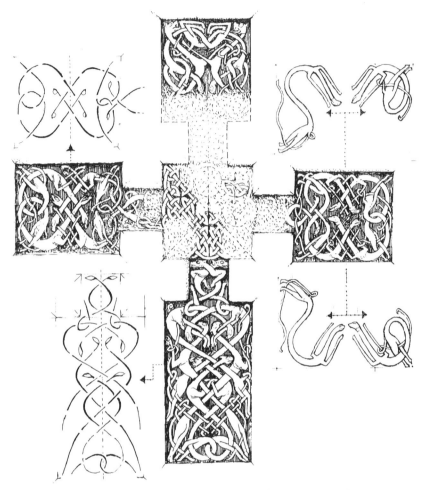

Fig. 8.1. Cross-slab, Nigg, Ross and Cromarty: animal ornament on the cross-head, with left arm and lower arm articulation and right arm animals dissected. Drawing by permission of Ian G. Scott; drawing copyright Ian G. Scott.

THE LEFT ARM

The design on the left arm of the cross has also a quatrefoil structure, with heads at the center and hindquarters at the corners. Again we have six animals, with four heads at the center and two heads belonging to the animals in the constriction. On this arm, the four necks do not simply cross and meet, but interlace to form a compact center. Again we have two types of animal pose. On this arm, all four animals have coiled hindquarters linked together in the manner of the linked hindquarters of the coiled animals on the right arm. The analytical drawing in fig. 8.1 shows the underlying symmetrical structure of the animals' bodies. But here, on the left arm, the arrangement of the stick-like forelimbs is varied, and is markedly more animated than the lizard-like pose of the animals on the right arm. The lower animals spring forward with the offside forelimb outstretched and the other raised, to lie parallel to their straight necks. They, as it were, salute, and cross forelimbs. The animals above this pair hold their forelimbs in a perky "hands up" position. These interlace to form a tighter, but similar, lattice, to that created by their tongues and the nearside forelimbs of the lower pair. All these animals have well-defined, virtually outlined, pear-shaped shoulders, a feature also found in the depiction of the animals in the Paul and Anthony scene in the pediment above the cross-head.[7]

The overriding characteristic of these panels of ornament vis-à-vis each other, and within the individual panels, is balanced asymmetry—a deceptive symmetry created by using the same motif within symmetrical constructions that support markedly varied internal arrangements. The variety embraces body pose and the treatment of the fine strand interlace made from tails. This, of course, is exactly how the pairs of panels of snake-boss ornament, and bossed spirals, on either side of the cross-shaft relate to each other. A common theme is varied and yet the pairs of panels are kept in balance.

THE LOWER ARM

The eye takes in the zoomorphic ornament on the lower arm as trellis work, opening and closing over a bed of interlace of the same density as the background interlace of the cross-arms. D. Wilson described this panel as being "symmetrical" and "disciplined" and there is indeed symmetry along a vertical axis as the analytical drawing in fig. 8.1 shows.[8] There is, however, no symmetry within the panel, in the sense that the design grows out of the six sets of hindquarters massed in the lower portion, to end with heads at the top. The main construction lines are created by two elongated animals with straight bodies and hanging hindquarters. Their bodies cross so that their raised forelimbs lie on the edge of the panel. Within their hind-quarters two smaller sets of coiled and linked hindquarters belong to the curved bodies of a pair of smaller animals whose necks cross, and whose forelegs (one each only depicted) grasp the bodies of the larger pair. This change of scale is within the design and is not simply due, as it was in the constrictions of the cross-arms, to restricted space. The small animals, are interlocked with, inhabit, as it were, the larger ones. Immediately above the hindquarters of the main pair are yet another set of hindquarters that belong to larger animals whose bodies cross above the necks of the small creatures. Their acutely bent shoulders are fitted into the upper corners of the panel. Their necks cross and reach down back into the design to form a heart shape. Their forelimbs, both of which are shown, nip the necks of the main ascending pair.

The constriction of the lower arm is filled with two small creatures whose bodies hook on to the necks of the animals below. Their single forelimbs are sharply bent at the elbow. One has its forelimb tucked behind its back, the other has it laid over his body. This slightly fantastic arrangement recalls the beasts with the forelimbs in the "hands up" position on the left arm. The lizard-like display of forelimbs in the right arm is therefore merely the most conservative version of a variety of forelimb poses.

THE UPPER ARM

The ornament in the fragmentary upper arm is rather different in that heads flank hindquarters instead of being kept apart (fig. 8.1). Noteworthy also is the introduction of naturalistic animal heads with prick ears, open, fanged, jaws, and markedly blunt muzzles. Different, too, is the chest to chest pose of the animals, with long necks thrust back to form a V-shape. Within this shape are interlocked hindquarters with limbs sharply bent to finish off the panel. This arrangement of hindquarters and legs contrasts with the otherwise uniformly limply hanging legs of the animals in the rest of the ornament. These interlocked hindquarters belong to animals whose elongated and curved bodies enter another set of coiled hindquarters to have their necks nipped by the hips. These animals have the more usual reptilian head and no doubt were met by two other heads of identical type from the design in the lost section of the arm.

The zoomorphic ornament on the Nigg cross-head has the controlled invention and technical brilliance displayed in the rest of the monument. Many of its characteristics seem similar to, indeed to reflect, plant-scroll ornament—a decorative motif present in other sculpture in the area, and used by the Nigg sculptor for illustrative purposes in his depiction of St. Paul's date-palms, which frame the narrative within the pediment and spread over the top of the slab. The animals are organized like a medallion plant-scroll with the main confronted animals arranged like two stems with their "root" hindquarters widely separated from their "shoot" heads. The animals on a smaller scale are comparable to enclosed, opposed, small tendrils.

THE ST. ANDREWS SARCOPHAGUS PANELS

The Nigg slab is not, as some writers have implied, atypical, an episodic masterpiece standing out with the normal line of development of Pictish sculpture.[9] On the contrary, there is a substantial group of high quality monuments in the vicinity, all with passages of comparable zoomorphic ornament. In this paper, I shall concentrate attention on a monument in the south of the Pictish area, the St. Andrews Sarcophagus, which, as is well-known, has a number of specific links, stylistic and iconographic with the decorative and figurative art of the Nigg cross-slab.

Decorative animal ornament survives on two panels bordering the figurative scene, and on two end panels.[10] One of the end panels, most of which is missing, has two animal motifs. One is the familiar Insular motif of two U-shaped animals with their feet resting on each other's shoulders and the other, a single animal whose body makes a figure-of-eight shape and whose hindlegs display the reversed position typical of Pictish coiled-animal designs.[11]

In this connection, I am concerned only with the two side panels. Again Allen failed to use his descriptive powers, being content to observe that the designs on these panels were "composed of animal forms intertwined in a most complicated manner."

The construction of the sarcophagus requires further investigation. In modern times, the panels have been variously positioned to the left or right of the front panel with the David scene, and in reverse position as to top and bottom. Nor is it absolutely certain that these two panels were on the same side of the sarcophagus. They certainly do not match each other, but, on the other hand, this is precisely what one would expect. They have exactly the same degree of similarity and difference as the pairs of decorative panels that flank the cross-shaft on the Nigg slab. My description refers to the current reconstruction of the Sarcophagus.

THE LEFT "DEER-HEAD" PANEL

The panel facing left (pl. 8.2) has been damaged and is restored at the upper end so the drawing reproduced here is of the design on the surviving section of the panel (fig. 8.2). The design consists of two symmetrical, roughly square units each made up of two large and two small animals. The units are linked to each other by the hindlegs of the four large animals. As at Nigg, the main quadrupeds have naturalistic drooping hindlegs. Their elongated bodies cross in three places. The arrangement is the same as the S-shaped animals on the right arm at Nigg, but the bends are tighter. Their

Pl. 8.2. Sarcophagus, St. Andrews, Fife: the "deer-head" panel. Copyright: the author.

Fig. 8.2. The St. Andrews Sarcophagus: animal ornament on the surviving portion of the front, left panel as mounted, and articulation of the basic motif. Drawing by permission of Ian G. Scott; drawing copyright Ian G. Scott.

deer-like heads are a quotation from the adjacent hunting scene, and this matching feature may justify the present location of the panel. The animals appear to have decorative, fringed feet forming a kind of foliate bunch.

As on the lower arm of the Nigg cross, smaller creatures occupy the interstices made by the undulating bodies of the larger animals. Their meek heads meet with necks uncrossed and their curved bodies enter a dense mass of interlace some of which may be made with their tongues.[12] In spite of some differences (and there is always a creative element in zoomorphic ornament), these creatures are clearly related to the decorative device of making small animals inhabit spaces made by the bodies of larger animals, such as we saw at Nigg.

THE RIGHT "LION-MANE" PANEL

On the right panel (pl. 8.3) naturalism is not apparent in the heads of the animals, but is vividly expressed on the shoulders and forelegs, which

Pl. 8.3. Sarcophagus, St. Andrews, Fife: the "lion-mane" panel. Copyright: the author.

Fig. 8.3. The St. Andrews Sarcophagus: animal ornament on the front, right panel as mounted, with articulation. Drawing by permission of Ian G. Scott; drawing copyright Ian G. Scott.

are given naturalistic body hair. This echoes the treatment of the manes of the lions in the David scene. Such matching detail between the figurative art and the ornament has already been seen in a less dramatic form in the use of outline pear-shaped shoulders for the animals in the Nigg pediment scene and in the zoomorphic ornament on the cross-head.

The drawing shows the whole panel (fig. 8.3). The design is again made up of two symmetrical square units. The junction between the two is achieved by the overlaying of four sets of hindquarters at the center. The location of the maned shoulders at the corners of the panel parallels exactly the arrangement of the uppermost animals in the Nigg lower arm. Like the Nigg creatures their necks reach down, but the collecting of hindquarters at the center, rather than at the lower end of the panel is a variation. The legs hanging from the hindquarters are interlaced, on analogy with the bodies of the small creatures on the "deer-head" panel, but here the legs are radically shortened, and clearly defined feet clutch together. Two roughly V-shaped animals meander through the arched bodies and forelegs of the maned animals. Their heads are seen from above. They have ears and a central furrow runs from the back of the head to the snout, as it does in the griffin's head, also seen from above, on the figurative panel. Their legs hook on to each other's necks in a manner similar to the junction of the symmetrical units in the "deer-head" panel.

Both ends of the "lion-mane" panel are very clotted. The very rounded relief allows neither balance nor symmetry. The basic structural shapes, two heart shapes with a lozenge in between, articulate the otherwise somewhat clumsy appearance. The collecting of hindquarters so that they lie like bossed shapes on a mat of fine interlace made of extremities is a variation of the theme of the snake-boss motif dominant on the Nigg slab and present on one of the end panels of the sarcophagus. Because the St. Andrews designs divide in the middle to create symmetry on a horizontal plane, the feeling of plant-scroll organization is not so strong as it is on the lower arm of Nigg. Nonetheless the bodies of the deer-headed and maned animals are arranged like interlaced medallion scroll. The sculptor of the sarcophagus was familiar with plant-scroll forms, for he used them in his depiction of the branches of the tree in the top left corner of the figurative panel.[13]

In spite of the Nigg sculptor's greater success in choosing the thickness of the interlacing strands of animal anatomy suited to the space available, Nigg and the sarcophagus are as closely related in respect of these zoomorphic designs as they are in other aspects, namely, David iconography, snake-bosses and spiral-covered knobbed bosses. The relationship between the two implies common knowledge of models used to disseminate both figural art, and decorative motifs, which included an animal style outside the boss tradition. As the accomplished creations of an inventive sculptor, the two monuments could conceivably be the work of one man, but if, as is more probable, different sculptors were at work, then the monuments are surely contemporary and do not stand in any necessarily dependent relationship.

COMPARABLE ORNAMENT ON OTHER SCULPTURE

The earliest example of panelled zoomorphic ornament in Pictish sculpture is the animalized interlace on the cross-arms of the Glamis 2 (Manse) slab.[14] Only its location on the cross links it with animal ornament on the Nigg cross-head. In genre, the unpanelled ornament to the right and left of the shaft of the cross on the Aberlemno 2 (Churchyard) slab is much closer.[15] The motif to the right of the top of the shaft is made up of two symmetrically interlocked (heads opposite hindquarters) creatures with coiled necks and long straight beaks. This discrete motif has an archaic look and has been related to the earliest phase of Northumbrian sculpture.[16] The animal ornament to the left of the shaft is not an appliqué motif but is skillfully designed to fill a tapering field. C. L. Curle was the first to relate this animal strip to the confronted animals which fill the background of the cross on f. 26v of the Lindisfarne Gospels.[17] For our purpose, the significance of the analogy is that it reveals knowledge on the part of Pictish sculptors of the motif of confronted elongated animals with coiled hindquarters—knowledge sufficiently assimilated to allow an adapted extract to be made from it.

Confronted animals are used to fill three panels on the shaft of the cross on the Meigle 2 (Daniel) slab.[18] These pairs are ultimately related to the paired animals on Northumbrian sculpture, but other features of their composition are distinctive. The top panel is structured by the bodies of large affronted blunt-muzzled animals. A single line defines the meeting point of their chests. They have the high groins, pear-shaped hips, and stick-like legs with forelimbs sharply bent, of the Nigg confronted animals. Small deformed creatures are placed within their legs and their necks are drawn back by biting animals whose coiled bodies fill the upper corners of the panel. The space thus created between their necks is filled with a boss-like mass of fine interlace, possibly made by their tongues. Fine interlace made by anatomical extremities runs through the panel linking the six creatures. The panel below is badly worn but its organization is broadly similar. It is varied by keeping the main animals apart and by introducing a twist of long, animal necks ending in reptile-like heads between them. The hindquarters of these animals may be compressed within the curved necks of the main animals or they may extend into the upper corners of the panel. The lowest panel may have swung the heads of the main creatures to the upper corners, but it is too worn to be certain of the arrangement. All three panels were clearly variants of the same theme.

Animals of this Meigle type appear in Easter Ross on either side of the cross-shaft of the Easter Ross Shandwick cross-slab, and there is no doubt that animal ornament even more closely related in organization to that on the Nigg cross-head is carved on the cross-slabs at Rosemarkie and Forres (Sueno's Stone), both in this northern area, but comparative analysis of all this ornament cannot be made until it is described and drawn out.[19]

The constriction of the upper arm on the front of St. Oran's cross on Iona is filled with addorsed rampant creatures reminiscent of the Meigle panels.[20] The design is a conflation of the two surviving Meigle pairs; a small animal is tucked between their legs and their tails create a twist between their necks. There are only traces of the finely carved intricate animal ornament of the Nigg cross-head on the Iona crosses. The reptiles emerging from some of the bosses have the lizard-like forequarters of the Nigg quadrupeds and these are bitten by other reptiles with neatly carved, gaping, fanged jaws.[21] One very delicate piece of animal ornament—four pairs of entwined animals edging a diagonally placed miniature boss on the west face of the St. John's cross—recalls the delicacy of the Nigg ornament[22] but in terms of what has survived it can be said that there is nothing on the Iona sculpture that can account for these panelled animal compositions at Nigg and St. Andrews.

The St. Andrews panels have been compared to a panel of animal ornament at the base of one of the narrow faces of the Rothbury cross-shaft.[23] They share the roundness of the relief, and the structural similarities of the designs are striking. At Rothbury, three pairs of creatures create clearly defined geometrical shapes.[24] A lozenge-shaped void towards the center of the panel contains the crossed tails of the uppermost creatures. All have lizard forequarters. All interlink, and the design "grows" from the bottom, with symmetry along the vertical access only—a feature it shares with Nigg rather than St. Andrews. The creatures are inhabited by small quadrupeds, an isolated head and a naked human figure. There are important differences, however. The main animals are of mixed types being both reptiles and quadrupeds. The quadrupeds are not elongated but have compact and well-proportioned bodies. There is no background formed by interlacing extremities. Rosemary Cramp has suggested that the reptile panel on Rothbury could be an illustration of Hell rather than a decorative panel of zoomorphic ornament.[25] Such a conflation, of plant-scroll, zoomorphs and narrative, would certainly be comparable to the methods of the designer at St. Andrews but other features of the Rothbury panel, particularly the appearance of reptiles, set it apart from the Pictish panels under discussion.

COMPARABLE ORNAMENT IN THE BOOK OF KELLS

Significantly, another, earlier, parallel that has been suggested for the St. Andrews panels is the ornament in rectangular panels set in the corners of the cross-carpet page on f. 138v of the Lindisfarne Gospels.[26] The four-animal motifs in all four panels are basically the same, but the lower two have more complex fine interlace extremities and the coiled bodies are linked in order to make a denser, more integrated design. One can appreciate the force of the analogy, particularly the way in which the forelegs hook onto necks, but within all four panels in the manuscript the long, straight necks of the creatures are the controlling factor. The undulations and free movement of tiered animals of differing scales, such as we find at Nigg and St. Andrews, show that this Lindisfarne animal motif had also been fully assimilated by Pictish sculptors, and was now being developed in different ways under different influences.

Quadrupeds with flowing elongated bodies, coiled necks, or hindquarters set in a bed of fine interlace made of extended lappets, eye-trails, and tails are used throughout the Book of Kells to fill panels of all shapes and sizes. The typical Kells quadruped used for this purpose has a rounded snub-nosed head, either lion-like or reptilian. It has a long straight neck, and a foreleg (only one depicted) running parallel to it. The body is ribbon-like, of equal thickness, except for the forequarters where a thickened section, sometimes spiralled, engages with a well-defined shoulder. The back of the body coils with varying degrees of tightness to end in a pear-shaped hip from which the back leg emerges to end in a heavily taloned foot. This animal type is a descendant of the animals on the back of the Tara brooch and in the Lindisfarne Gospels. Its almost exact counterpart in sculpture is found on the Irish Bealin Cross.[27] That particular variant is not found in surviving Pictish sculpture. There are, however, features of panelled zoomorphic ornament in the Book of Kells that suggest that the Nigg sculptor and the Kells artists shared the same artistic mentality, the result no doubt of shared familiarity with a whole range of objects in different media decorated in the Insular style and made in the years between the completion of the Lindisfarne Gospels and the completion of the Book of Kells—a period which could be the equivalent of two or three generations' work.

Contrary to what is often said, the Book of Kells is full of plant-scroll ornament. Most of it is inhabited with birds and quadrupeds, and is in a minute scale hidden away in panels and frames. Obviously, by the time the book was being decorated, plant-scroll ornament had become part of the Insular repertoire and no longer has significance for provenance or direct influence. It is not surprising therefore that the panelled animal ornament in Kells, like the Pictish carvings under discussion, shows signs of being influenced by plant-scroll. Examples of this and other features shared with the Pictish work are given below.[28]

FOLIO 7V: THE VIRGIN AND CHILD MINIATURE

The frame is filled with typical Kells quadrupeds as defined above. A frieze is created by pairs linking hindquarters. The link is clearly seen at the center of the top frame. The loose, rounded swing of the hindquarters is the one used for the pairs on the Nigg cross-head and can be contrasted with the rigidity of the animals in the panels on f. 138v of the Lindisfarne Gospels mentioned above.

FOLIO 28V: THE PORTRAIT OF MATTHEW, AND
FOLIO 32V: THE PORTRAIT OF CHRIST

The more tightly coiled animal motif with reptilian head and straight neck interlacing through the spring-like coils of its body is used for the border of the portrait of Matthew on f. 28v. On 28v the motif is almost out of control. This is the same animal as is used for the frame of the portrait of Christ on f. 32v but here it has been provided with guidelines. This motif is reminiscent of circular knotwork, but resembles even more spiraliform, plant-scroll. The effect is achieved by subordinating the anatomy of the quadruped.

FOLIO 3V: CANONS II AND III

Each of the four capitals of the Canon Table columns is filled with a pair of confronted animals set in fine interlace made of their own extremities. The bodies arch towards each other with their forelegs raised and crossing. Their elongated bodies cross, and their coiled hindquarters cross and link. Each pair is treated differently. The pair in the capital third from the left corresponds closely to the small animals within the larger ones on the lower arm of the Nigg cross-head.

FOLIO 29R: THE BEGINNING OF THE GOSPEL OF MATTHEW

The small panel below the four discs of ornament on the letter L contains a pair of affronted animals with necks and forelegs crossing and thickened foreshoulders. Their ribbon bodies cross, coil, and link, and end in a pear-shaped hip and sharply bent hind leg. Comparable pairs of affronted animals fill the outermost frame of this page. The pair to the right of the horizontal section of the frame shows the composition clearly. There the animals meet chest to chest like those in the upper arm of the Nigg cross-head.

FOLIO 114R: THE ARREST OF CHRIST

The avoidance of rigid symmetry in Kells can be seen at a glance in the comparatively simple example of the cruciform panels, which form the capitals on the columns framing the scene. The one to the left is a simple design of four snakes whose looped bodies fill the arms of the cross and whose heads collect round a disc at the center of the panel. The one on the right has the same elements, but here the snakes' bodies loop twice. The sculptor of the cross-arms of the Nigg cross-head shows exactly the same preoccupation with varying his ornament. The collecting of heads together at one point in the design, as opposed to the symmetrical juxtaposition of heads and hindquarters is a pervasive feature of panelled animal ornament in the Book of Kells.

Folio 27v: the Symbols of the Four Evangelists in Matthew

The T-shaped panels at the center of each side of the frame are filled with animal ornament. The bodies of the creatures on the side panels are looped in figure-of-eight curves whereas those at the top and the bottom have more angular trellis-like shapes. This is the clearest indication that the animals differ. The upper and lower panels are filled with quadrupeds and minute birds. The side panels are filled with snake ornament; both follow roughly the same looping system but are drawn freestyle. All four panels share with the Pictish sculptors a fondness for intricacy within clearly defined structures created by animal bodies. Looking at this page it is easy to imagine what the Nigg and St. Andrews ornament would have looked like when painted.

Folio 129v: the Symbols of the Four Evangelists in Mark

The cruciform panel at the center of the page provides a very clear example both of the use of attenuated animals to make shapes and of the extent to which the arrangement of animals in panels is affected by plant-scroll organization. A quatrefoil arrangement of coiled necks with minute heads occupies the center of the cross shape. Coiled hindquarters ending in pear-shaped hips emphasize the ends of the cross-arms. The undulating S-scrolls of the animals' bodies each has a blue-feathered bird sitting within the coiled hindquarters. What appears to be an undulating inhabited plant-scroll is on close inspection seen to be inhabited undulating animal bodies.

There is no evidence that the Pictish sculptors at Nigg and St. Andrews extracted designs for their panelled zoomorphic ornament directly from panels in the Book of Kells. A comparison of the two, however, reveals the presence of animal ornament at a similar stage of development, and bears out other arguments that would attribute these Pictish monuments to the Kells phase of Insular art.

COMPARABLE ORNAMENT IN THE ST. NINIAN'S ISLE TREASURE

All the animal ornament in the Treasure is fully described and illus-trated by Wilson in the St. Ninian's Isle publication. An important part of his analysis drew attention to parallels in Pictish sculpture for both forms and expertise. One of these was the zoomorphic ornament on the lower arm of the Nigg cross-head. Wilson's belief that the ornament on the treasure could be related to the ornament on Nigg can be strengthened.

The pieces with ornament most closely comparable to Nigg and St. Andrews are the cone-shaped mounts (nos. 12 and 13) and the pommel (no. 11).[29] All these pieces are decorated with quadrupeds with naturalistic hindquarters, long-reaching necks, and elongated coiled bodies. Heads and hindquarters are frequently widely separated. The heads are either reptilian or dog-like with blunt muzzles. The animals are paired, necks or bodies cross and interlock, heads meet but do not bite. Anatomical extensions create a background mesh. All these traits feature in the animals at Nigg and St. Andrews.

Cone no. 13 has the simplest decorative ornament.[30] The surface is divided into four panels two of which contain designs made up of a pair of quadrupeds whose hatched bodies cross below a scroll-jointed shoulder so that their heads and necks are back to back. Like the pair on Meigle 2 a single line expresses this meeting point. The coiled hindquarters create an inverted heart shape at the bottom of the panel. The background is filled with festoons of loosely knotted strands made from tails and head extensions. Although otherwise identical, one panel has the hindquarters less tightly coiled, and a nearside hind leg kicks upwards under the body. This freedom recalls the minor variations which we have seen characterize ornament on the Nigg cross-arms.

The animal motif on cone no. 13 invites comparison with the sym-metrically arranged animals on f. 26v of the Lindisfarne Gospels and with the related pair of animals on the back of the "Tara" brooch. The overriding characteristic of Lindisfarne animal ornament is the introduction of natural-istic heads and hindquarters to animals with ribbon bodies of uniform thickness. The "Tara" pair and the Aberlemno singletons have the same features. The St. Ninian's pair have decoratively coiled hindquarters but their bodies expand and they have sturdy canine heads and shoulders. The animals at Nigg and St. Andrews are undergoing the same development towards naturalism.

The spectacular ornament on the cone-shaped mount no. 12, in its weight and disposition, can be compared closely to the ornament on the

Nigg cross-head.[31] Unlike cone no. 13 the surface has no fields so that an allover pattern is laid over the entire surface. The pattern consists of four pairs of animals. Two pairs create the principle structure and two pairs of smaller animals interlock with them. All eight heads meet at the crest of the cone. The main animals have their forelegs outstretched. Their shoulders taper to a ribbon body which coils twice to end in pincer-like back legs. Their long necks swing back so that the heads face each other with the blunt muzzles meeting. The heart shape created by their necks and bodies contains their own back legs and the crescent-shaped hindquarters and legs of the lesser pair of animals. These smaller animals are similar in form to the main pair except that their bodies extend to a ribbon long enough to create a mat of interlace at the crest of the cone. Their necks cross and their shorter forelegs and taloned feet interlace tightly. Their heads meet within the space created by the necks of two main animals, one each from the addorsed pairs, that create from another viewpoint, an affronted pair. The animals on mount no. 12 grow from an onion-like layering of hindquarters precisely in the manner of the animals in the lower arm of the Nigg cross-head. The animals in the upper arm of the cross, where linked hindquarters are contained within a space created by the long swung back necks of creatures with blunt muzzles is also markedly similar to the design on this mount. The meeting of heads round a central point has already been described as a feature of small panels of ornament in the Book of Kells. Massing of hindquarters and heads at opposite ends of a field is characteristic also of our sculptors.

Wilson characterized the ornament on mounts nos. 12 and 13 as "well-disciplined" in contrast to the looser, more distorted, even "wild" ornament on the pommel. This "wildness" becomes even more marked in the panels of zoomorphic ornament on the uninscribed chape.[32] The raffish look to the forelimbs of the animals in the central fields of the pommel has a parallel in the "hands-up" and akimbo elbows of creatures on the Nigg cross-head. Their sharply bent legs also recall the treatment of limbs of animals in the top panel of the Meigle 2 shaft, and in the constrictions of the cross-arms and the upper arm of the Nigg cross-head.[33] The silversmith responsible for the St. Ninian's Isle pieces could easily have adapted the sculptors' paired animal compositions on the Nigg and St. Andrews monuments for his purposes, or vice versa.[34]

In his analysis of the ornament in the St. Ninian's Isle treasure, Wilson draws attention to the elements in the animal style which hark back to the Lindisfarne Gospels, but he also associates it, more firmly, with animal ornament in the Book of Kells and in the southern English books of the later eighth century. One might add to his comparisons ornament in two works in other media published after his account, a panel of animal ornament in the embroidered *casula* of St. Harlindis and St. Relindis at Maaseik and a bronze ornament found at Canterbury.[35] It is significant, however, that the Southumbrian books have a wide range of animal types which indicate a change of taste or repertoire not present in Pictish sculpture or in the panelled ornament of the Book of Kells. For example, the pair of animals that fill the central capital of the Canon Table columns on f. 12v of the Leningrad Gospels are almost entirely naturalistic.[36] In contrast, those in the fourth capital of the column on f. 16r of the same manuscript are fantastic; their heads, seen from above, have Kells-like ear-trails and stick-like forelegs held in the looser version of the lizard pose.[37] Without access to the manuscript, it is difficult to see whether they are tailed reptiles or quadrupeds. In these books coiled and linked naturalistic hind-quarters are less common and the decorative zoomorphs are frequently given tails which intertwine or interlace. An example of this transformation can be seen in the animal ornament in the central column of Canon I on f. 1r of the Barbarini Gospels.[38] The forequarters of the creatures look like our Pictish animals, but there are no tailed creatures of this type at Nigg or St. Andrews, or in the St. Ninian's Isle treasure.[39] This is the type of creature in the Rothbury panel, however. The Chi-Rho page of the Barbarini book displays a range of animal types, naturalistic and fantastic.[40] The animals in panels are bizarre paired creatures with no anatomy to structure the fine-spun interlace created by their now thread-like legs, lappets, and tails.

The paired or unpaired, naturalistic or fantastic animals scattered through the text pages of the Book of Kells are, of course, symptomatic of these changes, but for filling panels the Book favors animal types still rooted in the animal ornament of the early eighth century. Their disposition, however, is not the rigidly interlocked, head-opposite-tail, biting animals of that period. Above all they reflect the artists' freedom and capacity to draw freestyle, but they also reflect, as has been described above, a thoroughly assimilated knowledge of plant-scroll compositions, compositions exploited superbly in other panels and frames in the Book. Plant-scroll permeates the southern English manuscripts also, but in a more disintegrated form. The development and ultimate degeneration of the motif in relation to animal ornament has been discussed recently by Ryan and signalled by Wilson.[41]

The panelled ornament in the Book of Kells and in the sculpture at Nigg and St. Andrews combines conservatism with freedom and creativity. The deer heads and naturalistic body hair of the decorative animals at St. Andrews do not herald a new style. They are the product of the sculptor's freedom to exercise his ingenuity. It is a quality readily recognizable on every page of the Book of Kells and in such quirks as the animal-head initials in the Barbarini Gospels.[42] We have seen the same quality in the sculpture of the Hell panel on Rothbury, where a plant-scroll is transformed into a tangle of creatures inhabited by vulnerable men and small beasts.

The animal ornament at Nigg and St. Andrews can be recognized as a development of the Tara/Lindisfarne/Aberlemno animal style, and the presence of this phase of animal ornament in Pictish metalwork and sculpture needs stressing. This attempt to "place" the complex animal ornament at Nigg and St. Andrews may require modification, but awareness of its nature may help to integrate these remarkable monuments into more general assessments as knowledge increases.[43] Animal ornament is a common factor which should be able to help chart developments in Insular art in all media, but as Ryan has stressed recently, significant progress cannot be expected until more of the material is fully published.[44]

NOTES

1. I. Henderson, "Pictish Art and the Book of Kells," in D. Whitelock, R. McKitterick, and D. Dumville, eds., *Ireland in Early Medieval Europe: Studies in Memory of Kathleen Hughes* (Cambridge: Cambridge University Press, 1982), 79–105, at 85–89; "The Book of Kells and the Snake-boss Motif on Pictish Cross-slabs and the Iona Crosses," in M. Ryan, ed., *Ireland and Insular Art A.D. 500–1200* (Dublin: Royal Irish Academy, 1987), 56–65; É. Ó Carragáin, "The Meeting of Saint Paul and Saint Anthony: Visual and Literary Uses of a Eucharistic Motif," in G. Mac Niocaill and P. Wallace, eds., *Keimelia: Studies in Medieval Archaeology and History in Memory of Tom Delaney* (Galway, Ireland: Galway University Press, 1988), 1–58; D. Mac Lean, "Snake-bosses and Redemption at Iona and in Pictland," in R. M. Spearman and J. Higgitt, eds., *The Age of Migrating Ideas: Early Medieval Art in Northern Britain and Ireland* (Edinburgh: National Museums of Scotland, 1993), 245–53.

2. J. R. Allen, *The Early Christian Monuments of Scotland . . .* , part III (Edinburgh: Society of Antiquaries of Scotland, 1903), 76–77.

3. Henderson, "Pictish Art and the Book of Kells," and "The Book of Kells and the Snake-boss Motif."

4. The drawings published here are not definitive in the sense that further study of both monuments could add detail and make refinements. The drawing of the Nigg cross-head reproduces the current state of the monument. Lost sculpture in the constrictions of the cross-arm is present in the cast (acquired in 1894) on display in the Victoria and Albert Museum. Allen's photograph in *Early Christian Monuments* (fig. 72) is of a cast in Edinburgh. A drawing including this lost ornament will be published on another occasion. The slab is now housed within Nigg Church. The photograph published, chosen for its sharp focus, shows the disfiguring struts that held it together when it was in the churchyard. For its present appearance see the excellent photograph in A. Ritchie, *Picts* (Edinburgh: H.M.S.O., 1989), 35.

5. Allen, *Early Christian Monuments*, fig. 72A.

6. From the cast it appears that these animals in the right constriction have only one short, fin-like, foreleg that emerges from their bodies at the point before the bodies cross to lie within the inner corners of the constriction.

7. The cast makes it quite clear that the lower animals have the offside leg stretched forward as described above. The use of extended tongues is a marked feature of the snake-boss ornament on the slab. The cast also shows that the creatures in the left constriction had forelimbs that project at right angles to the bodies and then bend sharply at the elbow to fill the corners.

8. D. Wilson, "The Treasure," in A. Small, C. Thomas, and D. Wilson, *St. Ninian's Isle and its Treasure*, 2 vols. (Oxford: Oxford University Press, 1973), 45–148, at 141.

9. C. L. Curle and F. Henry, "Early Christian Art in Scotland," *Gazette des Beaux-Arts*, 6th ser. 24 (1943): 257–72.

10. Allen, *Early Christian Monuments*, fig. 365; D. Hay Fleming, *St. Andrews Cathedral Museum* (Edinburgh: Oliver & Boyd, 1931), 3–10 and figs. 1–3; I. Henderson, *The Picts* (London: Thames & Hudson, 1967), pls. 62–63 with the Nigg slab, pl. 61, facing.

11. Henderson, *The Picts*, pl. 63.

12. Ian G. Scott suggests that the interlace may also contain the legs of the animals.

13. Henderson, "Pictish Art and the Book of Kells," 97–98.

14. Ritchie, *Picts*, 32.

15. D. Wilson, *Anglo-Saxon Art from the Seventh Century to the Norman Conquest* (London: Thames & Hudson, 1984), pl. 138.

16. Henderson, "Pictish Art and the Book of Kells," 82–84.

17. C. L. Curle, "The Chronology of the Early Christian Monuments of Scotland," *P.S.A.S.* 74 (1939–40): 60–116, at 76 and fig. 5b and c.

18. Ritchie, *Picts*, 56.

19. Allen, *Early Christian Monuments*, figs. 66B, 60, 151. For a description of some of the Rosemarkie ornament see I. Henderson, *The Art and Function of Rosemarkie's Pictish Monuments* (Inverness: Groam House Museum Trust, reprint, 1991).

20. R.C.A.H.M.S., *Argyll: An Inventory of the Monuments*, IV, *Iona* (Edinburgh: H.M.S.O., 1982), 194, 196.

21. Ibid., 198F.

22. Ibid., 203B.

23. C. L. Mowbray (later C. L. Curle), "Eastern Influence on Carvings at St Andrews and Nigg, Scotland" *Antiquity* 10 (1936): 428–40, at 433 and pl. 3.

24. R. Cramp, *Corpus of Anglo-Saxon Stone Sculpture in England*, vol. 1, *County Durham and Northumberland* (Oxford: Oxford University Press, 1984), pl. 215.1224.

25. Ibid., 220.

26. Mowbray, "Eastern Influence," 433, pl. 3; J. J. G. Alexander, *Insular Manuscripts, 6th to the 9th Century* (London: Harvey Miller, 1978), ill. 34.

27. H. Crawford, *Irish Carved Ornament*, 2nd ed. (Dublin: Mercier Press, 1980), 49 and pl. 33. no. 91.

28. F. Henry, *The Book of Kells* (London, 1974): The Virgin & Child, pl. 10; Portrait of Matthew, pl. 22; Portrait of Christ, pl. 26; Canons II and III, pl. 6; beginning of the Gospel of Matthew, pl. 23; Arrest of Christ, pl. 45; Symbols of the Four Evangelists in Matthew, pl. 20; Symbols of the Four Evangelists in Mark, pl. 50.

29. For excellent photographs of the cone-shaped mounts see S. Youngs, ed., *"The Work of Angels": Masterpieces of Celtic Metalwork, 6th–9th Centuries A.D.* (London: British Museum Publications, 1989), 153.

30. Wilson, "The Treasure," pl. 28b.

31. Ibid., fig. 32.

32. Wilson, "The Treasure," 137, figs. 30, and 31. Distinctive animal ornament links the pommel and the uninscribed chape inextricably. It has been suggested that these objects might be English imports. See J. Backhouse and L. Webster, eds., *The Making of England: Anglo-Saxon Art and Culture, A.D. 600–900* (London: British Museum Press, 1991), 223–24. The undeniably English and Irish traits in the art of the St. Ninian's Isle Treasure is an indication of the existence of an Insular art style and not of provenance. The occurrence of the animal heads that decorate the crest of the inscribed chape on one of the brooches supports the view that the treasure is coherent. See also, in this connection, the mould from Orkney for a brooch that had animal terminals that closely parallel those of the uninscribed St. Ninian's Isle chape. C. L. Curle, *Pictish and Norse Finds from the Brough of Birsay, 1934–74* (Edinburgh: Society of Antiquaries of Scotland, 1982), 27, ill. 14.

33. The elongated tongues and tails which are such a feature of the animal ornament on the silver bowls (see Wilson, "The Treasure," pl. 18) are another link between the animal ornament on the Nigg cross-head and the St. Ninian's Isle treasure. Wilson further noted the similarity between the animal head on the spoon and the animal heads in the Nigg pediment. See Wilson, "The Treasure," 114, n.1.

34. Such a view begs the question of the extent to which there was an exchange of motifs between craftsmen working in different media. By the late-eighth century, the period under discussion, there seems ample evidence that metalwork and manuscript styles were interacting, and there seems no necessity to exclude sculpture from this free exchange.

35. M. Budny, "The Anglo-Saxon Embroideries at Maaseik: their Historical and Art-Historical Context," *Mededelingen van de Koninklijke Academie voor*

Wetenschappen, Letteren en Schone Kunsten von België; Klasse der Schone Kunsten 45.2 (1984): 57–133, pl. IIa; M. Budny and J. Graham-Campbell, "An Eighth-century Bronze Ornament from Canterbury and Related Works," *Archaeologia Cantiana* 97 (1981): 7–25.

36. Alexander, *Insular Manuscripts*, ill. 188.

37. Ibid., ill. 190.

38. Ibid., ill. 173.

39. The small animals at the center of the "deer-head" panel at St. Andrews may be an exception, but see the view of Scott n. 12.

40. Alexander, *Insular Manuscripts*, ill. 170.

41. M. Ryan, "Links between Anglo-Saxon and Irish Early Medieval Art: Some Evidence of Metalwork," in C. Karkov and R. Farrell, eds., *Studies in Insular Art and Archaeology*, A.E.M.S. 1 (Oxford, Ohio: American Early Medieval Studies, 1991), 117–26; Wilson, *Anglo-Saxon Art*, 64–61.

42. Wilson, *Anglo-Saxon Art*, pl. 194.

43. One such assessment must concern the provenance of Insular pieces of metalwork from Norwegian contexts.

44. M. Ryan, "Some Aspects of Sequence and Style in the Metalwork of Eighth- and Ninth-Century Ireland," in M. Ryan, ed., *Ireland and Insular Art: A.D. 500–1200*, 66–74.

CHAPTER NINE

Carol Neuman de Vegvar

THE ECHTERNACH LION

A Leap of Faith

The lion as Evangelist symbol at the opening of Mark in the Echternach Gospels (Paris, Bibliothèque Nationale, MS lat. 9389, f. 75v), (pl. 9.1), is one of the most compelling works in Insular art. The dramatic energy of the moving lion against the static rectilinear frame constitutes a design that haunts the memory of nonprofessionals who at some point in their careers took a survey course in art history. One question that has never been satisfactorily answered, however, is the meaning of this image: what did the illuminator intend to express by the dynamic opposition of energies of figure and frame? Why is so energetic, curvilinear, and organic a figure displayed against so rigid a framework; moreover, why is the lion free to overlap the frame at some points, notably the front and hind paws, and carefully contained by the frame at nose and tail? Is this merely a demonstration of the keen awareness of visual energies, of the tensions of confinement and release of dynamic forms with which Insular illuminators were certainly familiar, (we may think also of the Chi-Rho page of the Lindisfarne Gospels)?[1] Or is there possibly some underlying meaning in this tension, and in the very compelling nature of the image as a whole?

The provenance of the Echternach Gospels is currently controversial: Dáibhi Ó Cróinín arguing for Ireland, George Henderson suggesting a connection to Iona or to Egbert and the monastery of Mayo, Rupert Bruce-

167

Pl. 9.1. The Lion of Mark, Echternach Gospels, Paris, Bibl. Nat., Ms. Lat. 9389, f. 75v. Photograph courtesy of Bibliothèque Nationale.

Mitford and Nancy Netzer endorsing in various degrees Julian Brown's original assertion of strong paleographic ties to Lindisfarne, and Rosamond McKitterick proposing a continental site, possibley Echternach itself.[2] I will surely disappoint some readers by refusing to provide iconographic fuel for this conflagration, and by looking for evidence of the meaning of this image on both sides of the Irish Sea, since an origin circa 700 at an Insular center or at a relatively new continental site under strong Insular influence seems probable.

A fuller exploration of visual information in the design of the lion page is in order. The lion leaps upward diagonally from left to right. Wayne Dynes, who first worked extensively on the possible iconographic meaning of this page, was uncertain whether the lion should be understood as running, leaping, or flying.[3] However, walking or running would no doubt be indicated by horizontal rather than diagonal movement.[4] Flight seems improbable; the wingless lion (part of what Nordenfalk called the "terrestrial" series of Evangelist symbols) does not have the equipment of flight, and the diagonal pose primarily suggests leaping.[5] The probable imported model, whether we accept Dynes's zodiacal coins or Henderson's textiles (with reference to the Shroud of St. Victor) or some as yet untraced model, seems to have been chosen for its potential to suggest action.[6] George Henderson, in discussing possible Pictish elements in the Echternach Evangelist symbols, reached the very probable conclusion that the illuminator of the Echternach Gospels was not working from a complete set of Evangelist symbols but rather synthesizing a variety of models; this would allow also for extensive iconographic manipulation of the types.[7] Another visual factor is the strongly active curvilinear forms used for the curls of the lion's pelt and for the lion's body as a whole. The selection of yellow and orange for the lion's pelt is also intentionally striking; in combination with the use of red/orange and with the curves of the body and of the individual locks, the overall impression is of flame.[8] The frame that surrounds this highly active and curvilinear figure is static and rectilinear, a matrix that forms both a container for the form of the lion and a foil against which the lion leaps free. Nordenfalk called the frame "labyrinthine," but nothing of the lion's free leap across this carefully constructed structure, nor of the layout of the lines themselves, actually suggests a maze.[9] Rather, the lines encroach upon the lion from above and below, but do not hinder his leap. At one point where the lion's form and the frame coincide, at the lion's tail, it is not clear whether the frame is to be read as being bent by the lion's anatomy or bending to accommodate it.[10] The deliberacy of the use of mathematical ratios in the structure of the frame has been clearly demonstrated by Robert Stevick; the ratio of 3-to-1 is the predominant feature of the system.[11] The outer perimeter and inner structure of the frame are red/orange, with the exception of the four corner squares outlined in purple.

The lion in the Echternach Gospels is not the only example of an "active" full-length lion in the Insular world, but usually the action is much less dramatic, as in the Book of Durrow (Dublin, Trinity College, MS A.4. 5. [57], f. 124v).[12] In other examples, as in the Lichfield Gospels four-symbols page (Lichfield, Cathedral Library, p. 219), the upward "flight" of the lion, like that of the calf on the same page, seems to result from rotating a horizontal-format "walking" figure into the vertical to make efficient use of the available rectangular section of the grid of the page, and adjusting the position of the paws accordingly.[13] In the Trier Gospels four-symbols page (Trier, Domschatz, Cod. 61, f. 1v), the poses of all four symbols are probably derivative of the Echternach symbols, but without the same level of complexity in terms of relationship to the frame or potential meaning.[14] In the Book of Kells (Dublin, Trinity College MS A.I.6 [58]), the true leaping lion reasserts itself on the four-symbols page at the opening of Matthew (f. 27v); here and in the Lichfield Gospels the lions are winged.[15]

The lion in the Echternach Gospels is also not the only example of an Evangelist symbol overlapping the frame. The Echternach calf (f. 115v), (pl. 9.2) also breaks the perimeter of one of the intrusive crosses of the margin with one of its forehooves, but seems much more confined by its frame, a point to which I will return. Elsewhere, frame breaking seems much less deliberate, as is the case with the wings of the man in the four-symbols page in the Lichfield Gospels, and the wings of the calf in the Evangelist portrait of Luke in the same manuscript (p. 218), where the wing tips outside the frame don't even line up with their origins on the back of the calf inside the frame.[16] Here, we seem to be dealing with less talented artists who finished outside the frames parts of figures that would not fit inside, as seems also to be the case on the overcrowded four-symbols page in the Book of Armagh (Dublin, Trinity College Lib. MS 52, f. 32v).[17] In Kells, figure-frame relations are more expressive and are used with probable iconographic intent, notably in the case of the head, hands, and feet of what may be the crucified Christ protruding from the frame of the Evangelist portrait of John (f. 291v).[18] Later Anglo-Saxon manuscripts show remarkably expressive and often meaningful relationships between figure and frame.[19] In its time, however, the Echternach lion is unique in the dramatic interaction of figure and frame; this dynamic balance is most probably intentional not only as a design element but as a bearer of meaning.

Before exploring possible meanings in this powerful image, a word on methodology is obligatory. In his insightful review of Werckmeister's *Die Irisch-Northumbrische Buchmalerei und die monastische Spiritualität,* Paul Meyvaert presented two fundamental principles for iconographic analysis of early Insular illumination.[20] First, such analysis must be founded on the specific realities of monastic spirituality in the Insular context. To this end, the following analysis will be based not only on exegetical sources either written in the Insular context or known to have been widely available there, but also on what is known of the Insular liturgy that was the bedrock of monastic life. Éamonn Ó Carragáin has described the link between visual form and the liturgy:

Pl. 9.2. The Calf of Luke, Echternach Gospels, Paris, Bibl. Nat., MS lat. 9389, f. 115v. Photograph courtesy of Bibliothèque Nationale.

> Both literature and the visual arts in this period draw on, and are to be understood within, the liturgical life of the monasteries which produced patrons, writers, scribes and sculptors. . . . Liturgical performance must quite naturally have nourished imaginations which . . . visualized scenes so as to call to mind scriptural and liturgical texts. [21]

Second, Meyvaert warns the iconographer to bear in mind that there is "nothing inevitable about a chosen interpretation."[22] There is, however, a potential array of interpretations, or what Spiro Kostof once called an "atmosphere of meanings" about medieval non-narrative religious images, arising from their social and religious context and rendering them intelligible at several levels to the trained medieval viewer.[23] Multivalent imagery is equally possible in the Insular context: the Old Irish *Treatise on the Psalter* refers to the "four stories," the manifold sense of scripture: historical, allegorical, typological and moral; there is no reason why imagery for a monastic audience should be less complex.[24]

At first glance the lion, readily explicable as the symbol of Mark, serves in the Echternach Gospels primarily as an indicator of the opening of Mark's Gospel.[25] However, the association of the lion with the Evangelist Mark was from its inception more or less tangential to the identification of the lion and the other three symbolic creatures with the various aspects of the nature of Christ. Irenaeus, in his *Adversus haereticos* (Bk. III, XI:8), in discussing the four faces of the cherubim under the throne in Ezekiel, identified the four symbolic creatures with the Evangelists as a group, but then proceeded to identify them as "the images of the virtue of the Son of God. The first creature is that of a lion; that symbolizes Christ's strength, leadership, and His kingdom."[26] Epiphanius of Konstantia (ca. 392) saw the lion as symbolizing the writings of Mark, that, "as a lion rises up from the Jordan so also will the Lord as a lion from the Jordan rise up."[27] Jerome encodified the pairings for the West in his *Commentary on Matthew* (398), where the lion is assigned to Mark, in conjunction with the voice crying out in the wilderness.[28] These pairings were a fundamental part of Christian education in the early medieval period; in the Roman *Ordines* and the Gelasian rite they formed part of the third *scrutinium* for catechumens during Lent, and they also appeared in an instruction for catechumens in the Gallican rite of the Bobbio Missal.[29] Given this background, it seems probable that the Evangelist symbols continued to carry with them some element of Christological reference, and that the Echternach lion should be read as a reference to Christ in Mark and not as Mark alone.

Interpretations of the Evangelist symbols in the Echternach Gospels to date have been less than completely satisfactory. Werckmeister's highly complex cosmological and numerological approach to the man of Matthew, although adopted recently by Hutter and Holländer, was demonstrated by André Grabar and Paul Meyvaert to be highly problematic.[30] Wayne Dynes's 1981 study of the lion is the only close iconographic examination of this illumination to date.[31] Dynes associated the lion with the Resurrection on the basis of the *Physiologus*.[32] He then linked Evangelist portraits of Mark with the resurrected Christ in Byzantine and Ottonian manuscripts; in one case, an eleventh-century Gospel Book from the Bamberg Cathedral Treasury (Munich, Staatsbibliothek, clm 4454, f. 20v), Mark, the lion and the resurrected Christ appear together. Tentatively reading the frame as an allusion to city plans, Dynes also suggested that the image might refer to the ascending Christ, rising from the earthly Jerusalem or toward its heavenly counterpart.

However, Dynes's association of the Echternach lion with the theme of the Ascension has several potential problems, besides those already pointed out by Dynes himself with regard to the identification of the frame as an earthly or heavenly Jerusalem.[33] The visual connection between Mark and the resurrected Christ is found primarily in Byzantine and Ottonian manuscripts, neither in the Insular context nor in western Europe in the period of the illumination of the Echternach Gospels. The identification of the scene with the Ascension is also problematic within the context of the manuscript itself. First, why would a frontispiece to an entire Gospel make reference primarily to one event, which in Mark is confined to a single verse, Mark 16:19, the second-to-last verse in the text? Certainly a reference to the Ascension is possible, but if present it may not be the only allusion here.

If the image of the lion was identified in the minds of viewers with Christ, but no specific narrative was its primary focus, it seems probable that its intent may have been to evoke the presence of Christ himself through an evocative statement of his nature. William Loerke has examined the experiential nature of Early Christian art in the fifth and sixth centuries; he has proposed a hypothesis of the evolution of style based on the premise that art was not only a rendition of a past event, but also an evocation intended to render the subject "present."[34] The sermons of Leo the Great, used by Bede in composing his homilies, repeatedly refer to the visionary response of the faithful to hearing the reading of the Gospel narrative, "for committed and devout hearts to hear what is read is to see what was done."[35] In considering the apse mosaic of the Transfiguration in the church of St. Catherine on Mt. Sinai, Loerke suggests that the next step, achieved in the context of the monastic spirituality of the sixth century, was "to carry this sense of being an eyewitness beyond earthly events into the representation of a vision or theophany such as Christ's Transfiguration. . . . To represent it at all required an art capable of displaying, or suggesting, a vision of Christ in successive states, human and divine."[36] It will be my contention that this is also the primary intention of the illuminator of the Echternach lion.

That such a visionary presence would be evoked in an illumination of a Gospels volume as well as in the larger and more easily visible format of an apse mosaic reflects the role of the Gospel book within the liturgy. The Gospels were particularly honored and reverently treated in the early

Western liturgy. It was the only object permitted to share the altar with the consecrated Host, and its reading was one of the high points of the ceremonial of the Mass. The process of moving the Gospels to the altar and from the altar to the locus of the reading (in the Roman rite, the ambo) usually involved a procession with lights; in the seventh-century Gallican rite, the procession included not only the reader, usually the deacon, also but two acolytes with torches and two sub-deacons, one with a *thymiamaterium*.[37] The reading was often allocated to the deacon as the highest-ranking clergyman assisting at the Mass. J. A. Jungmann explains the honor paid to the Gospels as reflecting the idea that in the Gospels book, containing Christ's word, "Christ himself is honored and His entry solemnized."[38] The enthroning of the Gospels at synods, indicating that Christ was thought to be presiding (as at the Council of Ephesus in 431), suggests an identity between Christ as Logos and the Gospel as Word, an identification also indicated by the acclamations associated with the Gospel reading at Mass.[39] The strength of the identity of the Gospels volume itself with the presence of Christ may possibly have inspired, in the hands of an artist of no small degree of subtlety, a treatment of the lion as an expression of the nature of Christ. Since the Evangelist symbol is presented to us with no extensive text, only the words, *imago leonis*, the artist is dependent on the associations that the viewers of the image, the members of the monastic community for which the codex was destined, might bring to mind in viewing his image: the image must stimulate by its form the associations which give it meaning. What references would such a community have brought to this highly visually charged motif of the lion? The specific nature of Christ was a matter of no small concern in early Insular churches and was reflected in the devotions of the faithful.

The Athanasian Creed, a product most probably of Gaul towards the end of the fifth century, was known to and possibly authored by Caesarius of Arles, whose work was widely known and appreciated in the Insular world.[40] By the early sixth century, it began to emerge as a formula to be memorized by clergy and others.[41] It was imposed as a test of faith by the Synod of Autun around 670 and became widely known in the eighth century. The earliest extant text of the creed is found in Ambrosian MS 0 212 sup., which came to Milan from Bobbio and was written in an Irish hand of the late-seventh or early eighth century, suggesting a possible early conduit for Irish contact with this creed, and Columbanus may have referred to it in his description of the two natures of Christ in his fifth *Epistola*, written in the late-sixth century. The earliest extant manuscripts of the Fortunatus *Commentary* on the creed are connected to St. Gall, also an Irish missionary foundation on the continent. It can also be traced with relative certainty in Anglo-Saxon England by 798 at the latest, when bishop-elect Denebert of Worcester cited it as evidence of orthodoxy at his consecration.[42]

The Athanasian Creed summarizes and seeks to enforce under threat of damnation the conclusions on the nature of Christ reached by the Synod of Chalcedon of 451, and stated in the Chalcedonian Definition of the Faith; it was probably the most commonly known statement of the faith on this subject known in western Europe at the time of the illumination of the Echternach Gospels.[43] In part, it states:

> He is God from the Father's substance, begotten before time; and he is man from his mother's substance, born in time. Perfect God, perfect man composed of a rational soul and human flesh, equal to the Father in respect of his divinity, less than the Father in respect of his humanity.
>
> Who, although he is God and man, is nevertheless not two but one Christ. He is one, however, not by the transformation of his divinity into flesh, but by the taking up of his humanity into God (*adsumptione humanitatis in deo*); one certainly not by confusion of substance but by oneness of person.[44]

To a monastic viewer for whom the Athanasian Creed may have been a complete statement of faith, the partial freedom and partial confinement of the Echternach lion, as a symbol of Christ, may have embodied both divinity outside time and flesh bound by time, the leap upwards possibly the *adsumptione humanitatis in deo*. Thus, the image may have referred to the Incarnation, of which the entire Gospel speaks, rather than only the Ascension, which is but one aspect of theophany.

In what other contexts would this imagery have found echoes in the minds of Insular monastic viewers? The *Homilies on Ezekiel* of Gregory the Great were known to Anglo-Saxon homilists from Bede on, and consequently probably quite familiar to the Anglo-Saxon monastic audience.[45] They were also known as a source to the Hiberno-Latin poets, and their Irish listeners.[46] In *In Hiezechihelem* I, *Homilia* IV 1, Gregory follows the Hieronymian pairings and then links the lion of St. Mark very specifically to the two natures of Christ:

> Ipse enim unigenitus Dei Filius veraciter factus est homo, ipse in sacrificio nostrae redemptionis dignatus est mori ut vitulus, ipse per virtutem suae fortitudinis surrexit ut leo. Leo etiam apertis oculis dormire perhibetur, quia in

ipsa morte in qua ex humanitate Redemptor noster
dormire potuit, ex divinitate sua immortalis permanendo
vigilavit.[47]

In the Irish context, liturgical hymnody and its exegetical roots provide the most direct clues as to the possible interpretation of the Echternach
lion. Two of the hymns in the *Antiphonary of Bangor,* "Turba Fratrem," and
"Praecamus Patrem," may provide insight into the meaning of the
illumination.[48]

The *Antiphonary* opens with the "Turba fratrem," a hymn which
appears in ten extant manuscripts from the seventh to the thirteenth century, all either Irish or linked to Irish tradition. Curran suggests that it may
be sixth-century and Irish in composition, inspired by Prudentius and other
continental Latin hymnodists; the hymn opens with a call to praise Christ as
king, followed by a string of honorifics for Christ rare in Latin hymnody but
parallelling Irish litanic-type prayers in structure.[49] The third verse reads:

Tu dei de corde verbum, tu via, tu veritas,
Iesse virga tu vocaris, te leonem legimus.
Dextra patris, mons et agnus, angularis tu lapis,
Sponsus idem vel columba, flamma, ianua.[50]

The juxtaposition here of Christ's role as king and Logos and his close link
to God the Father with his earthly ancestry in Jesse suggests the presence of
some of the same concerns with the duality of Christ's nature also seen in
the Anglo-Saxon homiletic context.[51] The references to both the lion and the
flame in the same context are also suggestive of the Echternach illumination. "Turba fratrem" is a hymn for the predawn service, *ad matutinam,*
and its references to Christ as flame are not atypical for hymns of this
function, in Ireland and elsewhere.

"Praecamus patrem" is a complex hymn on the subject of the life of
Christ, thought at the time of the *Antiphonary of Bangor* to be of apostolic
origin, but Curran has determined it to be of "clearly Irish" origin.[52] The first
half of the hymn makes use of a protracted metaphor of Christ as the rising
light, on the precedent of morning and evening hymns of the Latin liturgy,
including works by Ambrose, Caesarius, and Aurelian of Arles, and Gregorian
evening hymns. The second half starts at verse 16 with the Incarnation:

In fine mundi post tanta miseria
adest salvator cum granda clementia.[53]

In fine is a phrase often used to speak of the Incarnation or the Second
Coming by Biblical commentaries either written or commonly in use in

Ireland, notably Pseudo-Jerome, and suggests a particular awareness of boundaries or frames.[54] Verse 18 concerns the dual nature of Christ:

> Natus ut homo mortali in tegmine,
> non deest caelo manens in trinitate.[55]

Here in describing Christ's dual nature, the hymnodist may refer to Columbanus (*Epistola* 5, 13):

> Christus enim salvator noster verus Deus aeternus sine tempore et verus homo absque peccato in tempore est, . . . qui natus in carne nequaquam deerat caelo, manens in trinitate.[56]

In this sixth-century reference, we find Christ's duality, as both confined by and outside of time, as defined in the "*Tome*" of Leo, which may also have been known in Ireland.[57]

The hymn "Spiritus divinae lucis," a hymn for matins on Sundays, besides providing a full array of references to Christ as light, casts additional light on Trinitarian thinking in Ireland or in the Irish monasteries on the continent. It is based on the writings of Victorinus in founding the assertion of the consubstantiality of the Trinity on the belief that they are one spirit. Victorinus's theology is premised on the identity of the Son as *forma Dei*: the Father's being is visible in the actions of the Son.[58] The eighth verse of the hymn, concerning the Incarnation, reads:

> Quia nunc cepit qui semper fuit naturae tuae
> Filius divinae lucis gloriae tuae
> Qui est forma et plenitudo divinitatis tuae frequens.[59]

No doubt an upward-leaping lion the color of the rising sun would bring to the minds of persons familiar with this hymn the figure of Christ not only as the new day, but also as the action of God in the world. References to Christ as light in the *Antiphonary of Bangor* are not restricted to the hymns but are found also in the collects, especially those for *ad matutinum*, before dawn, and *secundum*, at the beginning of the working day.[60] There is nothing unusual here in the persistent reference to Christ as light, for *lumen verum* is a frequent honorific for Christ in early liturgies, most notably in the Ambrosian and Spanish versions.[61] It is also a preeminent feature of matins hymnody in Anglo-Saxon monastic practice, although the earliest preserved collections of hymns from the Anglo-Saxon context are eleventh-century.[62]

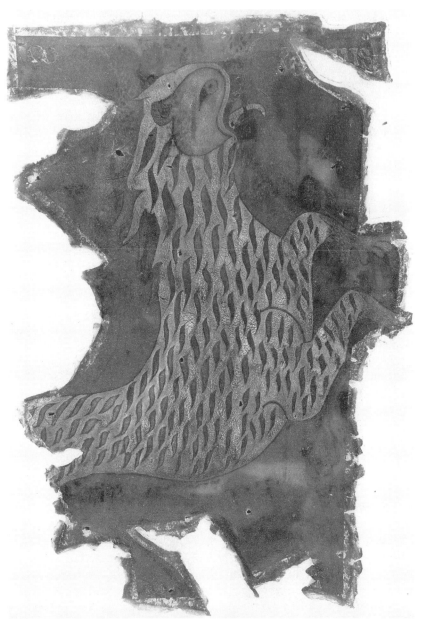

Pl. 9.3. The Lion of Mark, Corpus-Cotton Gospels, London, B.L., Cotton MS Otho C.V., f. 27. Photograph by permission of British Library.

Pl. 9.4. The Man of Matthew, Echternach Gospels, Paris, Bibl. Nat., MS lat. 9389, f. 18v. Photograph courtesy of Bibliothèque Nationale.

The Echternach lion seems to have been thought as compelling an image in its own time as it is today. This is suggested by the repetition of the leaping lion in the sister manuscript of the Echternach Gospels, the Corpus-Cotton Gospels (London, B.L., Cotton MS Otho C.V., f. 27) (pl. 9.3),

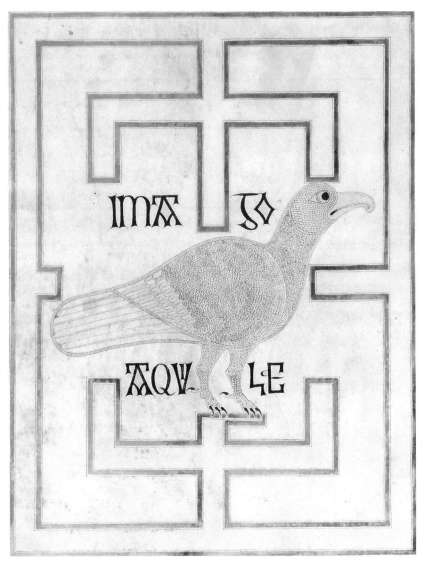

Pl. 9.5. The Eagle of John, Echternach Gospels, Paris, Bibl. Nat., MS. lat. 9389, F. 176v. Photograph courtesy of Bibliothèque Nationale.

with only the single change that the hanks of hair are more flamelike in the Cotton lion.[63] Sadly, most of the frame of the Cotton lion perished in the 1731 Ashburnham House fire, and only a fragment of the upper half of the lion himself remains, although there is a suggestion of a frame to the right of the lion that the right front paw may have crossed. The calf in the

Pl. 9.6. The Eagle of John, Corpus-Cotton Gospels, Cambridge, Corpus Christi College, MS 197B, f. 1. Photograph by permission of Master and Fellows, Corpus Christi College, Cambridge.

Echternach Gospels interacts with the frame, but more passively; here the frame seems to control, even to oppress, the humbly walking animal, suggestive of the sacrificial role of Christ. A similar reference to mortality may be construed in the compressive role of the frame of the man of Matthew (f. 18v) (pl. 9.4).[64] The eagle varies between Echternach and its sister codex. In Echternach (f. 176v) (pl. 9.5), it is reminiscent of a dove and perches on the frame; in Corpus MS 197B (f. 1) (pl. 9.6), the Eagle is clearly a raptor, linked by Henderson to the Pictish eagles of Burrian and Knowe, and is placed on an angle like the lions, perhaps to suggest flight.[65] Here, too, the relationship with the frame is dynamic, perhaps derivative from, although not nearly as powerful as, that of the Echternach lion page, which retains today its unique power to move the beholder.

NOTES

1. J. J. G. Alexander, *Insular Manuscripts 6th to the 9th Century* (London: Harvey Miller, 1978), 24; and M. Schapiro, "On some Problems in the Semiotics of Visual Art: Field and Vehicle in Image-signs," *Semiotica* 1 (1969): 228.

2. D. Ó Cróinín, "Pride and Prejudice," *Peritia* 1 (1982): 352–62; D. Ó Cróinín, "Rath Melsigi, Willibrord, and the Earliest Echternach Manuscripts," *Peritia* 3 (1984): 17–49; G. Henderson, *From Durrow to Kells; The Insular Gospel Books 650–800* (London: Thames & Hudson, 1987), 94–95; R. Bruce-Mitford, "The Durham-Echternach Calligrapher," in G. Bonner, D. Rollason, and C. Stancliffe, eds., *St. Cuthbert, His Cult and His Community* (Woodbridge, England: Boydell Press, 1989), 175–88; N. Netzer, "Willibrord's Scriptorium at Echternach and its Relationship to Ireland and Lindisfarne," ibid., 203–12; T. J. Brown, "The Lindisfarne Scriptorium," in T. D. Kendrick et al., *Evangeliorum quattuor Codex Lindisfarnensis, Musei Britannici Codex Cottonianus Nero D. IV* (Olten and Lausanne: Urs Graf, 1960), II, 89–106; R. McKitterick, "The Diffusion of Insular Culture in Neustria between 650 and 850: the Implications of the Manuscript Evidence," in H. Atsma, ed., *La Neustrae, Les pays au nord de la Loire de 650 à 850*, vol. 2 (Sigmaringen: Jan Thorbecke, 1989) 423–26.

3. W. Dynes, "Imago Leonis," *Gesta* 20 (1981): 35–41.

4. As in the Book of Durrow, Dublin, Trinity College, MS A.4.5. (57), ff. 124v, 151v; Alexander, *Insular Manuscripts*, pls. 15, 16.

5. Ibid., 31. In the Insular context, E. Kitzinger, "The Coffin Reliquary," in C. F. Battiscombe, ed., *The Relics of St. Cuthbert* (Oxford: Dean and Chapter of Durham Cathedral; Oxford University Press, 1956), 230–33, traced what he called the "naked" series of Evangelist symbols to Ravenna. Although the concept of the series as a whole may well have Ravennate roots, the leaping Echternach lion is completely different in pose from the staid walking lions of Ravenna (and the Book of Durrow), and so most likely has another individual source.

6. Dynes, "Imago Leonis," 37–38; Henderson, *From Durrow to Kells*, 76, and pl. 45.

7. Henderson, *From Durrow to Kells*, 73–79.

8. I do not agree with Dynes ("Imago Leonis," 39–40) that the yellow is to be read as an enhancement of the color of the parchment itself. C. Eggenberger, "Der Farbakkord Orange-Violett. Beobachtungen zur Farbwahl in der spätantiken und frühmittelalterlichen Buchmalerei," in *Von Farbe und Farben, Albert Knoepfli zum 70. Geburtstag* (Zurich: Manesse Verlag, 1980), 283–91, suggests that the orange of the lion and the purple of the frame are colors associated through the symbolism of liturgical vestments respectively with life and death, an interpretation that could be construed to fit with a theme of the Resurrection, or of the dual nature of Christ as both human (confined by death) and divine (free of death), motifs which will be explored later in the present paper.

9. C. Nordenfalk, *Celtic and Anglo-Saxon Painting: Book Illumination in the British Isles 600–800* (New York: George Braziller, 1977), 52.

10. Dynes, "Imago Leonis," 38.

11. R. D. Stevick, "The Echternach Gospels Evangelist-Symbol Pages: Forms from 'The Two True Measures of Geometry,'" *Peritia* 5 (1986): 284–308. It is tempting to speculate whether the choice of a 3:1 ratio in the structure of the frame was intended as a reference to the Trinity.

12. Alexander, *Insular Manuscripts*, pl. 15.

13. Ibid., pl. 81.

14. Ibid., pl. 114; N. D. Netzer, "The Trier Gospels (Trier, Domschatz MS 61): Text, Construction, Script and Illustration" (Ph.D. diss., Harvard University, 1987), 205–52.

15. Alexander, *Insular Manuscripts*, pl. 231.

16. Ibid., pls. 81, 82.

17. Ibid., pl. 230.

18. Ibid., 251.

19. H. R. Broderick, "Some Attitudes toward the Frame in Anglo-Saxon Manuscripts of the Tenth and Eleventh Centuries," *Artibus et Historiae* 5 (1982): 31–42.

20. P. Meyvaert, review of O. K. Werckmeister, *Irisch-Northumbrische Buchmalerei des 8. Jahrhunderts und monastische Spiritualität* (Berlin: de Gruyter, 1967), *Speculum* 46 (1971): 408–11.

21. É. Ó Carragáin, "The Meeting of Saint Paul and Saint Anthony: Visual and Liturgical uses of a Eucharistic Motif," in G. Mac Niocaill and P. F. Wallace, eds., *Keimelia: Studies in Medieval Archaeology and History in Memory of Tom Delany* (Galway, Ireland: Galway University Press, 1988), 38.

22. Meyvaert, Review of Werckmeister, *Irisch-Northumbrische Buchmalerei*, 411.

23. S. K. Kostof, *The Orthodox Baptistry of Ravenna* (New Haven and London: Yale University Press, 1965), 92. Potential intentional multivalency has been increasingly recognized by art historians as an obligatory consideration in iconographic analysis over the past two decades; see, for example, C. Harbison, "Sexuality and Social Standing in Jan van Eyck's Arnolfini Double Portrait," *Renaissance Quarterly* 43 (1990): 249–91.

24. M. McNamara, "A Plea for Hiberno-Latin Biblical Studies," *Irish Theological Quarterly* 39 (1972): 348. É. Ó Carragáin, "Christ over the Beasts and the Agnus Dei: Two Multivalent Panels on the Ruthwell and Bewcastle Crosses," in P. E. Szarmach and V. D. Oggins, *Sources of Anglo-Saxon Culture* (Kalamazoo, Mich.: Medieval Institute, 1986), 377–403, explores multivalent iconographic analysis in an Insular context, premised on reference to the liturgy.

25. Irenaeus, *Adversos haereticos* Bk. 3; XI:8, P.L. 7, col. 885; A. Roberts and W. H. Rambaut, *The Writings of Irenaeus* I, (Edinburgh: T. & T. Clark, 1868), 293–94.

26. Hippolytus, *Treatise on Christ and Antichrist* 7, in S. D. F. Salmond, *The Writings of Hippolytus, Bishop of Portus* (Edinburgh: T. & T. Clark, 1869), 8. Augustine also pairs the lion with Matthew (*De consensu evangelistarum*, I:6, P.L. 34, 1046ff.), and is followed in this association by Bede (*Explanatio apocalypsis* IV, P.L. 93, 144, and *Epistola ad Accam*, P.L. 92, 305ff.), but this pairing has no apparent influence in Insular art. See also: W. Neuss, *Das Buch Ezekiel in Theologie und Kunst bis zum Ende des XII Jahrhunderts* (Münster-in-Westfällen: Aschendorff, 1912), 88, 107.

27. Epiphanius of Konstantia, *De Mensuris et Ponderibus*, 35, quoting Jeremiah 49.19; in Neuss, *Das Buch Ezekiel*, 46–47.

28. Jerome, *Comment. in Ezechielem*, i.I, P.L. 25, col. 21; Kitzinger, "The Coffin Reliquary," 228.

29. B. Teyssèdre, *Le Sacramentaire de Gellone* (Toulouse: E. Privat, 1959), 100; M. Andrieu, ed., *Les Ordines Romani du haut moyen age* (Louvain: Spicilegium sacrum lovaniense, 1971), 2, Ordo 11, 427–33; and E. A. Lowe, ed., *The Bobbio Missal; A Gallican Mass-Book* (MS Paris Lat. 13246) (London: Henry Bradshaw Society, 1920), 54–59.

30. I. Hutter and H. Holländer, *Kunst des Frühen Mittelalters* (Stuttgart and Zurich: Belser, 1987), 165–67. Meyvaert (Review of Werckmeister, *Irisch-Northumbrische Buchmalerei*, 408–11) critiqued Werckmeister's hypothesis by questioning the relative availability of sources in the Insular context, and took issue with the exclusivity of Werckmeister's interpretation. Grabar (Review of Werckmeister, *Irisch-Northumbrische Buchmalerei, Cahiers archéologiques* 18 [1968]: 254–56) also critiqued Werckmeister's close linkage of texts and images and suggested that such parallels offer possibilities rather than absolute realities. He also stressed the potential polyvalence of images.

31. Dynes, "Imago Leonis," 38–40.

32. It is not clear that the *Physiologus* itself was well-known in early Anglo-Saxon England; however, J. D. A. Ogilvy (*Books Known to the English: 597–1066* [Cambridge, Mass.: Medieval Academy of America, 1967], 222) suggested that some passages were known to Anglo-Latin writers, such as Aldhelm, primarily via Isidore, Pliny, or Solinus. Isidore quotes the relevant passage on lions (Isidori Hispalensis Episcopi, *Etymologiarum sive originum*, Lib. 12:ii:3–6; ed. W. M. Lindsey [Oxford: Oxford University Press, 1957], n.p.). *The Bestiary*, another possible conduit of *Physiologus* material, may also not have been available in its entirety, although Latin notes on the *natura* of the lion among other animals are found in a possibly tenth-century Anglo-Saxon manuscript (Cambridge: Corpus Christi College, 448), (Ogilvy, *Books Known to the English*, 100). The date of arrival in Ireland of the *Physiologus'* information on lions, regardless of context, is also problematic. Stags and snakes, described as mortal enemies in the *Physiologus*, occur together on Gallen Slab T 27 (Co. Offaly), and the ninth-century Derrynaflan Paten (M. Ryan, "The Menagerie of the Derrynaflan Paten," this volume); the passage could again have been transmitted via Isidore, whose works arrived early in Ireland (B. Bischoff, "Die europäische Verbreitung der Werke Isidors von Sevilla," *Mittelalterliche Studien* I [Stuttgart: Anton Hierseman, 1966], 171–94). The *Physiologus* may provide more than one clue to the meaning or meanings of the Echternach lion. As Dynes pointed out, the Echternach design places special emphasis on the confinement of the lion's tail, which according to the *Physiologus* is used by the lion to conceal its spoor.

33. Dynes, "Imago leonis," 39.

34. W. Loerke, "'Real presence' in Early Christian Art," in T. G. Verdon, ed., *Monasticism and the Arts* (Syracuse, N.Y.: Syracuse University Press, 1984), 29–51.

35. Ibid., 38; and Ogilvy, *Books Known to the English*, 193.

36. Loerke, "'Real Presence' in Early Christian Art," 41.

37. J. A. Jungmann, *The Mass of the Roman Rite: Its Origins and Development*, vol. 1 (New York: Benziger, 1951), 442–47.

38. Ibid., 446.

39. Ibid., 446–47, and n. 26.

40. J. N. D. Kelly, *The Athanasian Creed* (New York and Evanston, Ill.: Harper & Row, 1964), 35–37, 112–13; and J. B. Trahern, "Caesarius of Arles and Old English Literature: Some Contributions and a Recapitulation," *A.S.E.* 5 (1976): 105–19.

41. Kelly, *Athanasian Creed*, 15.

42. Ibid., 16, 41–42.

43. Ibid., 113–14; P. Schaff, *A History of the Creeds of Christendom* (London: Hodder & Stoughton, 1877), I, 35; J. Stevenson, *Creeds, Councils and Controversies: Documents Illustrative of the History of the Church A.D. 337–461* (New York: Seabury Press, 1966), 334–39.

44. Kelly, *Athanasian Creed*, 19–20. One of the forebears of the Athanasian Creed, the *"Tome" of Leo* (Leo, *Epsitola 28*, Stevenson, *Creeds, Councils and Controversies*, 315–24), equally stresses time as a frame or confinement for the Incarnate Christ. Leo's text was intended as a directive to the Council of Chalcedon, which produced the *Definition* that in turn inspired the Athanasian Creed. In the *"Tome,"* Leo states the essence of the Incarnation as follows:

> In a new order—because invisible in what belongs to himself he became visible in what belongs to us, and he, the incomprehensible, willed to be comprehended, abiding before time, he began to exist in time . . . . (Ibid., 318)

There is some possibility that the *"Tome"* was known to Bede, as were some of Leo's other texts, (Ogilvy, *Books Known to the English*, 192–93; and J. D. A. Ogilvy, "Books known to the English, A.D. 597–1066: *Addenda et Corrigenda*," *Medievalia* 7 [1981]: 305). In his *Homilia 2: In Adventu (Ioh. i, 15–18)* (D. Hurst, ed., *Bedae Venerabilis Opera; Pars III: Opera Homiletica*, [Turnholti: Typographi Brepols, 1955], 7–13), Bede stresses the invisibility of God the Father and the intention of Christ of making his divinity visible to the blessed at their deaths, as well as to the elect at the Final Judgment, in contrast to the earthy visibility of the Incarnate Christ. Is this evidence of Bede's knowledge of Leo's mention of visibility and invisibility in the *"Tome"*? P. Meyvaert ("Bede the scholar," in G. Bonner, ed., *Famulus Christi* [London: S.P.C.K., 1976], 43) explores Bede's talent for critical source use and his preference for a literal interpretation of texts; Leo's reference to visibility may be the source of Bede's concept of visibility to the blessed. The issue of the visibility of Christ's two natures may indeed also inform the visual duality inherent in the design of the Echternach lion.

45. Ogilvy, *Books Known to the English*, 151. H. L. C. Tristram, "The Origins of the Rhetoric of Anglo-Saxon Preaching." Paper presented at the International Society of Anglo-Saxonists, University of Durham, 1989 discussed the question of originality and the use of quotations in the Anglo-Saxon homilitic tradition.

46. R. E. McNally, "The Evangelists in the Hiberno-Latin Tradition," in J. Autenreith and F. Brunhölzl, eds., *Festschrift Bernhard Bischoff* (Stuttgart: A. Hierseman, 1971), 116.

47. M. Adriaen, ed., *Sanctii Gregorii Magni–Homiliae in Hiezechibelem Prophetam*, C.C.S.L. 142 (Turnholti: Brepols, 1971), Homilia 4.1–3, 47–49; "For the only-born Son of God was himself truly made man, and himself considered it worthy to die as a calf for our redemption, and himself rose up as a lion by virtue of his strength. The lion is also said to sleep with its eyes open; thus, in the same death in which through his humanity our Redeemer was able to sleep, he was awake through being infused with his immortal divinity."

48. M. Curran, *The Antiphonary of Bangor and the Early Irish Monastic Liturgy* (Dublin: Irish Academic Press, 1984), 169–73, has hypothesized a single Irish monastic liturgy in this period, which would make the widespread use of

these hymns more probable. However, J. Stevenson, "Introduction," in F. E. Warren, *The Liturgy and Ritual of the Celtic Church*, 2nd ed. (Woodbridge, England: Boydell, 1987), xlvii–xlviii, has argued cogently in favor of a variety of liturgical practices in the eighth century. Despite the question of the number of liturgical sequences in use, the appearance of these hymns in manuscripts from a wide variety of centers and dates suggests their popularity in and familiarity to Irish monastic communities. I cite these hymns by the titles commonly given them by modern liturgists, not by the titles cited in the *Antiphonary*; respectively "Hymnum dicat turba fratrem," and "Ymnum apostolorum ut alii dicunt."

49. Curran, *Antiphonary of Bangor*, 22–26, 32.

50. Ibid., 26. "You are the Word from the heart of God, the Way, the Truth, / You are called the rod of Jesse, we call you the Lion. / The right hand of God, the Mountain and the Lamb, you are the Cornerstone, / the Bridegroom also and the Dove, the Flame, the Door."

51. This hymn itself was also known in England and may be construed as an available source on either side of the Irish Sea; Bede quotes it three times in *De Arte Metrica*; Ogilvy, *Books Known to the English*, 165.

52. Curran, *Antiphonary of Bangor*, 50.

53. Ibid., 53. "Into the borders of the world, after much suffering, / comes the Savior with great mercy."

54. Ibid., Pseudo-Jerome (*Commentarii in Evangelium Marci*, on Mark I:7): "Non est digna 'sola gratia' procumbens in baptismo solvere corrigiam calciamentorum eius, id est, mysterium incarnationis Dei. Calx enim extrema pars est corporis. *In fine* enim ad justitiam adest Salvator incarnatus." If, as according to J. F. Kelly, "The Venerable Bede and Hiberno-Latin exegesis," in P. E. Szarmach and V. D. Oggins, eds., *Sources of Anglo-Saxon Culture*, 69, the Venerable Bede may have used this commentary as his source in his *Commentary on Mark*, then it is also possible that this expression would also be known to a wider monastic audience in England as well as in Ireland.

55. Curran, *Antiphonary of Bangor*, 53. "Born as a man in the veils of mortality, / he was not absent from the sky, remaining in the Trinity."

56. Ibid., 52. "For Christ our Savior is true eternal God, without time, and true man without sin in time, . . . who born in the flesh was by no means absent from heaven, remaining in the Trinity."

57. See note 44.

58. Curran, *Antiphonary of Bangor*, 71; P. Hadot, "Introduction," in Marius Victorinus, *Traités Théologiques sur la Trinité*, P. Henry, ed. (Paris: Editions du Cerf, 1960), 79–86.

59. Curran, *Antiphonary of Bangor*, 70. "That which now began which always was a part of your nature, / the Son of the divine Light of your glory, / who is filled with the shape and the fullness of your divinity."

60. Ibid., 93, 96.

61. Ibid., 96.

62. J. Stevenson, ed., *The Latin Hymns of the Anglo-Saxon Church, with an Interlinear Anglo-Saxon Gloss* (Durham: G. Andrews, 1851), vii–x. In the present survey of the potential sources for the Echternach lion, I have not introduced literary material, as there is considerable question as to the availability of these materials in the period in question. However, similar concepts and source use may be noted in Ireland, both in Hiberno-Latin poetry (McNally, "The Evangelists in the Hiberno-Latin Tradition.") and in vernacular verse (J. Carney, ed., *The Poems of Blathmac Son of Cú Bretton* [Dublin: Irish Text Society; Educational Co. of Ireland, 1964], "Poem to the Virgin Mary," lines 200, 209, 211–12; 69, 71, 73).

63. Henderson, *From Durrow to Kells*, 78.

64. Schapiro, "On Some Problems in the Semiotics of Visual Art," 228.

65. Henderson, *From Durrow to Kells*, 76.

CHAPTER TEN

Susan Youngs

RECENT FINDS OF INSULAR ENAMELED BUCKLES

The discovery in Leicestershire in 1990 of two buckles with loops and plates enameled in Celtic style has added two distinctive examples to a small but remarkable group of early medieval buckles decorated with champlevé enamel. A third buckle was found in Lincolnshire in 1993, bringing the number of new and old finds of enameled buckles to fourteen, of which some are complete, while others survive only in part. Four of these have previously been published (the larger buckle from Lough Gara and numbers 7, 8, and 14 listed below). Although these buckles are remarkably varied, most fall into two main typological groups; continental derived forms, principally a loop with triangular or rectangular plate, or an apparently purely Irish type with a rigid rectangular frame comprising one or two plates with single or double integral openings. With the exceptions of the Leicestershire and Lincolnshire finds and an eleventh-century buckle from Cheshire, all the rest of the enameled buckles were found in Ireland. All, bar one, probably date from the period of the seventh to the ninth centuries A.D., although there is no firm contextual evidence for dating any one of these pieces.

The larger of the two Leicestershire buckles (pl. 10.1a) is of copper alloy cast in two parts only; one is the plate with an integral tongue and two projecting lugs, the other is the loop with a complementary pair of horizontal

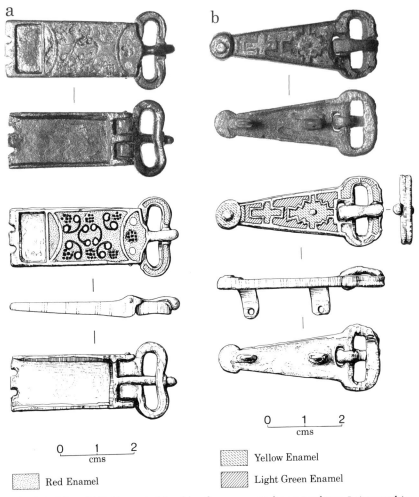

Pl. 10.1. (a) and (b) Enameled buckles from near Melton Mowbray, Leicestershire. Photographs courtesy of Leicestershire Museums, Arts and Records Service. Drawings by Lisa Reardon.

lugs. The two are joined by a slender pin through the four lugs. The length overall is 46mm, the plate is 15mm wide and 6mm deep where it widens to hold the pin. The buckle is recessed on the front and three of the panels are filled with opaque red enamel; the panel behind the tongue is a truncated segment and inlaid with two dots of opaque white enamel flanking a piece of millefiori glass; the main field has a pattern of six copper-alloy C-scrolls symmetrically arranged, each scroll ends in a small ring and resembles a pince-nez, each ring holds a dot of opaque white glass like those next to the tongue, while six more pieces of millefiori lie in and around the scrolls. All the millefiori is of the same type, opaque white glass appears to form a regular grid against an apparently black glass (probably dark blue or green). The third field of enamel is a segment of plain red. The last recess (internally 7 by 13mm) is empty but has on the base a blackened area and tiny scraps perhaps of silver foil against one edge. The end of the buckle-plate has two incomplete rivet holes and the back of the plate is recessed but is open at the end with the rivet holes (pl. 10.1a). The whole plate has three forward projections; two pierced lugs to engage the loop and the centrally placed tongue with a hooked tip. The loop is kidney-shaped with a gully for the tongue and recessed either side to hold red enamel. The buckle is on loan to Leicestershire Museums, Art Galleries, and Records Service, Jewry Wall Museum of Archaeology from a private collection.

The smaller buckle (pl. 10.1b) was also made from two principal parts of copper alloy, but here the buckle-plate and loop were cast in one piece and the tongue was made separately. Length overall is 43mm, the width of the loop 18mm. There are recesses for enamel on both loop and plate and the sides of the plate slope out slightly. The back of the piece (pl. 10.1b) is hollowed and has two pierced lugs lying along the main axis of the plate. These lugs are proportionally very deep, ca. 7mm, giving the buckle a total depth of ca. 10mm. The plate is sub-triangular and ends in a domed circular projection with opaque light green enamel set in a circle of opaque yellow. The main field has angular cells forming a stepped cross with a central metal dot and a simple cross towards the narrow end. Both crosses are filled with yellow enamel, against a background of light green. This green is consistent in color and does not appear to be decayed red. There is a small area of yellow against the wall of the circular terminal with no wall separating it from the main field of green. The buckle loop has a horizontal groove running part of the way round its vertical face; the upper surface has a gully to accommodate the tongue. There is a symmetrical arrangement of six enameled fields, three to each side of the tongue; the two flanking the tongue are slightly broadened and shaped to form stylized animal heads in profile and hold yellow enamel. The next pair of cells have green enamel, while the two larger cells which mimic attachment lugs held yellow enamel, but one is now empty. A rectangular hole was left to attach the tongue, the end of which was curled round. The metal of the buckle is grey-green and probably a high tin bronze.[1] The tongue is brown and is more corroded, roughly triangular in cross section and dips into the loop opening before resting on the bow. A group of three lines is scored across the back of the loop (pl. 10.1b). This buckle is also on loan to Leicestershire Museums, Art Galleries, and Records Service, Jewry Wall Museum of Archaeology from a private collection.

Both buckles were recovered by metal detectorists from fields south of Melton Mowbray, Leicestershire in an area that has produced finds from the Bronze Age to the post-medieval period (pl. 10.4). The fields in question lie south of the crossroads of an east-west road of almost certain Roman date and a north-south road of some antiquity, certainly medieval but probably earlier (W. G. Hoskins regarded it as prehistoric). A Roman occupation site and an early Anglo-Saxon cemetery (including seventh-century material) lie some 400m to the southwest of the crossroads. One of the buckles comes from the southeast quadrant, while an eighth-century coin, a porcupine *sceat* (Series E; Metcalf Class L, the "plumed bird" type), comes from the southwest quadrant some 300m away. Other finds which are generally located in this group of fields include the second enamel buckle, a strap-end with animal head terminal and a gilt-bronze disc brooch, both of ninth- to tenth-century date. The Melton Mowbray Archaeological Fieldwork Group has field walked the area but no further material from this period was recovered. In Leicestershire, finds of the eighth to tenth century are still uncommon and this group stands out.[2] There is no evidence for a furnished Saxon cemetery and it is tempting to consider this to be a possible "productive site," such as a market or meeting place, but the present coin evidence is insufficient to support this.[3]

The larger buckle is of particular interest because its form is based on a well-known type of seventh-century Germanic buckle with long rectangular plate and incorporating a tongue with a tongue-plate, a characteristic find from Anglo-Saxon and Frankish cemeteries. In this case, the tongue plate is a nonfunctional dummy and the complete buckle is very small. The empty rectangular field at the end appears to have held a panel of foil, a feature of some Anglo-Saxon rectangular buckle-plates.[4] Unlike the enameled buckle, most of the proposed models have separately articulated tongues. There is, however, one spectacular Anglo-Saxon polychrome buckle with a rectangular plate and integral tongue with false shield-on-tongue in gold and garnets, from the sword harness in mound one at Sutton Hoo in Suffolk.[5] It was normal to attach the backplate by three or more rivets through a flange, as on the enameled example, but this flange is invariably lower than the surface of the main plate. The rivet holes are not recessed on the Melton Mowbray buckle and it appears to be a variant of a Germanic, probably Anglo-Saxon model, but one that was not usually decorated with enamel.

The only parallel to the Leicestershire buckle is another equally diminutive example found subsequently at West Ravendale, Lincolnshire (pl. 10.2).[6] The precise context is unknown, the find place is about eleven kilometers southwest of Grimsby to the south of the Humber estuary (pl. 10.4). This is almost the same size, 46mm long, the plate 11mm and the

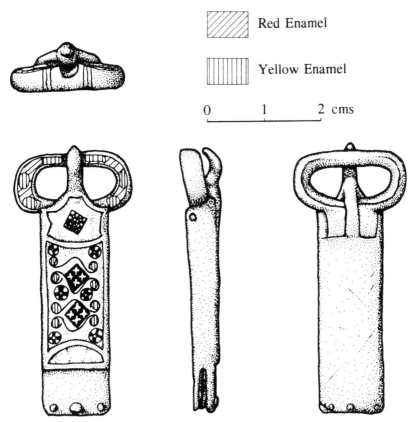

Red Enamel

Yellow Enamel

0   1   2 cms

Pl. 10.2. Enameled buckle from West Ravendale, Lincolnshire. Drawing by Julien Parsons.

loop 23mm wide respectively, and it has an almost identical construction except that the end of the main plate is split like a strap-end and was attached to a strap by three rivets. The enameling is in red and yellow on the loop, with yellow dots in the wire scrolls and complex millefiori inlays. The main fields are now an even yellowish color which is almost certainly decayed red. The circular platelets of millefiori are in translucent light blue and green glass, the rectangle in the tongue base is of translucent and bright pale blue glass in a chequer pattern, the two central panels have more complex a pattern of four opaque white crosses against a very dark blue or green glass. Here the segmental end panel is filled with plain enamel. The metal is a dark copper alloy with no sign of tinning or other surface enhancement apart from two groups of three vertical lines on the loop.

It is the proportionally large fields of opaque red enamel inlaid with millefiori and collared contrasting enamel which place the Melton Mowbray and West Ravendale buckles in the distinctive tradition of early medieval Celtic enameling.[7] While millefiori was used on sixth- and seventh-century Germanic jewelry it was cold-mounted in settings. The circular "sun-burst" type of rod is not known, it is peculiar to Celtic enameling. The use of a comparatively large field of opaque red enamel with millefiori pieces set without collars or enclosing walls is found on several types of sixth- and seventh-century Celtic metalwork and is seen, for example, on the last of the Irish series of zoomorphic penannular brooches and on some contemporary hand-pins.[8] It also occurs on the hinge plates of an Irish house shaped shrine found at Melhus, Norway, of seventh- or eighth-century date.[9] The enameled buckle excavated at Derry, County Down has the same feature (pl. 10.5c) but cannot be dated with any more precision. Some hanging bowl mounts also use enamel and millefiori in this way, so that a British origin remains a possibility for the buckles found in eastern England, accepting the possibility that enameled hanging bowl mounts were manufactured in Britain.[10] Although none of the buckles found in Ireland, enameled or otherwise, exactly matches the form or wire-inlaid enameling of this one some of them are also without parallel. The most likely area of manufacture for most of these enamels and the other buckles is certainly Ireland.

The unusual construction and small size of the Melton Mowbray and West Ravendale buckles support this cultural attribution, these are not typical Anglo-Saxon products with an unusual finish. There is one Anglo-Saxon buckle, excavated from grave 232 at Sarre, Kent, which was described as partly enameled; it had a rectangular plate with a broad diagonal cross made of panels reportedly inlaid with pale-green enamel and ivory, and had ivory and a garnet on the tongue-plate.[11] It appears otherwise to be a perfectly conventional Anglo-Saxon buckle of seventh-century date with an articulated tongue plate. Unless this buckle can be located and re-examined, the identification of both ivory and enamel remains very dubious. There are, however, Merovingian enameled buckles from the seventh century. Most of these have sub-triangular plates but the use of fields is very different and, more importantly, it appears that they may well not contain the same type of inlay.[12] Some Merovingian buckles do have plate and loop cast in one although these are not enameled and are usually openwork types. There is also a strong tradition particularly in earlier Visigothic metalworking, of extensive use of glass inlays on broad rectangular plates but these are significantly different both in design and technique where heat is not used to inlay the glass.[13]

The pince-nez inlay in wire is also found inlaid in red on some seventh-century Merovingian buckles, silver wire C-scrolls and a related motif occur on a much published example with triangular plate from

Amiens,[14] discussed below, but these buckles seem to belong to an independent enameling tradition. C-scrolls are a traditional element in the basic repertoire of gold and silver filigree work from classical times and usually made from beaded wire.[15] Both metalworking traditions may be looking back to common traditions inherited ultimately from the world of late antiquity. The four wires on the West Ravendale buckle are more elaborate variations of this simple C-motif. The traditional Celtic pelta also reduces to this form, for example, the smallest of the three Celtic hanging bowls deposited in the seventh-century Sutton Hoo ship burial has a four-pelta pattern in bronze against red enamel which can be read as eight interlocking scrolls of the Melton Mowbray type, that is of unbeaded bronze walls.[16] The classical filigree tradition was also well known to Irish craftsmen by the eighth century and beaded gold filigree C-scrolls were used to decorate glass studs on the finest pieces including the Ardagh chalice and Derrynaflan paten. On the Moylough belt-shrine (pl. 10.6a) two blue glass studs have inset unbeaded C-scrolls of silver thought to have originally held dots of contrasting red enamel inlay, a feature of the Melton Mowbray buckle.[17] Three loosely formed unbeaded pince-nez scrolls of gold, holding pale dots of enamel, decorate the blue enamel setting of a gold filigree ring published as Byzantine which was found in Ireland.[18] This enamel is cloisonné work. This raises the question of the technique used to create the small internal cells on the two buckles. They could be soldered to the base plate, forming cloisons or cells, but this technique is not known in early medieval Celtic enameling, or the design could have been left in reserve when the background was cut away, as in true champlevé. This was the method used on the third Sutton Hoo mound one hanging bowl and on a hand-pin from Craigywarren, County Antrim; in both these examples the pince-nez shape is part of a pelta design and the general design was probably cast and then tooled to give fine lines.[19] For the Melton Mowbray buckle this would require a large effort to create a small, discontinuous pattern, but it is more likely that the wires are simply embedded in the surface and this is more obviously the case on the West Ravendale example. Small amounts of surface wire inlay are found in eighth- to ninth-century Insular enameling; on a disc reused on a Viking weight from Kilmainham, County Dublin, a mount from Gjonnes, Norway, and a complex enamel disc from Aberdour, Fife, with possible Pictish affinities.[20] All apparently use unbeaded wire as on the buckle and the same technique is employed on niello on the eighth-century Steeple Bumpstead boss.[21]

The sub-triangular buckle from near Melton Mowbray, both in form and decoration, is a miniature version of a buckle found on the shore of Lough Gara, County Sligo (pl. 10.3).[22] The new buckle is much smaller, length 43mm as compared with 76mm and much simpler in construction.

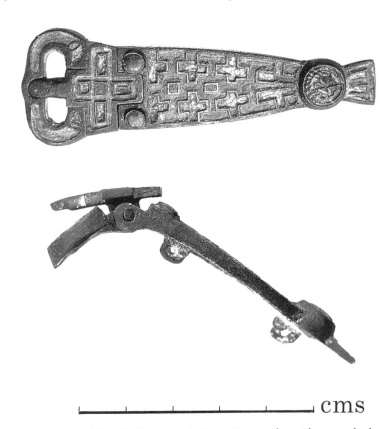

cms

Pl. 10.3. Enameled buckle from Lough Gara, County Sligo. Photographs by permission of the National Museum of Ireland.

The Lough Gara buckle has a separate loop and tongue with tongue-plate fully articulated, two circular studs inlaid with amber, as well as a larger terminal stud inlaid with reticella glass with a recessed grid pattern.[23] It has a further enameled panel projecting beyond the large stud. The two buckles have in common their overall design, a slight curvature and the use of cruciform cells; both employ yellow and green enamel, the larger one uses red also. Genuine green enamel is uncommon at this period and much green has proved to be discolored red. Recent examination of the pointed oval fields in the corners of the square escutcheons on the largest Sutton Hoo hanging bowl has confirmed that this enamel, too, is pale green and not stained white as previously conjectured.[24] The "green" enamel on a hinge plate in the Irish national collection under magnification appears to be deep blue fading to green where weathered, with one more consistently dark blue-green panel.[25] Green enamel on the Lough Gara buckle is confined to two central square cells and recent cleaning has confirmed the color is a strong green, deeper than that on the Melton Mowbray buckle. Use of this unusual color strengthens the impression that these two buckles were made in the same workshop tradition. The profile animal-heads with oval eyes on the loop of the Lough Gara find confirm the zoomorphic nature of the simple decoration on the Melton Mowbray piece, although on the latter the heads face the tip of the tongue and not its base. Both buckles were attached to a strap by large pierced lugs, although it does not seem correct to describe the tiny buckle from Leicestershire as a belt fitting (see also discussion below).

This type of buckle with a triangular plate also apparently has its origin in continental and Germanic models of the late-sixth and seventh centuries. The majority of these have inlaid, faceted or engraved decoration but Françoise Henry in her 1956 survey illustrated some enameled Frankish and Burgundian examples, and recent work has identified important Aquitainian groups.[26] It is significant however, that where these inlays have been tested they have turned out to be lead oxide and, in one case, degraded niello.[27] The red of the Amiens buckle was identified by the British Museum Research Laboratory as lead oxide and not cuprite, although it is not possible to prove whether this inlay was originally a compound of lead or a high-lead glass.[28] This limited evidence introduces the possibility that the enameled buckle-forms of the Celtic world represent an independent local, parallel development from Roman period buckles and need not depend directly on sixth- or seventh-century Merovingian or Anglo-Saxon exemplars, although this remains the most obvious source of influence.[29] The continued use of animal heads on the loops supports this suggestion, a tradition seen also in a gilt-bronze buckle loop from Knowth, County Meath.[30] Imported examples of both model-types are conspicuously absent from mainland Irish sites, but this is not surprising, nor is the physical presence of more than a very few necessary. An excavation at Randalstown, Meath, produced an unstratified, thick kidney-shaped buckle loop with bar of normal Germanic type but this is exceptional.[31]

Liam de Paor in his 1961 paper on Irish buckles and strap-mounts agreed with earlier writers that the belt-buckle was originally a non-Irish item of dress and briefly reviewed the evidence for its introduction, with particular reference to the Lough Gara find discussed above.[32] No general study has been published since this but a major survey was undertaken for a postgraduate degree which remains unpublished and has been a major source for this study.[33] Enameled buckles form a small part of the survey and are conspicuous for their variety and refusal to fit readily into tidy categories. De Paor's observation that the lack of grave goods and closed finds made dating difficult still holds good, although recently excavated workshop evidence at last offers a way forward. Excavations at the Dalriadic royal stronghold of Dunadd in Argyll have yielded the mould for a large buckle-tongue of Germanic type with stepped rectangular tongue-plate from a seventh-century context, traces of silver remained in the mould and in form it can be matched by an unpublished Anglo-Saxon example from Broadstairs, Kent; there was also a mould for a buckle loop with a flattened crossbar with dividing projections.[34] These moulds were found with many others for the manufacture of Celtic penannular brooches. The workshop of this important Irish colonial center in northwest Britain shows that the mixing and exchange of artefact types and techniques between Anglo-Saxon and Celtic traditions of metalworking in the seventh century already included buckles. If some buckles were originally copied in Ireland from the Late Antique world, luxuriously embellished belt sets were also visible on the princes and warlords with whom the British and Irish came into contact in Britain, Ireland, and on the continent in the sixth and seventh centuries. The Sutton Hoo burial has already provided an important example of a rectangular buckle with fixed tongue and also contained two imported Celtic hanging bowls with enameling related to the two enameled buckles of West Ravendale form.

Dating of the three buckles from Melton Mowbray and West Ravendale cannot be precise, it depends on the comparison of their design features with other objects which are themselves only broadly datable on art-historical or technical grounds. The triangular buckle may therefore date to the eighth century when polychrome enameling and imitation cloisonné cell work are eyecatching features of complex objects such as the Moylough belt shrine and the Ardagh chalice, although a date in the seventh century closer to the related Germanic forms is also possible, giving a range of 650 to 750 A.D. On the rectangular buckles, the extensive fields of red enamel with "floating" millefiori together with the use of the sunburst rods, tie them more closely to the late La Tène style decoration of the developed zoomorphic penannular brooches from Ireland and the largest hanging bowl from Sutton Hoo, indicating that these buckles, and with them the find from Derry, County Down (number 7 in the gazetteer) date to the seventh century.

The introduction of buckles as a new type of fastener in Ireland raises some interesting questions about function, whether decorated belt-buckles are evidence for a change in dress-style in the aristocratic, and therefore possibly more cosmopolitan section of Irish secular society. However, the continued development of distinctive Celtic brooch forms, which included absorption of design elements from very different Germanic models, shows a strong and vigorous native dress tradition, an impression borne out by scraps of pictorial evidence from illuminated manuscripts and sculpture.[35]

Barry Ager's observation that the triangular buckles are very narrow in comparison with their possible Germanic ancestors, combined with my own curiosity as to why many of these buckles are curved, and why there is a distinctive group with double openings and deep side flanges (numbers 10 to 13 in the gazetteer) which are best explained as strap-distributors, introduces the alternative possibility that these buckles were used for sword-scabbard and weapon harness mounts for which there are also Germanic models.[36] The early seventh-century "dummy" buckle from Sutton Hoo, mound one, with its narrow triangular plate, marked curvature and odd construction is perhaps representative of the type of model behind the Irish enameled triangular buckles.[37] Germanic belt and harness sets also include triangular counter-plates with prominent rivets.

It should be noted that distinctive triangular plates with domed rivet heads were also used elsewhere in later Irish metalwork and not only on buckles; for example, they appear richly decorated below the handles of the Ardagh and Derrynaflan chalices.[38] The sub-triangular hinge attachment plates on some of the Insular house-shaped shrines, particularly the Melhus shrine, should also be mentioned as enameled forms related to enameled buckles.[39] It might be assumed that the girdle which formed part of a monk's costume was a belt with buckle and that therefore with the spread of monasticism in sixth-century Ireland the buckle must have become a common and widespread artefact. However, it is not easy to identify buckles as distinct from belts in Old Irish or Latin sources, there appears to have been no specific word for a buckle.[40] Interestingly enough there is an early loan word from the Latin "fibula" alongside native words for brooch, could this perhaps have been borrowed to describe an unfamiliar type of dress fastener associated with the Christian church, such as a buckle?[41] This is pure speculation, to be dismissed or confirmed by those expert in the texts; the enshrined belt from Moylough (pl. 10.6a) is a relic of a saint or patron with a magnificent buckle suite in a style derived from the Late Antique, even though this is non-functional. From Irish sites there are indeed several simple buckles in bronze and iron suitable for belts, comprising a sub-rectangular loop with a tongue wrapped round the bar, but the narrow highly decorated enameled buckles perhaps belong to a separate tradition of body harness for weapons.

THE GAZETTEER

In addition to the four buckles discussed above (nos. 1–4 in the gazetteer, pl. 10.4), the corpus of early Irish enamel buckles now includes ten other pieces (pls. 10.5 and 10.6).[42] Only one, no. 7, is from an excavated

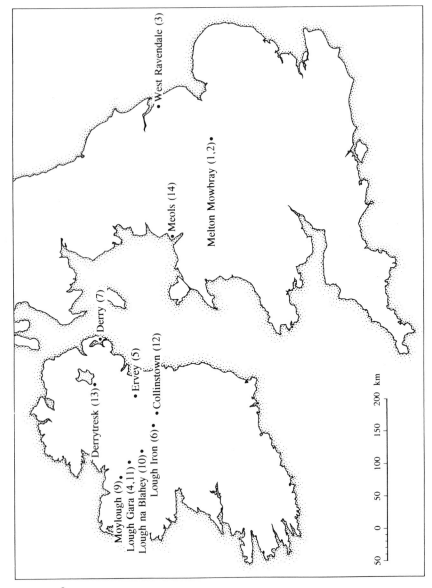

Pl. 10.4. Map of the
find places of
enameled buckles;
the numbers refer to
the gazetteer. Map
drawn by James
Farrant.

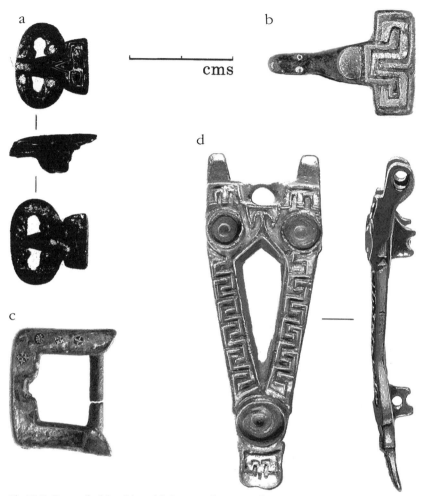

Pl. 10.5. Enameled buckles: (a) loop and tongue from Ervey, County Meath; (b) from Lough Iron, County Westmeath; (c) from Derry, County Down; (d) enameled buckle-plate, provenance unknown. Photographs by permission of: National Museum of Ireland (a–b, d); Ulster Museum (c).

context and that was an unstratified find. These are arranged in very rough chronological order: grouping 1 to 9, seventh- to eighth-century; 10 to 13, later eighth- to the ninth-, possibly tenth-century, (no. 13 is eleventh-century), divisions based on changes in form and inlays.

1. Melton Mowbray buckle with rectangular plate (discussed above)
2. Melton Mowbray buckle with triangular plate (discussed above)

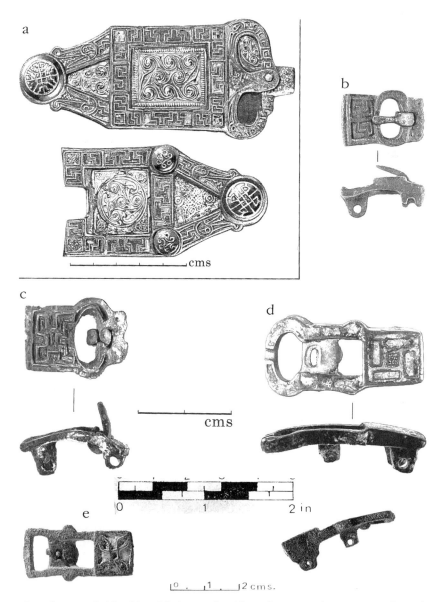

Pl. 10.6. Enameled buckles: (a) dummy buckle and counter-plate on an enshrined belt from Moylough, County Sligo; (b) with double plates from Lough na Blahey, County Roscommon; (c) with double plates from Lough Gara, County Sligo; (d) with two plates and double openings from Collinstown, County Westmeath; (e) with two plates and double openings from Derrytresk, County Tyrone. Original photographs: courtesy of National Museum of Ireland (a); by permission of National Museum of Ireland (b–d); courtesy of Ulster Museum (e).

3. West Ravendale buckle (discussed above)
4. Lough Gara, large buckle with triangular plate (discussed above)
5. Copper-alloy oval loop with a tongue with tongue-plate, both with champlevé cells of enamel (pl. 10.5a). Colors given as yellow and green. Loop width 17mm; tongue with plate length 15mm. This is possibly but not necessarily incomplete because without a plate it has no apparent means of attachment unless a strap was wrapped directly round the rod which originally joined the loop and tongue. From Ervey, County Meath (private collection).[43] This small buckle appears to copy sixth-century glass and garnet-inlaid Visigothic buckles, and there are not dissimilar Anglo-Saxon buckles.
6. Copper-alloy tongue plate with key pattern champlevé cells on the rectangular plate and a semicircular cell on the base of the tongue (pl. 10.5b). Traces of red enamel in both areas. Two small recesses on the tip of the tongue give it a zoomorphic appearance. The tongue is a flattened oval in cross-section. Plate 20.6 by 8.5mm, tongue and plate 29.3mm. The problem with this piece is that the back is completely plain with no means of fixing it to a cross bar and no sign to the naked eye that any such loop or lug once existed, it must have been soldered onto another fitting, which seems a rather weak construction. From Lough Iron, County Westmeath (National Museum of Ireland, E499:74). Although the shallow cross-section of the tongue is unparalleled, this shape of tongue plate is found on late-sixth to seventh-century Merovingian and Anglo-Saxon buckles.[44]
7. Copper-alloy rectangular loop with bar, tongue missing (pl. 10.5c). The loop is inlaid with enamel, originally red, and two types of millefiori glass. Maximum dimensions 24.1mm by 20mm. Excavated find but unstratified, Derry, County Down (HMBB.DoE Northern Ireland, 81/416).[45] This form is unique; the out-turned tapering panels are similar to those on a small enamel and millefiori mount, unprovenanced and unpublished, recently acquired by the British Museum (MLA, 1992, 5–3,1).
8. Copper-alloy buckle-plate with two lugs on the back for attachment, loop and tongue missing, secondary hole for a replacement tongue, length 63mm, maximum width 22.5mm (pl. 10.5d). The lugs also have secondary holes. The plate is sub-triangular with three circular settings, now empty, imitating studs on triangular Germanic buckles, as on the Lough Gara example (no. 4). The center is now empty but has a flange to retain an inserted panel, the outer frame has interlocking angular S- or Z-cells

originally filled with alternating red or yellow enamel, the color scheme reconstructed in an 1893 plate. Length 63mm, width 22.5mm. Unprovenanced, presented to Petrie by W. F. Wakeman (National Museum of Ireland, p. 616).[46] The source of these distinctive "tail" panels is not clear.

9. Dummy buckle with plate and counterplate in copper-alloy, silver, enamel and glass (pl. 10.6a). The well-known and published en-shrined belt from Moylough, County Sligo. Here the red and yellow enamel in angular cells frames repoussé foils, long-beaked bird heads in enamel flank the base of the tongue and animal heads support the composite glass studs at the apexes. Buckle length 119mm (the tongue is an ancient repair), width 50mm (National Museum of Ireland, 1945:81). The design of plate and counter-plate incorporates a triangular element, and they are much broader than the other Irish triangular plates. It is also the only example which is demonstrably a belt set. To the writer this piece shares more design characteristics with late-Roman belt suites than with later Burgundian buckles.[47]

10. Small copper-alloy buckle with decorated loop and plate cast in one, but also with a plain plate projecting beyond the loop from which the tongue is hinged (pl. 10.6b). Two curved fields for enamel on the loop, four "L" shaped cells on the larger plate, all now empty. On the back one attachment lug behind the enameled plate, one each side of the undecorated plate. Length 18mm, width 11.8mm. Provenance Lough na Blahey, Strokestown, County Roscommon (National Museum of Ireland, E499:106).[48]

11. Copper-alloy buckle with central opening and one plain, one decorated plate all cast as one, and with a separate tongue looped round a hole in the plain plate (pl. 10.6c). Decorated with one large stepped cell against a reserved field which also runs round the sides of the dummy loop. The fields are keyed for enamel but none survives. Length 14mm, width 17mm. From Lough Gara, County Sligo (National Museum of Ireland, E499:107). This is very similar to no. 10 in Gazetteer. These double-plated buckles with single openings are a very distinctive Irish form and can be seen, provisionally, either as precursors of the more elaborate double plate/double opening type (numbers 12 and 13 below) or more plausibly, as a contemporary but simpler type with a less complex function.

12. Copper alloy buckle-cum-strap-distributor with enameled plate, two openings and a central recessed plain plate, all cast in one (pl. 10.6d). The tongue is missing but was attached to a hole on the

reserved plain plate. A series of sub-rectangular champlevé cells decorate the border of the openings and the plate has four rectangular cells against an enameled background, surrounding a square cell holding millefiori. The millefiori is a common type with four white four-petalled motifs against a very dark background. All the enamel is yellow. The straps were attached by very deep twin lugs at the edge of the enameled plate and by a lug behind the recessed plain plate. Length 33mm, width 17mm. Found Collinstown, County Westmeath (National Museum of Ireland, E499:111). Very similar in shape and presumably function to 13.

13. Copper-alloy buckle-cum-strap-distributor, cast in one (pl. 10.6e). Rectangular buckle with central bar slotted for the tongue and an opening to either side, beyond on one side is a rectangular plate with a four-lobed decoration formed from intersecting arcs, originally inlaid with yellow enamel and with a contrasting color, now decayed, in the loops and central square (observed by Cormac Bourke). At each side of this panel are deep vertical flanges ending in pierced lugs, an arrangement probably designed to hold a second strap. Length 33mm, width 12.4mm. Provenance Derrytresk, County Tyrone (Ulster Museum, A5359). Very like buckle 12 in form. This distinctive type with double opening (numbers 10–13) appears to be unique to early medieval Ireland.[49]

14. A possible late example of an enameled buckle is an inlaid loop in Hiberno-Viking style from Meols in the Wirral, Cheshire, which is described as inlaid with enamel (unlocated).[50] It appears to be eleventh-century.

NOTES

My thanks to Peter Liddle and Robert Rutland of the Leicestershire Museums, Art Galleries, and Records Service for showing me the new buckles, much assistance and for allowing me to publish them, and also to Richard Knox for help with illustrations. I am also indebted to Cormac Bourke of the Ulster Museum, and to Eamonn Kelly, Mary Cahill and Paul Mullarkey of the National Museum of Ireland, Kevin Leahy of Scunthorpe Museum and Julien Parsons of Sheffield City Museum for access to new and old material, help, illustrations and permission to publish; to Orla O'Sullivan for kind permission to refer to her thesis; to my colleagues, Lisa Reardon for drawings and James Farrant for artwork preparation, Barry Ager, Cathy Haith, Dafydd Kidd, and Leslie Webster for references and guidance on buckle types.

1. W. A. Oddy, "Bronze Alloys in Dark Age Europe," in R. L. S. Bruce-Mitford, *The Sutton Hoo Ship-Burial*, edited by A. C. Evans, vol. 3 (London: British Museum, 1983), 945–62.

2. Information kindly supplied by Peter Liddle, Leicestershire Archaeological Survey Officer; for the distribution of early medieval material in the county see P. Liddle, "Anglo-Saxon Leicestershire," in J. E. Bourne, ed., *Landscapes in the East Midlands* (Leicester: Leicester Museum Arts and Records Service, 1996), 1–10. There is a shortened version of this present paper "Two Medieval Celtic Enamelled Buckles from Leicestershire," *Trans. of the Leicestershire Archaeological and Historical Society* 68 (1993): 15–22.

3. Productive sites are defined in M. A. S. Blackburn and D. M. Metcalf, eds., *Anglo-Saxon Productive Sites*, B.A.R. Brit. ser. (forthcoming).

4. G. Speake, *Anglo-Saxon Animal Art and its Germanic Background* (Oxford: Clarendon Press, 1980), pl. 9a–d.

5. R. L. S. Bruce-Mitford, *The Sutton Hoo Ship-Burial*, vol. 2 (London: British Museum 1978), 469.

6. Now on long-term loan to Scunthorpe City Museum and Art Gallery; a sketch was published in *The Searcher* 9, pt. 1 (Sept. 1993): 16.

7. G. Haseloff, *Email im frühen Mittelalter*, Marburger Studien zur Vor- und Frühgeschichte 1 (Marburg: Hitzeroth, 1991): 153–69.

8. H. E. Kilbride-Jones, *Zoomorphic Penannular Brooches* (London: Society of Antiquaries of London, 1980), nos. 84, 85, 96, 100, 103, 106, 111, 132, 133, 137; the Ballinderry, Crannog 2, brooch is a particularly fine example properly illustrated in M. Ryan, ed., *Treasures of Ireland, Irish Art 300 B.C.–1500 A.D.* (Dublin: Royal Irish Academy, 1983), no. 45; for a hand-pin see S. M. Youngs, ed., *"The Work of Angels" Masterpieces of Celtic Metalwork, 6th–9th Centuries A.D.* (London: British Museum, 1989), no. 4.

9. Haseloff, *Email*, Taf. 147, b, c.

10. Examples illustrated in R. L. S. Bruce-Mitford, *The Sutton Hoo Ship-Burial*, vol. III, fig. 205 (Sutton Hoo Bowl 3), fig. 217b (Northumberland), fig. 219 (Barlaston); for a recent survey of the debate on origins see J. Brenan, *Hanging Bowls and their Contexts*, B.A.R., Brit. ser. 220 (Oxford: British Archaeological Reports, 1991).

11. J. Brent, "Account of the Society's Researches into the Anglo-Saxon Cemetery at Sarr. Part 3," *Archaeologia Cantiana* 7 (1868): 307–21. I owe this reference to my colleague Cathy Haith.

12. F. Henry, "Irish Enamels of the Dark Ages and their Relation to the Cloisonné Technique," in D. B. Harden, ed., *Dark Age Britain* (London: Methuen, 1956), 71–88, see pages 73–75; S. Lerenter, "Nouvelle approche typologique des plaques-boucles mérovingiennes en bronze de type aquitain," in P. Perin, ed., *Gallo-Romains, Wisigoths et Francs en Aquitaine, Septimanie et Espagne*, Actes

des VIIe Journées internationales d'Archéologies mérovingiennes, Toulouse 1985, (Rouen: Association Française d'Archéologie Merovingienne, 1991), 225–57, see groups F, G, H.

13. Ariadne Gallery, *Treasures of the Dark Ages in Europe* (New York: Ariadne Galleries, 1992), 74–77.

14. Haseloff, *Email*, 110.

15. N. Whitfield, "Motifs and Techniques of Celtic Filigree. Are they Original?" in M. Ryan, ed., *Ireland and Insular Art A.D. 500–1200* (Dublin: Royal Irish Academy, 1987), 75–84, see 75–76.

16. R. L. S. Bruce Mitford, *Sutton Hoo*, 3, 257–63.

17. M. J. O'Kelly, "The Belt-Shrine from Moylough, Sligo," *J.R.S.A.I.* 95: 149–88; inlay discussed on p. 177, pl. 26.

18. C. C. Oman, *Catalogue of Rings in the Victoria and Albert Museum* (Ipswich: Anglia; Victoria & Albert Museum, 1930), 62, pl. 8, no. 223; Dr. Niamh Whitfield has kindly commented on the filigree work which is not typical of early Irish work but in a later tradition. The enamel, however, is not symmetrical and may be reused.

19. Bruce-Mitford, *Sutton Hoo*, 3, fig. 205; S. Youngs in Youngs, *"Work of Angels"*, 24–25, no. 5.

20. For the Kilmainham (Islandbridge) weight Haseloff, *Email*, 164, 186; for Gjonnes see ibid., 164, 186, and E. Wamers, *Insularer Metallschmuck in Wikingerzeitlichen Gräbern Nordeuropas*, Offa-Bücher Band 56 (Neumunster: K. Wachholtz, 1985), no. 119. The Aberdour disc is published on pages 232–35 of C. Bourke and J. Close-Brooks, "Five Insular Enamel Ornaments," *P.S.A.S.* 119 (1989): 227–37.

21. S. M. Youngs, "The Steeple Bumpstead Boss," in R. M. Spearman and J. Higgitt, eds, *The Age of Migrating Ideas: Early Medieval Art in Northern Britain and Ireland* (Edinburgh: National Museums of Scotland, 1993), 143–50.

22. National Museum of Ireland 1958:20; M. Ryan in Youngs, *"The Work of Angels,"* 58.

23. This revised description is based on information kindly supplied by Paul Mullarkey of the National Museum of Ireland after his recent cleaning of the buckle.

24. Report by Dr. Ian Freestone, British Museum Research Laboratory, clarifying Bruce-Mitford, *Sutton Hoo*, 3, 221, 303, 939.

25. R. Ó Floinn, "A Fragmentary House-shaped Shrine from Clonard, County Meath," *J.I.A.* 5: 53, pl. 3.

26. Henry, "Irish Enamels of the Dark Ages," pls. 7, 10; Lerenter, "Nouvelle approche typologique," groups F, G, H, 230–31.

27. E. Salin, *La Civilisation mérovingienne*, III, *Les Techniques* (Paris: A. et J. Picard, 1957), 231–32. I am grateful to Dafydd Kidd for bringing this information to my attention.

28. Comments by Mavis Bimson and Ian Freestone of the British Museum Department of Scientific Research, and see also Haseloff, *Email*, 75.

29. This approach was helpfully suggested by my colleague Dafydd Kidd.

30. F. Henry in G. Eogan, "Excavations at Knowth, County Meath, 1962–65," *P.R.I.A.* 66C (1968): no. 4, 359–60, pl. 60.

31. National Museum of Ireland, E149:671; O. O'Sullivan, "Buckles of the First Millenium a.d. from Native Irish Sites," 2 vols. (Master's Phil. thesis, University College Dublin, 1984), 92, 183.

32. L. de Paor, "Irish Belt-Buckles and Strap Mounts," *Bericht über den V. Internationalen Kongress für Vor- und Frühgeschichte Hamburg 1958* (Berlin: Verlag Bebr. Mann, 1961), 649–53.

33. O'Sullivan, "Buckles of the first Millenium."

34. Find 298, fig. 6.4b and find 1432, fig. 6.4a in E. Campbell and A. Lane, "Celtic and Germanic Interaction in Dalriada; a Seventh-Century Metalworking Site at Dunadd," in R. M. Spearman and J. Higgitt, eds., *The Age of Migrating Ideas*. My thanks to the authors for allowing me to see and discuss this material.

35. R. Ó Floinn, "Secular Metalwork in the Eighth and Ninth Centuries," in Youngs, ed., *"The Work of Angels,"* 72–91.

36. I would like to thank Barry Ager for bringing this information to my attention; W. Menghin, *Das Schwert im Frühen Mittelalter* (Stuttgart: K. Theiss, 1983), 102ff.

37. R. L. S. Bruce Mitford, *Sutton Hoo*, 2, 473–81, 572–74.

38. Ryan, *Treasures of Ireland*, 126.

39. M. Blindheim, "A House-Shaped Irish-Scots Reliquary in Bologna and its Place among the Other Reliquaries," *Acta Archaeologica* 55 for 1984 (1986): 1–53. They also have less sumptuous, hinged seventh-century Anglo-Saxon parallels, Speake, *Anglo-Saxon Art*, pl. 8f.

40. My thanks to Professor Fergus Kelly for his helpful comments on the Irish vocabulary.

41. D. McManus, "A Chronology of Latin Loan-words in Early Irish," *Ériu* 34 (1983): 21–71.

42. Most of these buckles were found by metal-detector users and have not been published. Fortunately, they have subsequently entered public collections.

43. O'Sullivan, "Buckles of the First Millenium," 135.

44. See p. 337, S. Chadwick Hawkes and M. Pollard, "The Gold Bracteates from Sixth-Century Anglo-Saxon Graves in Kent," *Frühmittelalterliche Studien* 15 (1981): 316–70.

45. D. M. Waterman, "The Early Christian Churches and Cemetery at Derry, County Down," *U.J.A.* 30 (1967): 53–69, see pages 55, 63–64; Bourke in Youngs, ed., *"Work of Angels,"* no. 203.

46. V. Ball and M. Stokes, "On a Block of Red Glass Enamel, Said to Have Been Found at Tara Hill. With Observations on the Use of Red Enamel in Ireland," *Trans. Royal Irish Academy* 30 (1893): 277–94, page 291, pl. 19,1.

47. O'Kelly, "The Belt-Shrine from Moylough, Sligo," 149–88; M. Ryan in Youngs, ed., *"Work of Angels,"* no. 47.

48. O'Sullivan, "Buckles of the First Millenium," 163–64, where the provenance is given as Dysart, County Westmeath.

49. I am indebted to Geoffrey Egan of the Museum of London for his comments on medieval buckles.

50. Page 22, fig.7b in J. D. Bu'lock, "The Celtic, Saxon and Scandinavian Settlement at Meols in Wirral," *Trans. Historic Society of Lancashire and Cheshire* 112 (1960): 1–27; I owe this reference to Leslie Webster. This piece is not with the other illustrated buckles in Grosvenor Museum, Chester.

CHAPTER ELEVEN

Niamh Whitfield

FILIGREE ANIMAL ORNAMENT FROM IRELAND AND SCOTLAND OF THE LATE-SEVENTH TO NINTH CENTURIES

Its Origins and Development

Microscopic study of the minute, intricate, gold filigree animal ornament from Ireland and Scotland of the late-seventh to ninth centuries has a three-fold interest. First, it shows details which reveal the long-lived influence of the Germanic prototypes. Second, the style of animal ornament on any one object is consistent, but as between objects it differs more than other motifs shown in filigree, so analysis of the designs makes it possible to comment on the idiosyncracies of particular workshops as well as on more general stylistic changes. Third, special care was generally lavished on animal panels, so they are often remarkable technically.

THE RELATIONSHIP WITH GERMANIC FILIGREE ANIMAL ORNAMENT

In recent papers, Michael Ryan has suggested that early medieval Celtic art is better studied against its Early Christian rather than its Germanic background. He argues that the use on the Derrynaflan paten from County Tipperary of filigree panels depicting beasts with birds, serpents, men, and deer can be traced directly to Late Roman or Byzantine church plate, available to Irish pilgrims to Gaul in Merovingian and Carolingian times.[1] Equally, he doubts the Germanic influence on the Derrynaflan chalice, commenting that the "abundance of animal ornament . . . owes a great deal not to a zoomorphic tradition of Salin's Style II but to Early Christian and Late Antique iconographies."[2] The case for Christian symbolism on the Derrynaflan chalice and paten is strong, and Ryan is right to point out that late-seventh- to ninth-century Celtic art generally must be seen in this context. Nevertheless, study of the decorative conventions and manufacturing techniques of Celtic filigree animal art demonstrates that Germanic goldsmithing traditions have considerable relevance to its design.

TRANSMISSION OF THE INFLUENCE OF
GERMANIC FILIGREE ANIMAL ART

Some details can be traced back to the origins of Germanic art in late-fifth-century Scandinavia. However, filigree was not made in Ireland or Scotland before the seventh century, and there is no evidence of a direct connection between early Scandinavian gold and the later Celtic work. Irish and Scottish goldsmiths seem to have learned how to make filigree from their Anglo-Saxon neighbors who, in their turn, were heirs to a long-standing Germanic tradition.[3] Three links in a chain are thus proposed: first, Scandinavian filigree animal ornament, second, that from Anglo-Saxon England, and third the Celtic version. This background must be taken into account to explain the appearance, if not the iconography, of Celtic filigree animal patterns.

As the immediate impetus to make filigree came from the Anglo-Saxons, it was their regional style which provided the point of departure for Celtic goldsmiths, and there are numerous parallels between seventh-century Anglo-Saxon zoomorphic filigree and Celtic work of the late-seventh to ninth centuries. These range from the way minute filigree animal patterns are used as just one element in a complex symmetrical scheme of ornament laid out on separate panels, each covered with dense ornament, to more specific details of their design and manufacture.

THE DEPICTION OF ANIMALS

The motif of the beast in profile with an interlaced ribbon-like body, which plays such an important role in Celtic filigree (figs. 11.2, 11.4a–c, and 11.5a), is generally agreed to derive from Germanic Animal Style II, whose roots lie in part in Scandinavia, but which flourished in Anglo-Saxon England in the seventh century. While the Celtic specimens have their own distinctive character, their Germanic ancestry is evident from a number of features.[4]

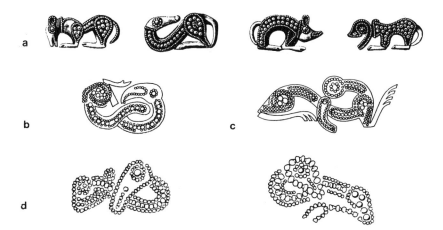

Fig. 11.1. Scandinavian and Anglo-Saxon filigree animal ornament: (a) collar from Ålleberg, Västergötland, Sweden (after Salin 1904), scale ca. 1.3:1; (b) brooch from Kitnaes, Sjaelland, Denmark (after Haseloff 1981), scale ca. 1.5:1; (c) brooch fragment from Elsehoved, Fyn, Denmark (after Haseloff 1981), scale 1.5:1; (d) shoulder-clasp from Sutton Hoo, Suffolk, England, scale ca. 3.75:1. Drawings by permission of: H. Haseloff-Bönning (b–c); N. Griffiths and N. Whitfield (d).

These analogies go beyond general anatomical appearances. One sees the recurrence of specific features such as a granule at the back of the mouth (cf. figs. 11.1c–d, and 11.2b–f; pls. 11.2b, and 11.3a–c) and pear-shaped hips (cf. fig. 11.1a–d, and Ryan, this volume, p. 252, pl. 12.2). Individual beasts strike similar poses with, for example, a backturned head (cf. figs. 11.1b, and 11.4a) or a raised foreleg (cf . figs. 11.1c, and pl. 11.4b). Paired animals may be confronted,[5] or interlaced in axial symmetry.[6] Furthermore, the device of the frieze, of which there is at present just one Celtic example in filigree (fig. 11.5b), is also found in Anglo-Saxon metalwork.[7] Another feature in common is the use of zoomorphic patterns to fill panels almost in their entirety (cf. pls. 11.1b, 11.2, and fig. 11.2).

FORMS OF WIRES USED TO DELINEATE ANIMALS

The influence of Germanic prototypes on Celtic work is also evident in the choice of types of ornamental wire used to "draw" animals. In each case beaded wire, or on some Celtic examples a compound strand involving beaded wire, delineates the motifs, while two- or three-strand cables never do so, but are used in a subsidiary role on panel borders or in decorative infills. Granulation may also form decorative infills, and is used for eyes and to highlight other focal points.

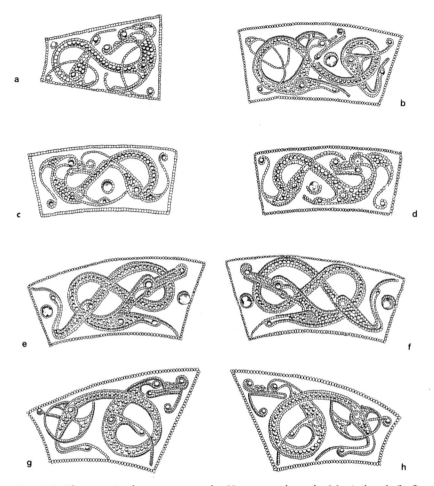

Fig. 11.2. Filigree animal ornament on the Hunterston brooch: (a) pin-head; (b–f) hoop; (g–h) terminals. Scale ca. 2:1. Drawings by permission of J. Longcrane and N. Whitfield.

DECORATION OF ANIMALS' BODIES

Another Celtic element which can be traced to a Germanic source is the decoration of the animals' bodies. Celtic filigree animals' bodies may be (1) speckled all over with granules, (2) delineated by bands of patterned wire which create hatching, or (3) plain and outlined by a single contour-line. All these interrelated traditions, which have counterparts in other metalwork techniques, can be traced back to Germanic prototypes.

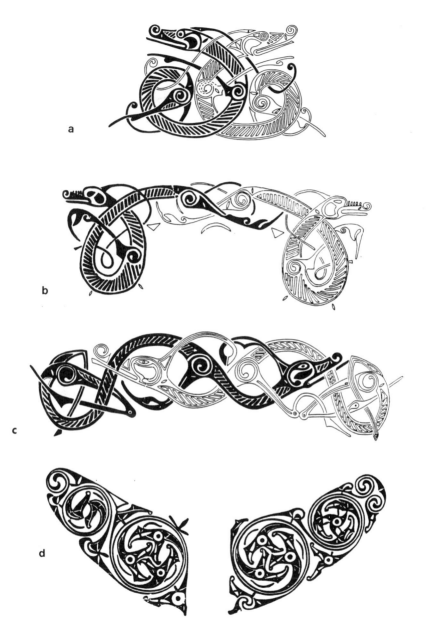

Fig. 11.3. Chip-carved ornament: (a) Steeple Bumpstead boss, scale ca. 2:1; (b) "Tara" brooch, reverse of pin-head, scale ca. 2.75:1; (c) Hunterston brooch, reverse of hoop, scale ca. 2:1; (d) Hunterston brooch, reverse of terminals (after Stevenson 1983), scale ca 1.25:1. Drawings by permission of: N. Griffiths and N. Whitfield (a,c); D. Dolinka-Korda and N. Whitfield (b); National Museums of Scotland (d).

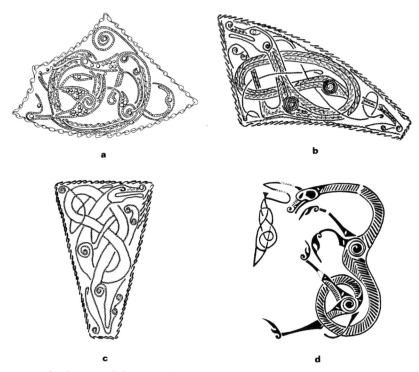

Fig. 11.4. Filigree and chip-carved animal ornament: (a) Westness brooch, terminal, scale ca. 2:1; (b) "Tara" brooch, terminal, scale ca. 2.5:1; (c) "Tara" brooch, pin-head, scale ca. 2.75:1; (d) "Tara" brooch, reverse, scale ca. 2:1. Drawings by permission of: J. Longcrane and N. Whitfield (a); D. Dolinka-Korda and N. Whitfield (b–d).

Speckled beasts. This convention is naturalistic in origin and ultimately derived from the late provincial Roman world. Thus, the fur of the beasts on late Roman chip-carved belt-fittings is often represented by punched or incised dots.[8] Early Germanic metalworkers sometimes also decorated the bodies of animals with dotting. Often such dots are punched as, for instance, on the incised parcel-gilt animals on the fifth-century Sarre quoit-brooch from Kent,[9] or an early Style I chip-carved brooch from Hardenberg, Sjaelland, Denmark.[10] On fifth-century Scandinavian filigree, however, they are represented by granules, though on these creatures there is often room only for a single row on the slender trunk (fig. 11.1a–c).

Curiously, no surviving seventh-century Anglo-Saxon filigree shows an animal with granules covering the beast's entire body, and we lack a link between the archaic Scandinavian filigree prototypes and their Celtic descendants. However, granules appear on the thighs of the Anglo-Saxon hatched

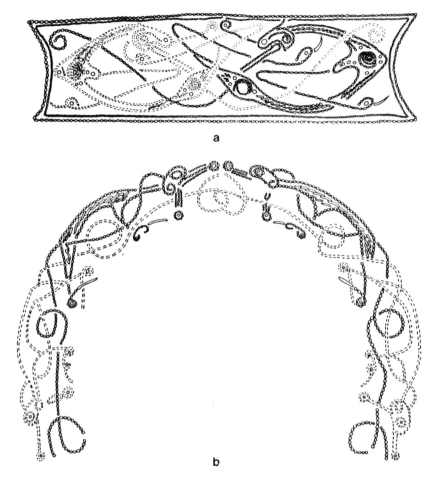

a

b

Fig. 11.5. Filigree animal ornament on the Ardagh chalice: (a) bowl girdle, scale ca. 2.5:1; (b) detail of panel under foot-cone, scale ca. 3:1. Drawings by permission of D. Dolinka-Korda and N. Whitfield.

beasts to be discussed below (pl. 11.2), and the archaeological record is far from complete. Moreover, punched speckling is found not only in a fifth-century Anglo-Saxon context, as mentioned above, but also on eighth-century Anglo-Saxon animal ornament, for example, on a fragmentary pin-head from Brandon, Suffolk,[11] and pins from the river Witham, at Fiskerton, Lincolnshire,[12] and Flixborough, South Humberside.[13] On these objects the animals' bodies may be elongated, and much of the dotting is laid out in single rows very reminiscent of the lines of granules on earlier filigree beasts.

A connection with Celtic filigree animal ornament is clear, since slender beasts whose trunks are decorated with a single row of granules

Fig. 11.6. Filigree and chip-carved animal ornament: (a) Dunbeath brooch, terminal, scale ca. 2:1; (b) Killamery brooch, reverse, scale ca. 1:1; (c) Large Ardagh brooch, reverse, scale ca. 1.3:1; (d) Derrynaflan paten, motif E (after Ryan 1991), scale ca. 2.3:1. Drawings by permission of: D. Dolinka-Korda and N. Whitfield (a–c); M. Ryan (d).

occur on the Hunterston brooch from West Kilbride, Ayshire, which comes early in the series,[14] being perhaps made before A.D. 700 (fig. 11.2; pl. 11.3). On Celtic filigree dotting composed of massed granules also appears on the bodies of creatures on the Dunbeath brooch from Caithness (e.g. fig. 11.6a). More sophisticated filigree speckling appears on the Derrynaflan paten, where beasts' bodies and thighs are coated with granules ringed by collars of beaded wire (so-called collared granules) (pl. 11.4a). Further still removed from the prototype are beasts found on the ninth-century Derrynaflan chalice, which may be infilled with even more elaborate dotting composed of wire cones (fig. 11.7a).

Hatched beasts. In this convention, massed granules are confined to broad areas such as the thigh, while each body is delineated by a narrow band of wires. There is a clear Anglo-Saxon prototype for the Celtic examples on the Sutton Hoo shoulder-clasps from Suffolk (fig. 11.1d; pl. 11.2), where the pear-shaped thighs are coated with granules, and each ribbon-like body is formed of a central beaded wire flanked by finer beaded wires (echoing, in a form which would be easier to solder, the lines of granules flanked by wire on earlier Scandinavian gold) (fig. 11.1a–c).

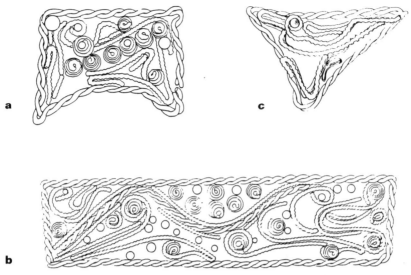

Fig. 11.7. Filigree animals in three conventions on the Derrynaflan chalice (after Ryan 1993): (a) speckled beast on the handle, scale 2.5:1; (b) hatched beast on the bowl girdle, scale 2:1; (c) plain beast on the handle escutcheon, scale ca. 2.75:1. Drawings by permission of M. Ryan.

On Celtic filigree the bands of wire delineating the beasts' bodies are more complex, and two-strand cables may create ribbing in the form of oblique hatching (fig. 11.5) or a herringbone pattern (fig. 11.4b and pl. 11.4b). There are precedents for this convention also, since two-strand cables are used to similar effect on a fifth- to sixth-century pendant from Skenänas, Vingåker, Södermanland, Sweden.[15] No surviving Anglo-Saxon filigree animal has such a body, but both oblique hatching and herringbone patterning is found, for instance, on *pressblech* animal ornament from Sutton Hoo.[16] Moreover, herring-bone patterns in filigree also occur on Anglo-Saxon work, for example, on the Acklam sword pommel from Yorkshire.[17] A development which seems to be peculiar to filigree animal ornament from Ireland or Scotland is that the wire bands delineating the bodies may not be flat as on the Sutton Hoo clasps, but of trefoil cross-section.

Like some Scandinavian antecedents, but unlike their Celtic descendants in filigree, the hatched beasts on the Sutton Hoo shoulder-clasps lack shoulders and forelegs. Nevertheless, the Sutton Hoo format is followed fairly closely on some pieces of Celtic filigree, for example, the Westness brooch, found in a Viking grave in Orkney, Scotland (fig. 11.4a), where the thighs of both the fore- and hindleg (and also the shoulder and snout) carry

a

b   c

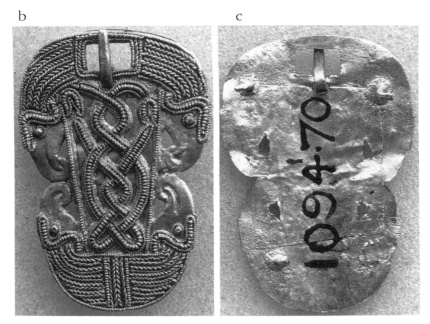

Pl. 11.1. Germanic filigree mounted on pierced impressed foil with flat foil beneath: (a) scabbard mount with opposed serpentine beasts from Bergsaker, Vest Agder, Norway. Length 5.4cm. Note that the loss of filigree from the head of the right beast reveals the flat-topped platform of the upper foil; (b) miniature bird-buckle from Faversham, Kent, England, with interlaced serpentine beasts resting on pierced impressed foil. Length of buckle ca. 3.2cm; (c) reverse of Faversham buckle, showing flat under-foil—marked with registration number. Photograph by G. Haseloff used by permission of H. Haseloff-Bönning (a); photographs by author (b–c).

a

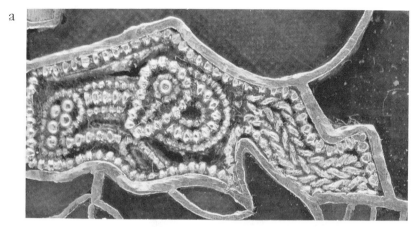

b

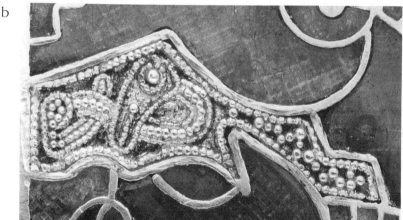

Pl. 11.2. Filigree animal ornament on shoulder-clasp from Sutton Hoo. Maximum length of panels: (a) ca. 1.3cm; (b) ca. 1.45cm. Photographs by permission of the Trustees of the British Museum.

massed granules, while the body consists of a band of wires. This convention is also adopted on the Derrynaflan paten, first on the panels depicting the deer confronted by a rearing serpent (see Ryan, this volume, p. 252, pl. 12.2b), where (as on the shoulder-clasps) the hip (and also the shoulder) are pear-shaped, and second, on the panels with two back to back kneeling beasts (fig. 11.6d), where the body is formed of a band of wires and each leg is speckled with granules.

Hatched beasts which follow the Sutton Hoo convention may also be identified on the Derrynaflan chalice, where the body may consist of three parallel wires, with sporadic granules on the thighs (fig. 11.7b). An object

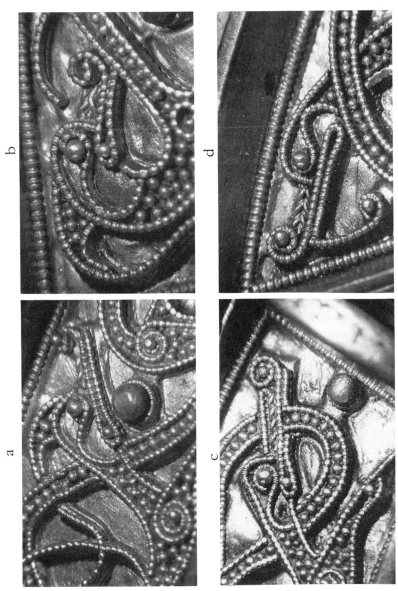

Pl. 11.3. Filigree animal ornament on the Hunterston brooch: (a–c) hoop; (d) terminal. Not to scale. Photographs courtesy of R. Bradley.

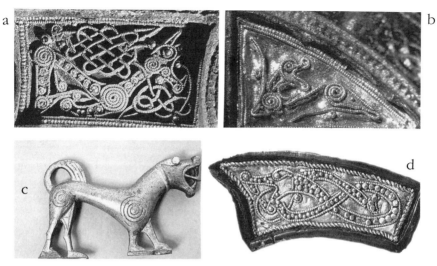

Pl. 11.4. (a) Filigree animal on the Derrynaflan paten (length of panel ca. 1.87cm); (b) filigree animal on the Mohill brooch (length of panel ca. 1.2cm); (c) zoo-morphic mount from Islandbridge, Dublin (maximum length ca. 5.8cm) (d) filigree beast-headed snake on the Dunbeath brooch (maximum length of panel ca. 2cm. Photograph by permission of National Museum of Ireland (a); photographs by author (b–d).

where very few granules survive on the thighs, but where the beasts' bodies are also delineated by a band of wires, is the recently discovered Mohill brooch from County Leitrim (pl. 11.4b).

Further removed from the prototype are the beasts on the terminal of the "Tara" brooch from Bettystown, County Meath, (fig. 11.4b) and the bowl girdle of the Ardagh chalice, from County Limerick (fig. 11.5a), where wires predominate, with few granules on the limbs. Granules were, however, sometimes dispensed with altogether, as in the procession of beasts under the foot-cone of the Ardagh chalice (fig. 11.5b).

Plain beasts outlined by a single contour-line. Further still from extant filigree precedents is a third type of beast with a blank body, like those on the pin-head of the "Tara" brooch (fig. 11.4c) and on the handle escutcheons of the Derrynaflan chalice (fig. 11.7c). An Insular analogue for these beasts is found on f. 95 of the Lindisfarne Gospels, where a pair of beasts with blank bodies is outlined by a dotted line, perhaps simulating beaded wire.[18] However, occasionally beasts on Anglo-Saxon metalwork have plain bodies and are outlined by a single contour-line, as in the case of those engraved in procession on the reverse of the Kentish Faversham composite disc-brooch.[19] The Celtic designers of plain filigree animals were thus following an established convention.

THE GOLD FOILS ON WHICH THE ANIMALS REST

On Celtic work filigree animal ornament is not attached directly to the object it decorates, but is soldered instead to small plates of gold foil, the discrete nature of each panel being emphasized by a wire border. Anglo-Saxon filigree animal ornament may also be mounted on foils, which are likewise edged by a wire border. Another shared characteristic is that the beasts are generally raised slightly above their background, the foil of the ground having probably been pushed back in repoussé after the wires were soldered in place.[20]

Impressed foils of two types, each of which is also found on earlier Germanic filigree work, occur on Celtic animal panels. The first type appears on, for instance, the Hunterston and "Tara" brooches (pl. 11.3b–c and fig. 11.4b respectively). Just one foil is used, with the wires delineating the beasts set on the crests of narrow flat-topped ridges set above a sunken, undecorated ground. There are numerous examples of such foil on seventh-century Anglo-Saxon filigree work; those on one of the Sutton Hoo shoulder-clasps are illustrated here (pl. 11.2).

With the second type, two superimposed backplates are used, an upper impressed foil pierced to reveal a lower flat one. Foils of this second type occur on objects of the highest quality, the Hunterston brooch (pl. 11.3a, and 11.3d), the Ardagh chalice[21] and the Derrynaflan paten.[22] They are also found in a late-sixth- to seventh-century Anglo-Saxon context on the Kentish Kingston brooch and Faversham bird-buckles (pl. 11.1b–c).[23] The technique has a long history, occurring on aristocratic continental Germanic filigree, as on the two matching bow brooches from an aristocratic woman's grave in Cologne, Germany,[24] dated by coin evidence to the second quarter of the sixth century, and (judging from photographs) on sixth-century Scandinavian sword and scabbard fittings (pl. 11.1a). It survived in Scandinavia, as well as in the Celtic West: it is typical of Viking Age Terslev brooches, as also of the Hiddensee filigree style.[25]

Just why such two-tiered foils came into being is not clear, but there may be a technical reason for their creation. When deep repoussé is applied it is difficult to avoid accidently piercing the foil, so the device may have been invented to overcome this problem, the goldsmith creating deliberate openwork and inserting a second foil behind the first. However, this may not be a complete explanation for the genesis of this convention, because on very early Scandinavian filigree individual animals may also be cut in openwork. There is, for instance, an openwork griffin on the Skenäs pendant from Sweden.26 Moreover, there is a beast on a discrete piece of impressed openwork gold foil attached to the flat foil base-plate of the fragmentary brooch from Elsehoved, Fyn, Denmark (fig. 11.1c).[27] The creation of openwork in the background to zoomorphic patterns on the two-tier foils may thus, in part, derive from a long-standing tradition.

While the recessed areas on Celtic foils are not normally faceted, it is likely that a chip-carving[28] tradition lies behind the relief on zoomorphic panels. On very early Scandinavian filigree, on the Ålleberg, Möne and Färjestaden collars from Sweden (fig. 11.1a), manufactured ca. A.D. 450–550[29] minute filigree animals are outlined on thin pieces of solid gold no more than ca. 5mm long, engraved with the ground cut away and the figure in false relief.[30] Moreover, on Anglo-Saxon filigree foils such as those on the Sutton Hoo shoulder-clasps, the recessed areas quite clearly mimic chip-carving (pl. 11.2),[31] as they do on some sixth-century Norwegian scabbard mounts (pl. 11.1).[32] Finally, though the recesses on Celtic zoomorphic foils are flat-bottomed, there is chip-carved style faceting on an interlaced panel on the "Tara" brooch.[33]

Conclusions on the Relationship with Germanic Filigree Art

Celtic goldsmiths, therefore, while not always bound by archaic conventions, were heavily indebted to Germanic goldsmithing traditions.

I now return to the issue raised by Ryan in connection with the animal ornament on the Derrynaflan hoard. How is one to reconcile the undoubted Early Christian influence on the Derrynaflan paten and chalice with the long lasting effect of Germanic art? I suggest that these two forces are not mutually exclusive. The Irish, as Christians since the fifth century, would naturally have looked to Christian models when designing liturgical vessels. However, in the early Middle Ages there was constant interaction between Classical and Germanic traditions of design. Moreover, while Early Christian and Byzantine art descended from Roman art, Germanic art itself stemmed in part from the art of the Roman provinces. Thus, a cousinly relationship existed between motifs executed in different styles in different areas, making craftsmen who were familiar with one idiom receptive to designs executed in the other.

Technical similarities between Germanic and Celtic filigree animal art go beyond coincidence. They indicate that when Celtic goldsmiths followed an Early Christian model they employed the idiom in which they had been trained, one heavily influenced by Germanic traditions of design.

THE STYLE OF THE FILIGREE ANIMAL ORNAMENT

Detailed study of Celtic filigree animal ornament shows that despite an inventive variety, each individual object has a consistent style of animal ornament, whether in filigree, chip-carving or engraving. The Hunterston brooch, which has eight filigree panels with individual beasts on its front face (fig. 11.2, and pl. 11.3), and an interlaced pair of chip-carved beasts on the reverse (fig. 11.3c), will be used to demonstrate the point.[34]

THE UNIFORMITY OF STYLE OF ANIMAL ORNAMENT ON THE HUNTERSTON BROOCH

To take the filigree first, while there are small differences between one panel and the next, the anatomy of each animal is essentially the same. It has a small head; a long decorated snout with a spiral at its tip; and a thin undecorated jaw. The mouth is always closed. The body is ribbon-like and there is a single-coil spiral at the shoulder and hip. Just one foreleg and hindleg is shown, each limb terminating in a ball-and-claw foot with a markedly long claw. It may also have an ear-lappet, tail or tongue, though no individual has all three features. Each creature is invested with considerable vitality and is also naturalistic in that the head, ears, neck, legs, feet, claws, and tail can always be distinguished, but it performs improbable athletic feats to form a complex interlaced knot.

There are further affinities, for the animal is always "drawn" in the same way. For example, the eye is a granule enclosed in an S-shaped hook linked to the neck, leaving a clear cheek beneath. The closed mouth is formed from a single wire, the upper end bent into a spiral, generally with a granule in its center. The fold at the back of the mouth bulges and also generally encloses a granule. The same strand forms the shoulder or hip spiral and the claw of the adjacent leg. On the other hand, the ball of the foot is a continuation of the body outline.

Thus, the goldsmith who cut the wires was working to a standard pattern. This differs from the standardized ways of cutting wire for filigree animal ornament on each other object in the corpus. The consistent way wires were cut to "draw" animals is one of the most interesting findings to emerge from detailed study of Celtic filigree, for like the study of calligraphy, it reveals idiosyncratic procedures and suggests differences between workshops.

The resemblances between the filigree and chip-carved beasts on the Hunterston brooch are less immediately obvious (cf. figs. 11.2 and 11.3c) partly because a different convention is used to decorate the bodies of the beasts executed in each medium: the filigree beasts are speckled, while the chip-carved ones are hatched. The different nature of each medium also affects the appearance of the animals, since it is harder to produce subtle effects with minute lengths of wire than when drawing with a fine point on the soft material of a chip-carving model.

The second factor accounts for the relative simplicity of the filigree beasts. Thus, simple spirals appear at the snout-tip, shoulder and hip of each filigree beast, but on the chip-carved creatures these are replaced by Ultimate La Tène trumpet-spirals complete with lentoid divisions of sub-triangular fields, while an additional chip-carved trumpet-spiral marks the tip of the rump.

However, once these differences are discounted, the motif in each case is very alike. The beasts' proportions and anatomy are the same, including the depiction of ball-and-claw feet (although curiously, each of the chip-carved creatures has, in addition, a more angular foot). The ear-lappets and tails are also similar, each expanding into a sub-triangular field at the junction with the body, then shrinking to a fine line before termi-nating in a further small swelling. Other minute details also correspond, such as the extra sub-triangular expansion on the ear-lappet of one filigree and one chip-carved beast (cf. figs. 11.2b, and 11.3c).

Turning to the layout of the design, one of its most striking charac-teristics is its regular geometry. The single filigree animals in corresponding positions on either side of the brooch are paired in mirror symmetry (fig. 11.2c–h), while the interlaced chip-carved pair also form a disciplined, axially symmetrical pattern (fig. 11.3c). It is to be concluded that a uniform style of animal ornament appears in each medium on the Hunterston brooch.

OTHER STYLES OF FILIGREE ANIMAL ORNAMENT

The filigree animal ornament on each of the other objects in question is also distinctive. I shall now consider their style, my aim being to identify the particular characteristics of the individual workshops and to distinguish traits which help to date each object.

The "Tara" brooch. The extant filigree ribbon-beasts on the "Tara" brooch closely resemble those on the Hunterston brooch. However, there are small anatomical differences which suggest that these two brooches were made in different workshops (cf. figs. 11.2, and 11.4b–c, and also fig. 11.3b, 11.3c, and 11.3d).

On "Tara" each filigree creature lacks the granule at the back of the mouth and has a claw and two paw pads (rather than a ball-and-claw foot).

The eyes and cheek in each case are also treated differently, as are the legs, which on Hunterston are rounded but on "Tara" incorporate an angle (probably representing the hock). Further the wires on the two brooches are cut differently to delineate the creatures. For example, on "Tara," as opposed to Hunterston, the jaw is formed of a double (rather than a single) line, which continues to outline the front of the neck (rather than ending at the tip of the jaw). Yet another distinction is that while on Hunterston the strand used to outline the body always continues to the foot pads, on "Tara" (except in one instance) separate curled strands are used to mark the foot pads.

Some filigree animal panels from the "Tara" brooch have been lost in modern times, but nineteenth-century illustrations show that an axial layout was as fundamental to the "Tara" as to the Hunterston animal ornament.[35] That on the Lindisfarne Gospels, made in ca. A.D. 698, is similar and both brooches were probably made at about that time, though, as argued elsewhere,[36] "Tara" may be the later. The chip-carved and incised animal ornament on the Steeple Bumpstead boss, found in Essex far from its place of manufacture (fig. 11.3a) and the Donore disc, from County Meath, belongs to the same stage in the history of style.[37]

The Westness brooch. Interlaced ribbon filigree beasts also appear on the Westness brooch (fig. 11.4a). These loosely drawn and rather ungainly creatures have characteristics in common with the beasts just discussed. For instance, the snout is broader than the jaw and (as on the "Tara" brooch) the eye is linked by a curved line to a spiral at the back of the head. However, details such as the massed granules on the snout, the bulbous tips of the snout and jaw, and the wide open mouths find no parallel on the filigree or chip-carved quadrupeds of either the Hunterston or "Tara" brooches.[38] In feel, the Westness creatures are closer to beasts on the St. Ninian's Isle silver bowl no. 2,[39] the Monymusk reliquary,[40] and the Aberlemno churchyard slab,[41] each of which is also from Scotland. On the basis of these comparisons it is likely that the Westness brooch was made in the eighth century. Stevenson's suggestion of the second quarter of the eighth century,[42] may be correct, but precision is impossible.

The Ardagh chalice. More elegant filigree animals appear on the Ardagh chalice, paired on four panels of the bowl girdle which show the same motif (fig. 11.5a) and grouped in a frieze of six on a ring-shaped panel under the foot-cone (fig. 11.5b). The beast on each area differs from that on the other, yet both types are treated in a way not hitherto reviewed.

The first impression of the zoomorphic panels on the bowl girdle (as of the adjacent ornithomorphic panels) is of an abstract interlace but, in fact, each displays a pair of attenuated creatures and no extraneous abstract elements. Those under the foot-cone, in contrast, are more naturalistic: they are not contorted to form interlace, and stand squarely confronting each other.

There are other small differences between the beasts on each area. For example, the bowl girdle beasts alone have a horn-like feature projecting from their foreheads, and a spiral and granules at the shoulder and hip. The feet and heads also differ, as do the mouths. In both cases, the snout and jaw are of equal width, a feature to which we will return. However, on the bowl girdle the mouth is tightly shut, while under the foot-cone it is menacingly wide open, perhaps indicating a roar.

Nevertheless, three distinctive mannerisms suggest that both types of animal panels are the product of a single workshop employing two different idioms. First (as on the chip-carved zoomorphic panel on the chalice), the body of each filigree beast is kept almost separate, and only the extremities intertwine. Second, the tail, which in each case is continuous with another element (the mouth on the bowl girdle, the ear-lappet under the foot-cone), extends to the furthermost point of the body of its partner. Third, close inspection shows that (as on the ornithomorphic panels) the claw at the tip of each foot is generally depicted not by the usual beaded wire but by a plain round wire. No other filigree animal ornament known to me combines these features. The last two occur only on the Ardagh chalice.

Both stylistically and technically, the filigree on the chalice seems more developed than that on the "Tara" brooch. The relative naturalism of the beasts under the foot-cone may also indicate that it was made at a time when the influence of Style II was receding. Another factor which points to this conclusion is the depiction of gaping (rather than closed) jaws on the beasts under the foot-cone, since mouths of this type predominate on later work.[43] Thus, the date of ca. 710–735 suggested by Rynne[44] seems rather early, though it cannot be ruled out, since it is impossible to gauge the pace at which the filigree style developed. My view is that the degree of development from the style of the "Tara" brooch together with other factors which cannot be examined here[45] suggest a date in the mid- to later eighth century, or just possibly in the early ninth century.

The Derrynaflan paten. Yet another distinctive style of animal ornament appears on the Derrynaflan paten. The paten and the Ardagh chalice have a number of features in common.[46] However, the animal ornament on each differs, suggesting that the two were made in separate workshops.

Only one motif on the paten will be considered, a stylized quadruped with a large head and gaping mouth, shown alone looking forwards (motif B) (pl. 11.4a) or paired, with confronted backturned heads and separate kneeling bodies (motif E) (fig. 11.6d)[47] (see also Ryan, this volume, p. 252, pl. 12.2). Like other filigree motifs on the paten, these beasts share space with great clusters of interlace. In the first case, this interlace springs from the creature itself and in the second is quite independent.

The stylistic interest of these creatures lies in the way some standard elements are enlarged. On Celtic work, focal points such as the snout tip, junction of the head and neck, shoulder and hip are often emphasized, usually by spirals. On the paten these elements are exceptionally prominent, particularly the shoulder, which on the paired beasts has a penny-farthing relationship with the hip (fig. 11.6d).

On the single beasts a large single-coil filigree spiral marks each focal point, although on the foil backplate, shoulder and hip are represented by three-coil spirals,[48] a device presumably too complex to reproduce in filigree. The paired beasts are even more complex and three elements occur: first, a single-coil spiral (at the snout and jaw tip); second, a roundel containing a triskele of C-scrolls (at the back of the head and at the shoulder); third, a roundel of massed granules (at the hip). Both types of roundel appear elsewhere in Celtic filigree, for example, on the County Cavan brooch,[49] but only on the Derrynaflan paten are they incorporated into an animal.[50] Here they are so prominent that they distort the beasts' proportions. Another mannerism which is peculiar to the paten is the overlapping of the elongated fore- and hind paws of each beast, a feature of both motifs B and E.

No filigree analogues for these creatures exist. However, some details are paralleled on cast animals. For instance, the roundels on the joints of the paired beasts (fig. 11.6d) are matched by plain roundels at the shoulder and hips of the beasts on the large Ardagh brooch (fig. 11.6c), an object which belongs at the earliest to the late-eighth century and may be ninth-century in date, as Ryan has pointed out.[51] Even closer parallels for some of these roundels occur on two ninth-century brooches, the Ardagh brooch no. 102 and the Killamery brooch, from County Kilkenny, since the "brambled" bosses at the joints of some of their marginal animals are clearly skeuomorphs of roundels of massed granules.[52]

Furthermore, stylistically the single beast especially is reminiscent of chip-carved beasts on the back of the Killamery brooch (fig. 11.6b). The similarities lie in the roughly similar proportions, the lack of interlacing of the body itself, the treatment of the head, and the prominence of the spirals at the focal points. While the fangs of the Derrynaflan beasts are lacking on the Killamery creatures, in both cases the mouth is open to receive a fine line (the tongue on one, the tail on the other). The snout and jaw are of equal width and conspicuous spirals appear not only at their tips, but also at the back of the head. Exceptionally large spirals appear at the shoulder and hip. A very significant shared feature is the multicoil spiral found on the foil of the Derrynaflan beast and (in the two-coil version) on the hip of the Killamery beast. Only single-coil spirals appear on beasts on the Hunterston and "Tara" brooches and closely related Steeple Bumpstead boss (fig. 11.3a–c) and Donore disc. On metalwork (though not on manuscripts)[53] two- or three-coil spirals appear to be a feature of the developed phase of the style,[54] as does the depiction of roundels in lieu of spirals and snouts and jaws of equal size.

The clusters of interlace on the Derrynaflan paten may also suggest that it may belong to a mature phase. Ryan has pointed out their relationship with eighth-century Anglo-Saxon derivatives of inhabited plant-scroll ornament;[55] but they also recall interlace on the Book of MacRegol,[56] written at Birr, County Offaly, not far from Derrynaflan, at some time before A.D. 822.[57] It is not necessary to date the paten as late as the Killamery brooch, whose filigree is simpler. Ryan suggests, a date roughly contemporary with the Ardagh chalice; I would place the emphasis on the later end of the bracket, that is, the later eighth and early ninth centuries (rather than the mid- to late-eighth century).

The Mohill and Dunbeath brooches and the Derrynaflan chalice. Beasts with non-interlaced bodies also appear on the Mohill brooch (pl. 11.4b), the Dunbeath brooch (fig. 11.6a) and the Derrynaflan chalice (fig. 11.7). A different variant is found on each, yet they have enough in common to allow them to be considered together here. All display the backturned openmouthed beast with a raised forefoot, also found on the ninth-century Killamery brooch (fig. 11.6b).

The depiction of a raised forefoot has a long history, occurring, for instance, on animal ornament on the late-fifth- to sixth-century Danish Elsehoved brooch (fig. 11.1c), on a seventh-century cloisonné mount from Tongres, Belgium,[58] and on a seventh-century Anglo-Saxon chip-carved mount from Barham, Suffolk.[59] This feature therefore is not associated exclusively with later work, but it became fashionable across Europe in the late-eighth to ninth centuries. It appears on Anglo-Carolingian metalwork, including the Tassilo chalice, made between 777 and 788,[60] and on Anglo-Saxon objects of the ninth century decorated in the Trewhiddle style.[61]

Other shared elements are the gaping mouths and the spirals at the tip of both the snout and jaw, represented in some panels on all three objects by a single splayed V-shaped strand with spirals at the end of each stem (cf. fig. 11.6a, 11.7a, and pl. 11.4b). Also suggestive of a later date is the representation of snouts and jaws of equal width, features found on both the Dunbeath brooch and on the Derrynaflan chalice.

The style of the animal ornament on each of these objects differs slightly. An "old-fashioned" characteristic of the Mohill beasts (pl. 11.4b) is that (as on the Hunterston and "Tara" brooches) the snout is distinguished from the jaw by the addition of a two-strand cable. However, the band of wires on the body and the conspicuous spirals at the shoulder and hip recall the Derrynaflan paten. Typologically, the Mohill brooch dates to the ninth century, a date also acceptable for its spindly but legible animal ornament.

The stockier Dunbeath beast (fig. 11.6a), unlike the other two, has four visible legs and appears to walk forwards. It is also distinguished by minuscule spirals at the shoulder and hip, and by the liberal application of massed granules not only to the body, but also to the snout, jaw, ear, and footpads. It has a collar, a feature also found on a zoomorphic mount from Islandbridge (pl. 11.4c), which consists of an animal that likewise walks forward on all four legs and has a similar eye and mouth. Further, the Islandbridge beast, like the beast-headed snake on the Dunbeath brooch (pl. 11.4d), has fangs and a tongue. This mount has been assumed to be Viking, but is more probably ninth-century and Irish not only because its curled leonine mane resembles that on the symbol of St. Mark in the Book of Armagh, made ca. A.D. 807,[62] but also because its legs are decorated with incised trumpet patterns. A peculiarity of the Dunbeath creature is that only the forefoot (as opposed to half of the leg) points upwards; a similar mannerism is found on the beast on the large Ardagh brooch, which is also four-legged and has a walking gait (fig. 11.6c). The combination of features found on the Dunbeath brooch suggests a late-eighth- or ninth-century date.

More crudely sketched beasts appear on the Derrynaflan chalice (fig. 11.7), which are often difficult to distinguish not only because some of the wires delineating their bold and simplified outlines may be slightly misplaced but also because of the plethora of tiny elements which surround them. Ryan's comparison of the animal ornament on the chalice with that on the back of the Killamery brooch is apt.[63] I would suggest a date of plus or minus A.D. 850.

CONCLUSIONS ON THE DEVELOPMENT OF INSULAR FILIGREE ANIMAL STYLE

Analysis of the design of filigree animal ornament reveals important differences from one object to the next. The style is diverse and the lack of firmly dated contexts make absolute dating impossible. Nevertheless, some general trends can be distinguished. Early in the period as on the Hunterston and "Tara" brooches, animals have interlaced ribbon-like bodies, but as time passed, probably towards the middle or end of the eighth century, there is a tendency for beasts to become more naturalistic. While interlace may be included in the design, the creatures' entire bodies are no longer contorted into knotwork and they stand in more realistic poses. However, more naturalistic beasts did not immediately banish interlaced ones and on the Ardagh chalice the two idioms coexist. At about the same time, a more mannered creature evolved on objects such as the Derrynaflan paten where spirals, in particular, became enlarged. In the ninth century animals with non-interlaced bodies seem to have become the norm.

TECHNIQUES OF MANUFACTURE OF CELTIC FILIGREE ANIMAL ORNAMENT

The basic elements of Celtic filigree are simple enough: first, the gold wires and granules used to outline the pattern; second, the gold foil to which these are soldered, which may be flat or in relief; third, the means used to fix the foil in the compartment in which it sits. However, within these limits a wide range of techniques was employed.

Those found on animal panels are not peculiar to them, but as animal motifs are elaborate, the panels are often particularly complex in construction. Two aspects of this topic[64] will be considered: first, the way animal ornament is treated in the group as a whole, and second, variations in its treatment on three objects, the Hunterston and "Tara" brooches and the Ardagh chalice.

TECHNIQUES IN THE GROUP AS A WHOLE

When depicting animal patterns, Celtic goldsmiths followed a set of conventions, but within these displayed considerable flexibility. For example, while beaded wire always outlines the beast, the type chosen varies not only between objects but sometimes also within an individual object. As on the Germanic prototypes, one simple beaded wire may be used, but more often than not a more complex form of wire is substituted—either a flattened beaded wire or a beaded wire placed on top of one or more wires. A spiral at the shoulder and hip may be flat or conical. Moreover, such spirals may be lacking altogether. Furthermore, the body may be plain or decorated. The foil backplate may be flat, impressed, or impressed with a pierced ground with or without a second flat foil beneath the pierced one. Finally, the foils on brooches are most commonly secured by overlapping burrs of metal gouged from the compartment wall, so-called "jewelers' stitches," but some are riveted, and others are held by a cement. On the paten and the chalices, they may also be pinned onto the object beneath an openwork frame.

Some of these elements have chronological significance, but sifting them out is a complex process. The general rule is that work which most resembles the foreign prototypes is likely to be earlier than that which departs from established conventions or includes new elements. However, its application is complicated by a number of factors. Many techniques are long-lived and it is typical of Celtic filigree that panels with different combinations of techniques are juxtaposed. No chronology can be based on the occurrence of a single element and the work therefore is best studied in its totality, always remembering that probably only a fraction of the filigree produced survives.

Nevertheless, some trends can be identified on panels with animal ornament. For example, on early objects such as the Hunterston and "Tara" brooches animal panels are technically more elaborate than those displaying other motifs. However, on the more developed Ardagh chalice and Derrynaflan paten, and also on the Derrynaflan chalice, animal panels are no more complex than various others.

Changes in the form of beaded wire used to outline the beasts are also detectable. For example, on the Hunterston and "Tara" brooches animals are outlined either by a flattened beaded wire on edge or by a simple vertical combination—a beaded wire on a ribbon on edge of a beaded wire on top of another. This latter combination also occurs on the Ardagh chalice. However, in addition a trefoil-sectioned combination of wires also appears there, as on the Derrynaflan paten and Mohill brooch. This form of compound strand appears to have been invented in the eighth century and is not peculiar to filigree from Ireland or Scotland, since it is also known in an eighth- to ninth-century Anglo-Saxon context (although not on animal ornament).[65] Filigree on other Irish and Scottish ninth-century work, however, is simpler. On the Derrynaflan chalice and Dunbeath brooch animals are outlined by a simple beaded wire, though the tradition of outlining the beast in a beaded wire on a ribbon on edge persists on the chalice handle filigree panels (fig. 11.7c).[66]

There are also innovations on later work. For instance, on the Derrynaflan chalice (fig. 11.7a–b) conical spirals are used far more liberally than on earlier filigree, and may be placed not just on the beast itself but also between it and the panel border. These may be made of plain or beaded wire. The use of cones of plain round wire may be a ninth-century phenomenon: they are also prominent on the Killamery brooch.

Another trend is for the relief on individual impressed foils to become lower with the passing of time. There are, in addition, changes in the treatment of openwork gold foils. Color contrasts may be introduced with a silver foil below, as on the Derrynaflan paten.[67] On the Dunbeath brooch, a crudely pierced foil is placed, not over a second one, but in a compartment with a gilt floor.

VARIATIONS IN THE TREATMENT OF
ANIMAL ORNAMENT ON INDIVIDUAL OBJECTS

An interest in variety for its own sake is characteristic of Celtic filigree at its best. On certain objects this is especially highly developed on animal panels. It is particularly evident on the Hunterston and "Tara" brooches and Ardagh chalice, but apparently is also found on the Derrynaflan paten, for Ryan reports slight differences in treatment between each version of motif B.[68] On as late an object as the Derrynaflan chalice, different elements are combined on animal panels, though here variations are less subtle than on earlier more exquisite filigree.

The Hunterston brooch. While the same type of beast appears on the eight filigree panels with animal ornament on the Hunterston brooch, the goldsmith produced so many playful variations in technique and design (fig. 11.2; pl. 11.3) that the filigree can only be described as virtuoso.

The following technical differences stand out. The animal may be outlined by one beaded wire on top of another (pl. 11.3a, 11.3c, and 11.3d), or by a flattened beaded wire on edge (pl. 11.3b). The impressed foil to which the filigree is soldered may be solid (pl. 11.3b–c), or pierced with a flat foil beneath (pl. 11.3a, and 11.3d). The foils themselves may be fixed in their compartments by one or two rivets, each of whose heads is ringed by a wire collar (pl. 11.3a, and 11.3c). Alternatively, there may be no visible means of support beyond traces of sparse "jewelers' stitches" (pl. 11.4d) and in these cases foils are probably held by a cement of beeswax with traces of chalk, a method identified on another filigree panel on the brooch.[69]

There are other variations in detail. The beast on each pair of matching panels is knotted to form a different interlace. Some creatures lack a tongue, an ear-lappet and a tail (fig. 11.2e–f); others have a tongue and a tail (fig. 11.2g–h); yet more have an ear-lappet and a tail, but no tongue (fig. 11.2a–d). Even the snouts are treated differently on each pair. These may consist of a two-strand cable (pl. 11.3a), a two-strand cable outside which is a beaded wire (pl. 11.3c), or a false plait composed of a pair of opposed two-strand cables (pl. 11.3b, and 11.3d). This last arrangement is found on two pairs of panels. An extraordinary detail is that it runs in a different direction on each.

These fine distinctions are all the more striking not only because they are not always in mirror symmetry, but also because of the small scale of the work. As no panel is more than ca. 22mm wide, the wires are very fine, no more than 0.3mm in diameter in the case of the beaded wires and ca. 0.25 x 0.55–0.56mm in the case of the flattened beaded wires. Close scrutiny is needed to identify the different techniques, but each produces a slightly different effect, if only in the way it reflects light.

The "Tara" brooch. On the "Tara" brooch only two panels with animal ornament now survive (fig. 11.4b–c), yet here, too, the goldsmith teased variations from a limited number of basic elements. First, although the creature on each area appears to leap, each is contorted into a different interlace pattern. Second, the body of the beast on the terminal is coated with wires and incorporates an Ultimate La Tène element in the hindleg, while the body of that on the pin-head is blank. Third, different forms of wire outline the beasts' bodies—one beaded wire on top of another on the terminals; a beaded wire on a ribbon on edge on the pin-head. Fourth, the border on each panel differs in composition. Fifth, the foil on the terminal is impressed (but unpierced), while the foil on the pin-head is flat, apart from dishing of the backplate to emphasize the head and feet.

The wire on the "Tara" brooch is even finer than that on the Hunterston brooch. The uppermost beaded wire on the terminal is under 0.25mm in diameter, that on the pin-head under 0.2mm. Since wires do not genuinely interweave on interlace, over seventy-seven short units were needed to delineate the minute pattern and border on the terminal.

The Ardagh Chalice. Beasts on the bowl girdle and under the foot-cone differ stylistically, as described above. They also differ technically, since trefoil-sectioned wire delineates those on the bowl girdle and a beaded wire on top of another those under the foot-cone.

WHY THESE VARIATIONS?

This taste for unexpected variations may, in part, reflect Germanic influence, because study of the Sutton Hoo shoulder-clasps shows that seventh-century Anglo-Saxon goldsmiths also created small variations of the same general type, as it seems, did their Vendel contemporaries in Sweden.[70]

There are two shoulder-clasps, each composed of matching halves. Not only do the filigree motifs vary from one clasp to the other, so do the details of patterns on each one. On that with animal ornament the beast on each half displays a number of small differences (cf. pl. 11.2a, and 11.2b). Each pair assumes its own pose. The shape of the heads also differs, as does the infilling of the narrow end panel—massed granules on one pair of panels, a carpet of wires on the other. A small detail is that there is a granule at the back of the mouth of one pair, but not of the other (cf. pl. 11.2a, and 11.2b). On the other clasp, filigree snakes show similar variations in design: their foil base plates also differ, one pair being flat, the other in relief.[71]

However, the Hunterston brooch, the "Tara" brooch, and the Ardagh chalice are far more complex. Moreover, such subtlety is not confined to their filigree. On the Hunterston brooch, for instance, the paired chip-carved panels with Ultimate La Tène decoration on the reverse (fig. 11.3d) also show small differences. For instance, there are two birds' heads in the smaller roundel on the left panel, but three on the corresponding roundel on the right. On the left there is a two-coil spiral in the corner next to the hoop, but in the equivalent corner on the right a more complex pelta. There are also different space filling devices on each side of the brooch.

Such virtuosity cannot be due just to outside influence. As Françoise Henry pointed out, dislike of exact symmetry is fundamental to La Tène art, which fastidiously avoids the obvious,[72] and such juggling with diverse patterns and techniques to produce a harmonious whole must surely reflect native Celtic taste. The mentality behind such subtle creations has perhaps been best characterized by Gerald of Wales some centuries after the works reviewed in this paper were made, when he described music in twelfth-century Ireland:

> They glide so subtly from one mode to another, and the grace notes so freely sport with such abandon and bewitching charm around the steady tone of the heavier sound that the perfection of their art seems to lie in the concealing of it, as if "it were better being hidden. An art revealed brings shame". Hence it happens that the very things that afford unspeakable delight to the minds of those who have a fine perception and can penetrate carefully to the secrets of the art, bore, rather than delight, those who have no such perception—who look without seeing, or hear without being able to understand.[73]

CONCLUSIONS

Microscopic study of techniques of manufacture and stylistic analysis of Insular filigree animal ornament suggest that Celtic goldsmiths derived their knowledge of filigree from Germanic art. However, these models were not followed slavishly and an elaborate form of animal ornament was developed distinguished by its technical virtuosity. The style of the animal panels show subtle changes which provide a guide to the date and the context of individual pieces. It is suggested that a consistent style of animal ornament appears on every major piece of Insular metalwork but that no two objects in the extant corpus were made in precisely the same milieu. This is hardly surprising since the historical records refer to numerous royal centers and monasteries and it is likely that the products of several of these would survive. No object can be dated precisely. However, the style seems to have flourished in Ireland and Scotland from approximately the end of the seventh to the middle or later ninth centuries.

NOTES

I am very grateful to Cormac Bourke and Ian Fisher who read the text in draft and to James Graham-Campbell, who commented on the work at an earlier stage. I would also like to thank Dr. Heidel Haseloff-Bönning who supplied drawings and a photograph by the late Professor Günther Haseloff, and Michael Ryan who permitted reproduction of drawings of motifs on the Derrynaflan paten and chalice by Ursula Mattenberger. I am also indebted to Barry Ager, Robert Baines, Trevor Cowie, Wladyslaw Duczko, Angela Evans, Lars Jørgensen, Peter Harbison, Catherine Johns, Adrian Kennedy, Jan Peder Lamm, Rebecca Lang, Susan La Niece, Margaret Lannin, John Leopold, Arthur MacGregor, Paul Mullarkey, Raghnall Ó Floinn, Uaininn O Meadhra, George Speake, Mike Spearman, the late Robert Stevenson, Françoise Vallet, Leslie Webster, Terry Weisser, Martin Welch and Susan Youngs. Drawings were prepared in collaboration with the writer by Darwin Dolinka-Korda (figs. 11.3b, 11.4b–d, 11.5, and 11.6b–c), Judy Longcrane (figs. 11.2, 11.4a, and 11.6a), and Nick Griffiths (figs. 11.1d, 11.3a, and 11.3c). Permission to reproduce fig. 11.3d was given by the National Museums of Scotland. Finally, I would like to thank the British Academy for a grant towards the funding of illustrations for a forthcoming catalogue of filigree-decorated brooches, some of which are used in this paper.

1. Ryan, "A Suggested Origin for the Figure Representations on the Derrynaflan Paten," in E. Rynne, ed., *Figures from the Past: Studies on Figurative Art in Christian Ireland in Honour of Helen M. Roe* (Dun Laoghaire: Glendale Press; Royal Society of Antiquaries of Ireland, 1987), 62–72.

2. Ryan, "Some Aspects of Sequence and Style in the Metalwork of Eighth- and Ninth-Century Ireland," in M. Ryan, ed., *Ireland and Insular Art A.D. 500–1200* (Dublin: Royal Irish Academy, 1987), 66–74.

3. G. Speake, *Anglo-Saxon Animal Art and its Germanic Background* (Oxford: Clarendon Press, 1980), 46–51; J. Hines, *The Scandinavian Character of Anglian England in the pre-Viking Period*, B.A.R. Brit. Ser. 124 (Oxford: British Archaeological Reports, 1984); D. Leigh, "The Kentish Keystone-Garnet Disc Brooches: Avent's Classes 1–3 Reconsidered," *A.S.S.A.H.* 3 (1984): 67–76.

4. For a more fully illustrated discussion of this point see N. Whitfield, "Formal Conventions in the Depiction of Animals on Celtic Metalwork," in C. Bourke, ed., *From the Isles of the North: Early Medieval Art in Ireland and Britain* (Belfast: H.M.S.O., 1995).

5. Compare fig. 11.2g–h, showing a confronted pair on the Hunterston brooch, and animals on the Sutton Hoo shoulder-clasps, details of which appear on pl. 2, fully illustrated in R. Bruce-Mitford, *The Sutton Hoo Ship-Burial*, vol. 2 (London: British Museum, 1978), pls. 15–16.

6. Compare the paired filigree beasts on the lost panels from the "Tara" brooch in N. Whitfield, "The Original Appearance of the Tara Brooch," *J.R.S.A.I.* 106 (1976): 5–30, fig. 7a–d, and those on the Sutton Hoo maplewood bottle in A. C. Evans, *The Sutton Hoo Ship-Burial*, vol. 3 (London: British Museum, 1983), fig. 261a.

7. Speake, *Anglo-Saxon Animal Art*, fig. 8.

8. See G. Haseloff, "Salin's Style I," *M.A.* 18 (1974): 1–15, pl. 1a–b.

9. See R. Jessup, *Anglo-Saxon Jewellery* (Aylesbury, Buckinghamshire: Shire, 1974), pl. 7.

10. See Haseloff, "Salin's Style I," pl. 3c.

11. L. Webster and J. Backhouse, eds., *The Making of England: Anglo-Saxon Art and Culture A.D. 600–900* (London: British Museum, 1991), no. 66e.

12. Ibid., no. 184.

13. See B. Whitwell, "Flixborough," *Current Archaeology* 126 (1991): 244–47, col. illus. p. 245.

14. R. B. K. Stevenson, "The Hunterston Brooch and its Significance," M.A. 18 (1974): 16–42; N. Whitfield, "The Filigree of the Hunterston and 'Tara' Brooches," in R. M. Spearman and J. Higgitt, eds., *The Age of Migrating Ideas: Early Medieval Art in Northern Britain and Ireland* (Edinburgh: National Museum of Scotland, 1993), 118–27.

15. Own observation. See J. P. Lamm, "Ett filigransmycke från folk-vandringstiden, funnet i Söndrum socken, Halland," *Fornvännen* 88 (1993): fig. 4.

16. There is oblique hatching on the drinking horn, and herringbone hatching on the maplewood bottles, see Evans, *The Sutton Hoo Ship-Burial*, vol 3, figs. 239a and 261a.

17. B. Ager and B. Gilmore, "A Pattern-welded Anglo-Saxon Sword from Acklam Wold, North Yorkshire," *Yorkshire Archaeol. J.* 60 (1988): 17–18 (no illustration).

18. See J. Backhouse, *The Lindisfarne Gospels* (Oxford: Phaidon, 1981), pl. 29.

19. See Speake, *Germanic Animal Art*, fig. 8c.

20. I would like to thank Robert Baines for discussing this technique with me.

21. R. Organ, "Examination of the Ardagh Chalice: A Case History", in W. J. Young, ed., *The Application of Science in the Examination of Works of Art* (Boston: Museum of Fine Arts, 1973), 238–71, fig. 39–40.

22. M. Ryan, ed., *The Derrynaflan Hoard I: A Preliminary Account* (Dublin: National Museum of Ireland, 1983), 18, col. pls. 11–12.

23. Own observation.

24. J. Werner, "Frankish Royal Tombs in the Cathedral at Cologne and Saint-Denis," *Antiquity* 38 (1964): 201–16, pl. 31, 10a–b. I would like to thank Birgit Arrhenius for confirming the identification of pierced foils on these brooches.

25. I would like to thank Wladyslaw Duczko for this information.

26. Own observation. See Lamm, *Filigransmycke från folkvandringstiden*, fig. 4.

27. Own observation.

28. This technique was originally derived from woodworking and passed on to Germanic craftsmen via late Roman sources. It is normally associated with cast animal art, the model from which the cast is taken being carved with the figure in false relief with the ground cut away at sharp angles.

29. G. Haseloff, *Die germanische Tierornamentik der Völkerwanderungzeit. Studien zur Salins Stil I*. Vorgeschichteliche Forschungen 17 (Berlin: de Gruyter, 1981), 231–35, figs. 136–39.

30. B. Arrhenius, "Technical Properties as a Discriminant in Migration Period Jewellery," in L. Webster, ed., *Aspects of Production and Style in Dark Age Metalwork* (London: British Museum, 1982), 1–19, fig. 1, pls. 1–5. I would like to thank Jan Peder Lamm for discussion and for allowing me to examine these panels.

31. Another case in point is the great gold buckle from Taplow, Buckinghamshire, see Bruce-Mitford, *The Sutton Hoo Ship-Burial*, vol. 2, fig. 437.

32. See also Haseloff, *Die germanische Tierornamentik*, pls. 34–38.

33. See N. Whitfield, "Motifs and Techniques of Celtic Filigree: Are they Original?" in Ryan, ed., *Ireland and Insular Art*, 75–84, fig. 1k.

34. For the uniformity of style of animal ornament on the "Tara" brooch see N. Whitfield, "Animal Ornament on Insular Metalwork of the late 7th–8th Centuries: Its Character and Development," *Medieval Europe 1992: Art and Symbolism, Pre-printed Papers*, vol. 7, 9–15. For that on the Derrynaflan hoard see M. Ryan, "The Menagerie of the Derrynaflan Chalice," in Spearman and Higgitt, eds., *The Age of Migrating Ideas*, 151–61.

35. Whitfield, "Original Appearance of the Tara Brooch," figs. 4a and 7a–d.

36. Whitfield, "Filigree of the Hunterston and 'Tara' Brooches."

37. Whitfield, "Animal Ornament on Insular Metalwork," 11, fig. 3; N. Whitfield and J. Graham-Campbell, "A Mount with Hiberno-Saxon Chipcarved Animal Orna-

ment from Rerrick, near Dundrennan, Kirkcudbright, Scotland," *Trans. Dumfries. Galloway Natur. Hist. Antiq. Soc.* 67 (1992): 9–27.

38. However, while all the complete beasts on "Tara" have closed mouths, the mouths of some marginal beasts' heads are wide open, see N. Whitfield, "Animal Ornament on Insular Metalwork," fig. 4a.

39. D. M. Wilson, "The Treasure," in A. Small, C. Thomas, and D. M. Wilson, *St. Ninian's Isle and its Treasure* (Oxford: Oxford University Press, 1983), 131, fig. 21.

40. Ibid., 129–31, fig. 41.

41. Ibid., pl. 55; I. Henderson, "Pictish Art and the Book of Kells," in D. Whitelock, R. McKitterick, and D. Dumville, eds., *Ireland in Early Medieval Europe* (Cambridge: Cambridge University Press, 1982), 79–105.

42. R. B. K. Stevenson, "The Celtic Brooch from Westness, Orkney and Hinged-pins," *P.S.A.S.* 119 (1989): 239–69.

43. P. Harbison, "The Antrim Cross in the Hunt Museum," *N. Munster Antiq. J.* 20: 17–40.

44. E. Rynne, "The Date of the Ardagh Chalice," in Ryan, *Ireland and Insular Art*, 85–89.

45. N. Whitfield, "Celtic Filigree from the Seventh to Ninth Century A.D. with particular reference to that on Brooches" (Ph.D. diss., University College London, 1990), vol. 2, 370–76.

46. Ryan, "Aspects of Sequence and Style," 68.

47. This is the nomenclature employed in M. Ryan, ed., *The Derrynaflan Hoard I: A Preliminary Account*, 19.

48. I would like to thank Michael Ryan for this information.

49. S. Youngs, ed., *"The Work of Angels": Masterpieces of Celtic Metalwork 6th–9th Centuries A.D.* (London: British Museum, 1989), no. 73, col. illus. p. 80.

50. A similar roundel is incorporated into the body of a late-sixth-century Merovingian filigree bird from Ste. Claire sur Epte, Val d'Oise, France (Musée des Antiquités Nationales, Reg. No. 72430), but this is probably too early to be relevant to the Derrynaflan paten.

51. M. Ryan, ed., *Treasures of Ireland: Irish Art 3000 B.C.–1500 A.D.* (Dublin: National Museum of Ireland, 1983), no. 51c, 129.

52. Ibid., no. 51e, 130 and no. 63, col. pl. p. 42 respectively.

53. Three-coil spirals occur, for example, on f. 94v of the Lindisfarne Gospels (Backhouse, *The Lindisfarne Gospels*, fig. 28).

54. E.g., on the gilt bronze mount from Romfohjellen, Möre, Norway (G. Haseloff, "Insular Animal Styles with Special Reference to Irish Art in the Early Medieval Period," in Ryan, ed., *Ireland and Insular Art*, 44–55, figs. 14–17). Two-

and three-coil spirals also appear on some pieces of Anglo-Saxon metalwork dated to the eighth century, e.g. the Coppergate helmet from York (Webster and Backhouse, eds., *The Making of England*, no. 47), and a die from Canterbury, (ibid., no. 174).

55. M. Ryan, "Links Between Anglo-Saxon and Irish Early Medieval Art: Some Evidence of Metalwork," in *Studies in Insular Art and Archaeology*, ed. C. Karkov and R. Farrell, A.E.M.S. 1, (Oxford, Ohio: American Early Medieval Studies, 1991), 117–26.

56. H. Richardson, "Number and Symbol in Early Christian Irish Art," *J.R.S.A.I.* 114 (1984): 28–47, fig. 12a–c.

57. J. J. G. Alexander, *Insular Manuscripts 6th to 9th Century* (London: Harvey Miller, 1978), no. 54.

58. R. Bruce-Mitford, *Aspects of Anglo-Saxon Archaeology: Sutton Hoo and Other Discoveries* (London: Gollancz, 1974), 273–75, pl. 91.

59. Webster and Backhouse, eds., *The Making of England*, no. 39.

60. D. M. Wilson, *Anglo-Saxon Art from the Seventh Century to the Norman Conquest* (London: Thames & Hudson, 1984), figs. 162–64.

61. Ibid., fig. 104.

62. Alexander, *Insular Manuscripts*, no. 53, illus. 229.

63. Ryan, "Aspects of Sequence and Style," 68.

64. For fuller discussion of the manufacture of Celtic filigree see Whitfield, "Motifs and Techniques of Celtic Filigree," and N. Whitfield, "Some New Research on Gold and Gold Filigree from Early Medieval Ireland and Scotland," in C. Eluère, ed., *Goldsmiths' Tools and Workshops Worldwide from the Vth Millennium B.C. to the XVI Century A.D.* (Paris: Société des Amis des Musée des Antiquités Nationales et du château de Saint-Germain-en-Laye, 1993), 125–36.

65. I have seen the following trefoil-sectioned combinations: (1) three square rods in the base of the inner cup of the late- eighth-century Ormside bowl (Webster and Backhouse, eds., *The Making of England*, no. 134 [no illustration]); (2) a beaded wire resting on a pair of opposed two-strand cables on the silver trefoil ornament from Kirkoswald, Cumberland, deposited ca. 855 (D. M. Wilson, *Anglo-Saxon Ornamental Metalwork 700–1100 in the British Museum* [London: Trustees of the British Museum, 1964], no. 28, pl. 19); (3) ditto on the "carpeting" on the eighth- to ninth-century Bossington finger-ring (D. Hinton, *Catalogue of the Anglo-Saxon Ornamental Metalwork 700–1100 in the Department of Antiquities Ashmolean Museum* [Oxford: Clarendon Press, 1974], no. 4).

66. Ryan, *The Derrynaflan Hoard*, 9.

67. Ibid., 18.

68. Ibid., 19.

69. Stevenson, "The Hunterston Brooch," p. 26.

70. See the minor differences between the animal ornament on the similar shield strips from the Vendel 12 boat grave from Sweden, Bruce-Mitford, *The Sutton Hoo Ship-Burial*, vol. 2, fig. 53.

71. Ibid., fig. 436a, and b.

72. F. Henry, *Irish Art in the Early Christian Period (to 800 A.D.)* (London: Methuen, 1965), 211–16.

73. J. J. O'Meara, *The First Version of the Topography of Ireland by Giraldus Cambrensis* (Dundalk: Dundalgan Press, 1951), 87–88.

CHAPTER TWELVE

Michael Ryan

THE MENAGERIE OF THE DERRYNAFLAN PATEN

The Derrynaflan paten was found in a hoard of altar plate in the monastic site of that name in County Tipperary, Ireland in 1980. The find was published in preliminary form in 1980 and more extensively in 1983.[1] The objects found included a chalice, a sieve, and a basin together with an ornamental hoop which has been interpreted as a foot-ring for the paten. In its restored form the paten measures 35.6–36.8cm in diameter and stands 3.35cm in height excluding the foot-ring (pl. 12.1). It is an extremely complex structure consisting of many separately manufactured components which have been elaborately assembled in a manner which would have enabled the piece to be dismantled for repair, cleaning and so forth.[2] There is evidence that the object was disassembled and reconstructed in antiquity at least twice. An assembly code of letters and symbols engraved on the components had evidently been modified in ancient times. It is not intended to discuss the constructional history of the piece here—the code has been studied in detail by Raghnall Ó Floinn and the letters and a faint inscription by Michelle Brown[3]—but it is important to note that decorative components have been moved from their original positions, or been found not to fit the positions already chosen—to judge by the code—for them and this must have a bearing on the question of whether a symbolic *sequence* had

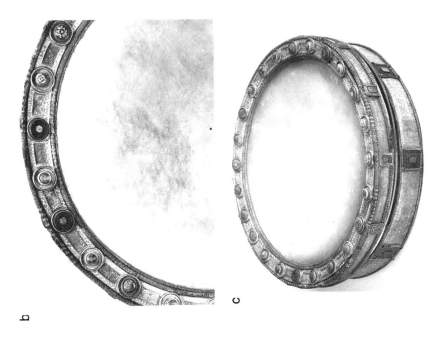

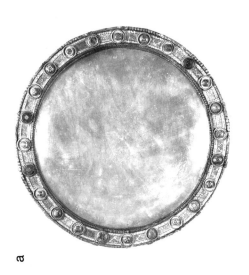

Pl. 12.1. (a) The Derrynaflan paten, general view; (b) the paten, detail of filigree panels and studs of about one-third circumference. Panels from lower left, clockwise: four crossed snakes, S-scroll with possible zoomorphic elements, interlocked peltae, kneeling beast, inverted stag, paired kneeling quadrupeds, eagle with snakes; (c) the paten and stand, conjecturally restored. Photographs by permission of National Museum of Ireland.

been originally intended by the craftsman and designer. As we shall see, if such a scheme had originally existed it is not now evident, nor does it seem to be mathematically recoverable although given the sophistication of the piece and the general tradition of paten-design throughout the early church the creators of the Derrynaflan communion plate are likely to have had something of the sort in mind.

It is enough to note that the paten is essentially a large silver plate with around its rim a series of filigree ornaments displayed in pairs in contiguous cast copper alloy frames. They are further embellished with polychrome glass studs, some in the familiar Insular pseudo-cloisonné manner, others with cast false-relief decoration and inset metal trays of filigree. The elaboration of the filigree, the stamped ornaments of the side of the paten, the glass settings, the knitted mesh of its rim, and the organization of the ornament place the paten clearly within the same aesthetic as the Ardagh chalice.[4] It belongs to the mainstream of Irish-style metalwork of the eighth century and is to date the most elaborate and accomplished piece to come to light from that tradition. I see no reason to modify the view which I expressed in 1987 that the two pieces stem from the same workshop tradition, a phrase carefully chosen so as not to imply that they were made by the same person nor indeed on the same premises. Although that fine distinction has often been missed in recent discussion, it finds new support in the comments of Brown about the significance of the lettered assembly code—there is no doubt that a literate person, almost certainly a cleric, was closely involved in the creation of the paten; an assembly code, perhaps also original, of Roman numerals, was noted on the Ardagh chalice during its restoration in the British Museum in the early 1960s.[5] I also maintain that it flies in the face of commonsense to deny that the two are "effectively contemporary" in so far as one may use the highly charged term "contemporary" in discussing phenomena which are essentially without dating indications independent of art-historical speculation.[6] Indeed, great care is needed in arriving at chronological conclusions about individual pieces—the implications of indentifying styles by period, region, workshop practice, and individual inventiveness must be very carefully weighed. The practice, still unfortunately to be seen, of assigning very precise dates to undated objects on stylistic grounds is quite unjustified.

There are twenty-four filigree ornaments placed in double frames around the rim. Of these, three are abstract and the remaining twenty-one are either anthropomorphic or zoomorphic. They may be tabulated as follows:

Table 12.1

Zoomorphic/Anthropomorphic

Two kneeling men	4
Kneeling quadruped	5
Two squatting addorsed beasts	3
Raptorial bird with snakes	1
Stag with snake	1
Interlaced snakes	2
Stag with interlace	1
Narrow-bodied quadrupeds	3
Interlace with bird-heads	1

Abstract

Plain interlace	1
Interlocked peltae	1
S-scroll with trumpet devices	1

Rynne has argued that the latter described by me as abstract is to be read as zoomorphic. The ornament of the panel consists of an S-scroll composed of interlocking spirals linked to the arms of miniature trisceles. The spiral endings contain pendant half-loops of wire with short lengths dividing them. These he argues are long-snouted beasts of general Salin Style II derivation, similar to those on the well-known belt-buckle from Lagore Crannóg and widespread in the curvilinear art of the Tara-Lindisfarne style.[7] This is not entirely to be ruled out although it is worth pointing out that the wire loop which forms the eye of the beast is precisely the same as that used to render the bell-mouths of the trumpet scrolls on the panel where the motif is undoubtedly an entirely abstract one composed of peltae.[8]

The motifs are executed with a variety of beaded wires and ribbons of gold, together with granules. These wires are built up in combinations to form more complex structures, designed to highlight detail, fill in bodies and create depth of field.[9] The filigrees are all executed on foil on which in some places, the motif has been previously traced by repoussé or stamping. In these cases, the background foil has been cut away and the motif displayed in its frame against a further foil sheet. The technique, known as hollow platform, is well attested on Insular pieces. It is not the purpose of this paper to discuss the filigree in great detail; suffice it to say that it is highly accomplished and extends the range already known from the major pieces of the period considerably.

Paired arrangements—more or less symmetrical—are the most common on the paten, six zoomorphic, one possible ornithopomorphic and four anthropomorphic are disciplined in that way. Only two motifs represent solitary beasts—the stag with interlace and the kneeling beast, of which there are five examples. The remaining panels depict either creatures of unlike type on the same panel—two examples—or interlaced serpents. It would seem reasonable to conclude that pattern was especially important in the design of the symmetrical motifs and that those with beasts of two different types represent—either overtly or by derivation—*scenes* or symbols which had been less subordinated to ornament.

The paired men panels (pl. 12.2d) have already been the subject of a detailed discussion by the writer in which it was argued that they derive in the main from the human figures frequently represented with beast motifs on the rim friezes of Late Antique silver plates from which it may be argued Christian patens derived.[10] This impression is reinforced by the use on vessels in several Gaulish finds of silver of paired back-to-back human heads (Janus?) and single human heads used in effect as scene dividers.[11]

Early Christian patens tended to carry complex iconographical symbols or figured scenes—the Riha and Stuma patens, for example, are well-known as is the later fifth-century Plate of Paternus now in the Hermitage in St. Petersburg. The latter bears a rim ornament of doves, chalices, and vines to which secondary settings for applied ornaments are soldered; the dished interior bears a large Chi Rho monogram.[12] Later medieval patens in western Europe often carry elaborate engraved scenes. The majority of surviving early medieval Western patens are small examples made en suite with grave- or traveling chalices and preserved because they were placed in tombs. The sample which survives is unrepresentative. References in inventories and documents such as the *Liber Pontificalis* make it clear that very large patens were once fairly common in the great churches of Western christendom and the Derrynaflan paten is of special interest because it is the only example of its type to survive from early medieval western Europe. The well-known inventories of the holdings of the Basilicas of St. Stephen and St. Germanus in Auxerre, recorded by Heiric in the ninth century make it clear that Western church treasuries sometimes held substantial amounts of silver vessels, many of them very large, of secular and even pagan, origin.[13] The significance of this for the evolution of communion vessels is obvious.

DISCUSSION OF THE MENAGERIE

The raptorial bird shares its panel with two snake-heads on a common body which forms the interlace within which it is displayed but with which it is not involved (pl 12.2a). The eagle is not shown in combat with the serpent. The form of the bird is clearly dependent on manuscript representations where the general type, usually and for obvious reasons, is the eagle a symbol both of the evangelist John and of Christ himself.[14] While bird and beast combinations are common, I know of no other Insular metalwork scene which specifically relates the eagle with the serpent although birds and serpents occur from time to time on the same piece, for example, the "Tara" brooch and the Hunterston brooch—in the latter case, bird heads only.[15] The serpent (because it sloughs off its skin and is renewed) in the *Physiologus* tradition may sometimes represent repentance. The eagle and snake in combat is a very ancient and widespread motif in both literature and the visual arts. In the Roman world, it appeared on tombstones and in medieval Christian art appears in manuscript illumination (in the Valerian Gospels, Munich, Staatsbibliothek, and the Douce MS 176 in the Bodleian Library) and on Byzantine and Romanesque sculptures. Its use as a Christian symbol can be traced continuously into modern symbolic systems.[16]

The serpents of the Derrynaflan scene (their two heads on a common body) provide an interlaced setting within which the eagle is placed. It seems reasonable to see it as nevertheless dependent on eagle and serpent combat scenes and as having therefore the same kind of christological symbolism.

The scene does occur in Insular and Anglo-Saxon stone sculpture—a very fine example dominates the head of the Keills cross and an unpublished Anglo-Saxon example in the south porch of the church of Bakewell in Derbyshire has been drawn to my attention by Dr. Jane Hawkes.[17] It is worth noting that motifs of two beasts—in this instance serpents—who share a common body composed of interlace seems to be a feature of the later eighth- and ninth-century Anglo-Saxon art which is reflected elsewhere on the paten.[18]

In his discussion of the Keills version of the motif, Doug Mac Lean proposes a particular and ingenious interpretation of the iconography. In his view, the eagle is the symbol of St. John who in an apocryphal tradition well-known in early Ireland survived a cup of poison given to him by the pagan, Aristodemus of Ephesus, having first offered a prayer to God whose power exceeded that of dragons, vipers, toads, and other venomous creatures. The prayer was known in Ireland and Anglo-Saxon England and, significantly, is referred to in the epilogue to the *Martyrology of Oengus* a tract produced in a monastery which had close links with Derrynaflan itself.[19] This presents an attractive alternative to the more usual interpretation of the import of the scene.

The stag and snake (pl. 12.2b) like the eagle and snake are not in combat nor are they interlaced together. The serpent rears up in front of the stag but is not grasped in its jaws, nor is it in the process of being ingested as described in the *Physiologus*. The motif appears on another Irish object of the same general period, a slab from Gallen Priory[20] and occurs widely on a number of Early Christian sources depicting the combat of the stag and snake from the *Physiologus* tradition.[21] The mosaic of the baptistery at Messaouda in Tunisia depicts on its central panel a pair of stags flanking a tree, each with a serpent grasped in the jaws. Parallels are not common, however: Puech[22] lists a detail on the apse mosaic of San Clemente, in a Romanesque baptistery at Freudenstadt, Würtemberg, a wall painting at Bawit, Egypt, and on a mosaic from the Imperial Palace in Byzantium. A mosaic fragment from Carthage now in the British Museum, also depicts a stag with a snake but Puech does not list it. He does point out that the stag and snake enmity was known to the Latin fathers and St. Ambrose refers to it twice in his *Breviarium in Psalmos* commenting on Ps. 41 ("As the hart panteth for fountains of waters") and in a sermon addressed to neophytes in which the stag is associated with baptismal imagery and the slaying of the serpent is given symbolic value. St. Augustine commenting on the same psalm also makes the same references to the stag and serpents, the latter he specifically identifies as sins; the serpents of iniquity must be consumed by those who desired the Waters of Life. In a number of liturgies, Ps. 41 was recited at the vigil on Easter Saturday night when the cathecumens achieved their initiation. The Mass of the cathecumens on Good Friday in the Roman rite still uses Ps. 139:2–10, 14 as the tract: "Deliver me O Lord from the evil man: rescue me from the unjust man. . . . They have sharpened their tongues like a serpent: the venom of asps is under their lips." Ps. 41 is the Tract for the blessing of the font during the Easter Vigil. It was chanted by Pope, clergy, and cathecumens in the early Roman Ordines. The symbolism of the stag and serpent is appropriate also to monastic life according to Puech because the stag ejects the snake from caves and clefts in the rock just as the anchorites and contemplatives destroy their enemy the allegorical serpent. Doubtless some of the Desert Fathers had to evict the real thing too—in Ireland St. Patrick had taken care of the problem.

The stag in the field of interlace (pl. 12.2c) is quite clearly an antlered beast not a horned one. Alone of all the animal panels found in situ in its frame, it was placed so as to be read looking from the inside of the plate outwards. It could be described as being inverted with respect to its neighbors. This beast has been tentatively identified by Michelle Brown with the ibex of the *Physiologus*, an animal which fell from a height and was stuck upright in the ground.[23] I am not convinced. First, its "inversion" on the paten may well be accidental—the result of haste in the assembly or reassembly of the piece. Secondly, it may not have been alone in

c

a

d

b

Pl. 12.2. (a) Eagle with snakes; (b) stag with snakes; (c) stag (inverted); (d) two kneeling men. Photographs by permission of National Museum of Ireland.

Pl. 12.3. Plain interlace organized so as to suggest a cross form. Photograph by permission of National Museum of Ireland.

appearing inverted—other panels were found detached and have been replaced in their frames on the assumption that they were read looking from the center outwards. Principally, however, we are dealing here with a beast with a fine and clearly shown rack of antlers. Whatever about the ibex, the stag was an animal well-known to the Irish in early medieval times. It is important to note that in Christian representations of deer, symmetrical pairs are often shown.[24] Is the Derrynaflan depiction of two, albeit on different panels and one accompanied by snakes, the other, not, a reflection of this tradition? Is it simply an autonomous representation of a stag much in the manner that examples are depicted on contemporary sculpture? Whatever interpretation one chooses, the baptismal[25] significance of the stag symbol is unquestioned and its appropriateness on a eucharistic dish is obvious and need not be labored.

The stag as a symbol without serpents is thus well known: examples occur on mosaics at St. John Lateran, S. Maria Maggiore, the mausoleum of Galla Placidia at Ravenna, and many more Christian scenes in a variety of contexts. In Ireland, the stag in a trap is especially well shown on the Banagher shaft, a sculpture dating probably to the ninth century. Its significance there may well be the soul caught for Christ. I take the stag on the paten to be an explicit reference to baptism and redemption.

The interlaced snakes need not detain us long. In Christian terms, the serpent is an ambivalent figure being both a symbol of evil and of renewal. Snake forms are fairly common on Insular metalwork and whether we should see anything more than conventional ornament in their use is arguable. I believe that we must accept the sophistication of the artists and their mentors and allow for the probability that the examples on the paten were not simply reproductions of conventional ornament but this is an open question. What is not questionable is their disposition to form an interlaced cross and this is reflected also in the panel of plain interlace (pl. 12.3) where there is a cross evident in the void created by the interlacements.[26] Some of the glass studs of the rim also repeat the cross theme.

The paired motifs do not lend themselves to quite such detailed interpretation. I have suggested for some time that they are closely related to paired beast patterns, inhabited plant-scroll derivatives which seem to emerge in a secondary phase in the Anglo-Saxon province of Insular art.[27] This has some chronological value: it might be taken to suggest that the paten belongs to the later rather than the earlier eighth century when equivalent motifs make their appearance in Anglo-Saxon art. Here I must continue to declare that the taste represented by the narrow strip of panelled ornament, alternating animal, curvilinear and interlace patterns is that identified by Professor Cramp in the Durham manuscript of Cassiodorus's commentary on the psalms and in the Breedon sculptures. It is not the aesthetic of the Tara brooch and the Lindisfarne Gospels of the late-seventh and early eighth centuries A.D. This suggests to me that the paten and the Ardagh chalice belong to a later phase of the Irish tradition. Having said that, I should add that I simply do not accept that there is any precision in this. Far too many certainties have been claimed in the field of early Irish art history.

The plant-scroll phenomenon is of course explicitly iconographical in import. I doubt, however, if we can see the entire corpus of Derrynaflan animal panels as an integrated scene, a procession of, say, the *tria genera animantium* of Genesis or a comprehensive illustration of an early bestiary. What I have suggested elsewhere is that the rim beast-motifs in a general way reflect the ornament of animals found on Late Antique silver dishes reinterpreted to suit contemporary taste and technology. This is no more than a re-emphasis of a truism about the origins of early altar plate as a whole. Individual scenes within the circle of the rim embody specific Christian themes, but it is difficult to see them married to form on the paten a coherent integrated symbolic cycle dependent on a single source of inspiration. It is an eclectic piece.

Notes

1. M. Ryan, "An Early Christian Hoard from Derrynaflan, Co. Tipperary," *North Munster Antiq. J.* 22 (1980): 9–26; Ryan, ed., *The Derrynaflan Hoard: A Preliminary Account* (Dublin: National Museum of Ireland, 1983), and with R. Ó Floinn in S. Youngs, ed., *"The Work of Angels": Masterpieces of Celtic Metalwork, 6th–9th centuries A.D.* (London: British Museum, 1989), 130–33.

2. Ryan and R. Ó Floinn in Ryan *The Derrynaflan Hoard*, 17–30.

3. Ó Floinn forthcoming; M. Brown, "'Paten and Purpose': the Derrynaflan Paten Inscriptions," in R. M. Spearman and J. Higgitt, eds., *The Age of Migrating Ideas: Early Medieval Art in Northern Britain and Ireland* (Edinburgh: National Museum of Scotland, 1993), 162–67.

4. M. Ryan, "Some Aspects of Sequence and Style in the Metalwork of Eighth- and Ninth-Century Ireland," in M. Ryan, ed., *Ireland and Insular Art A.D. 500–1200* (Dublin: Royal Irish Academy, 1987), 66–74, at p.68.

5. Brown, "Paten and Purpose," 163–64.

6. Ryan, "Aspects of Sequence and Style."

7. E. Rynne, "The Date of the Ardagh Chalice," in Ryan (ed.), *Ireland and Insular Art*, 85–89, at p. 89. His general conclusions as to the relationship of the paten and Ardagh and Derrynaflan chalices should be treated with reserve. Similar whorls are to be found in the ornament of *inter alia* the Lindisfarne Gospels and one of two discs from the Donore hoard. The presence of stylized zoomorphic elements does not affect the general arguments for dating the paten.

8. Compare Ryan, ed., *Derrynaflan Hoard*, 19–20, pls. 42, and 43.

9. See now N. Whitfield, "The Filigree of the Hunterston and 'Tara' Brooches," in Spearman and Higgitt, eds., *Age of Migrating Ideas*, 118–27, esp. 121, figs. 14.7, 14.8, and also this volume pp. 211–43.

10. M. Ryan, "A Suggested Origin for the Figure Representations on the Derrynaflan Paten," in E. Rynne, ed., *Figures from the Past: Studies on Figurative Art in Christian Ireland* (Dun Laoghaire: Glendale Press, Royal Society of Antiquaries of Ireland, 1987), 69–72.

11. Examples in F. Baratte and K. Painter, eds., *Trésors D'Orfèverie Gallo-Romains* (Paris: Ministere de la culture, 1989), nos. 24, 75, 88, 103, 104, 107, 125, 174, 184, 197, 201, 202 ranging in date from the first to the third centuries A.D.

12. E. C. Dodd, *Byzantine Silver Stamps*, Dumbarton Oaks Studies 8 (Washington: Dumbarton Oaks Research Library, 1961), nos. 20 (Riha), 27 (Stuma), 95, 108, and ibid., no. 2, 54 (Plate of Paternus).

13. J. Adhemar, "Le tresor d'argenterie donne par Saint-Didier aux eglises d'Auxerre" (viie siècle), *Revue archéologique* 6 ser. 4 (1934): 44–57; Ryan, "Suggested Origin," 69–70.

14. See E. Kirschbaum, ed., *Lexikon der Christlichen Ikonographie* (Rome, Freiburg, Basel, Wien: Herder, 1974), 70–76: the eagle may in addition symbolize the Resurrection of Christ. Christ in combat with the serpent may be taken as a depiction of his victory over Satan and so forth. The christological symbolism of the eagle is made very explicit on a number of Irish high crosses where the bird is placed behind the head of Christ, e.g., on the Crucifixion scene on the cross of Patrick and Columba at Kells.

15. See, for example, Whitfield, "Hunterston and 'Tara' Brooches," fig. 14.4

16. The motif has been surveyed in detail by R. Wittkower, "Eagle and Serpent," *J. of the Warburg Inst.* II (1938–39), reprinted in Wittkower, *Allegory and the Migration of Symbols* (London: Thames & Hudson, 1987), 16–44.

17. Douglas Mac Lean, "The Keills Cross in Knapdale, the Iona School and the Book of Kells," in J. Higgitt, ed., *Early Medieval Sculpture in Britain and Ireland,* B.A.R., Brit. ser. 152 (Oxford: British Archaeological Reports, 1986), 175–97.

18. D. Tweddle *The Anglian Helmet from Coppergate*, The Archaeology of York: The Small Finds 17/8: 1159–62; Ryan, "Suggested Origin."

19. Mac Lean, "Keills Cross," 176–77; on the links between Derrynaflan and the circle of Oengus see N. O'Muráile, "Notes on the History of Derrynaflan," in Ryan *The Derrynaflan Hoard*, 54–61.

20. F. Henry, *Irish Art in the Early Christian Period to 800 A.D.* (London: Methuen, 1965), 123, and pl. 64; Ryan, "Suggested Origin," 72. The interlaced cross, panelled ornament including a fretted frame for the stag and snake scene and the symmetrically placed beasts above it, perhaps also associated with snakes, make this sculpture an interesting parallel for the ornament of the Derrynaflan paten in other ways also.

21. G. L. Feuille, "Une mosaïque chrétienne de l'henchir Messaouda (Tunisie, région d'Agareb), *Cahiers Archéologiques* IV, 1949, 9–15, and H.-C. Puech, "Le cerf et le serpent note sur le symbolisme de la mosaïque découverte au baptistère de l'henchir Messaouda," ibid., 17–60. See also M. J. Curley, trans., *Physiologus* (Austin: University of Texas Press, 1979), 58–60 where the combat between the stag and the dragon is specifically likened to the Lord's defeat of the devil.

22. Puech, "Le cerf et le serpent," 26.

23. Brown, "Paten and Purpose," 164.

24. E.g., Henry, *Irish Art in the Early Christian Period*, 185, Fig. 24a.

25. Deer figure prominently on the Fount of Life scenes in the Soisson and the Godesalc Gospels: V. H. Elbern, "Der Eucharistische Kelch im frühen Mittelalter, Teil II Ikonographie und Symbolik," *Zeitschrift des Deutschen Vereins für Kunstwissenschaft* 17 (1963): 117–88 at 131; waterspouts in the form of stags are recorded among papal gifts to the churches of Santa Maria Maggiore and San

Vitale, the benefactions respectively of Popes Sixtus III and Innocent I, S. Duchesne, *Le Liber Pontificalis I*, Paris 1886, 220, 233.

26. R. B. K. Stevenson, "Aspects of Ambiguity in Crosses and Interlace," *U.J.A.* 44–45 (1981–82): 1–27.

27. "Links between Anglo-Saxon and Irish Early Medieval Art: Some Evidence of Metalwork," in C. Karkov and R. Farrell, eds., *Studies in Insular Art and Archaeology*, A.E.M.S. 1 (Oxford, Ohio: American Early Medieval Studies, 1991), 117–26, at 124–26.

CHAPTER THIRTEEN

Raghnall Ó Floinn

INNOVATION AND CONSERVATISM IN IRISH METALWORK OF THE ROMANESQUE PERIOD

This chapter deals with fine metalwork from Ireland during the eleventh and twelfth centuries. It suggests some parallels in form and decoration the origin of which is to be found on the mainland of Europe and in Britain and outlines the historical context in which such influences might have come about. The influences of Scandinavian and Anglo-Scandinavian art will not be examined here as this has been extensively reviewed elsewhere.

The eleventh and twelfth centuries in Ireland witnessed a true renaissance of artistic endeavor. This is most evident in the case of architecture where, unlike Britain, pre-Romanesque architectural sculpture is virtually unknown. As a result, it is very difficult to date the earliest Irish stone churches which on the whole tend to be plain, but it now seems that the majority are unlikely to be earlier than the eleventh or twelfth centuries.[1]

Cormac's Chapel at Cashel, County Tipperary, dedicated in 1134 is generally regarded as the earliest Irish building in the Romanesque style. In the case of the metalwork the position is less clear. Françoise Henry in her third volume on Irish art chose to define the Romanesque period as beginning with the battle of Clontarf in 1014 and ending with the coming of the Normans in 1169–1170.[2] It is easier to justify the end of the period in question: with the possible exception of a few crucifix figures,[3] there are no

259

major metalwork pieces of native manufacture which can be dated to the century after the Anglo-Norman invasion. For the purposes of this study we can take as a purely arbitrary starting point the early decades of the eleventh century when the first metalwork pieces which can be dated by their inscriptions appear. The earliest of these are two book shrines which have been redated recently on the basis of a reinterpretation of their inscriptions—in the case of the Soiscél Molaisse to the years 1001–1011[4] and of the Shrine of the Stowe Missal to the years 1026–1033.[5]

Unlike the products of the eighth and ninth centuries the fine metalwork of this later period is almost exclusively ecclesiastical—the manufacture of large brooches seems to have gone out of fashion in the tenth century and harness mounts or belt fittings, so common in the earlier period, are not represented. Hoards of ecclesiastical or secular plate are also unknown. Recent finds of swords with elaborate mounts from Lough Derg, County Tipperary and from the Irish Sea at Smalls Reef off the Pembrokeshire coast, and the recognition of a number of late drinking horn mounts are beginning to redress the balance.[6] The corpus is therefore more limited than that of the earlier period, consisting largely of enshrined objects associated with the saints of the early Irish church—associative relics—particularily bells, books, and croziers. These objects have survived through being entrusted to certain families in whose possession they have been preserved down to modern times and this would account for the bias in favor of shrines as opposed to other ecclesiastical or secular objects.[7] The peculiar devotion of the Irish to relics of an associative type was the subject of comment by contemporary foreign writers. The Anglo-Norman commentator Giraldus Cambrensis writing in his *Topographia Hibernica* at the end of the twelfth century declared, "I should not omit to mention also that the people and clergy of both Wales and Ireland have a great reverence for bells that can be carried about, and staffs belonging to the saints, and made of gold and silver, or bronze, and curved at their upper ends."[8] The Anglo-Saxon author of a *Passio* of St. Indracht—an Irish monk whose cult was established at Glastonbury—written sometime in the twelfth century makes a special mention of the fact that Indracht and his companions were carrying staffs or croziers "*ut Hybernensibus moris est*" (as is the custom of the Irish).[9]

These later reliquaries are often similar in form to those of the eighth and ninth centuries and these forms are largely unparalleled in Anglo-Saxon or continental metalwork. This is especially true of the book-shrines and croziers. As a result, this later metalwork has not received much attention from scholars outside Ireland except in so far as it relates to the later Viking art styles—particularily the Ringerike and Urnes styles. The implication of this neglect is that Ireland somehow lay outside the mainstream of fine art metalworking in northern Europe in the eleventh and twelfth centuries and that the metalwork styles practiced were somewhat archaic, harking back to the so-called Golden Age of the eighth and ninth centuries. It is the conservative nature of this later corpus that is stressed: the survival into the twelfth century of earlier forms such as book shrines and croziers and the continued use of designs based primarily on zoomorphic interlace and techniques such as champlevé enameling and millefiori. I hope to show that this view is only partly true and that the extraordinary revival in metalworking in Ireland in the eleventh and twelfth centuries took account of current European developments in terms of form, technique, and decoration.

There is one piece of evidence to show that the Irish goldsmith's skills were appreciated on the continent at this time. In the biography of Saint Bernward, Bishop of Hildesheim (+1022) by his tutor Thangmar, there is a passage in which it is stated that Bernward—himself an accomplished goldsmith, sculptor, and miniature painter—had a high regard for Anglo-Saxon and Irish metalwork which had been presented as gifts to the Emperor:

> adeo ut ex transmarinis et ex Scotticis vasis, quae regali maiestati singulari dono deferebantur, quicquid rarum vel eximium reperirit, incultum transire non sineret. (Thus, when he found a rare and exceptional piece among Anglo-Saxon and Irish vessels presented to his royal majesty as special gifts, he knew how to make use of it somehow.)[10]

It is interesting that a distinction is made between Anglo-Saxon and Irish metalwork and the fact that the vessels are described as gifts to the Emperor means that the text is referring to contemporary metalwork of the early eleventh century rather than to Insular objects of an earlier date such as the eighth-century house-shaped shrine preserved at Abbadia San Salvatore in Italy[11] which may have been preserved for centuries in a church treasury on the continent.

No Irish metalwork object of the tenth or eleventh centuries is known for certain to have survived on the continent but one could speculate that Thangmar may have had in mind something like the Irish ceremonial- or reliquary-horn dating to ca. 1100, formerly in the treasury of the Beguinage in Tongeren in Belgium, which is linked stylistically to Irish objects of Munster provenance such as the Shrine of St. Lachtin's Arm and the Lismore Crozier.[12] Such a drinking- or ceremonial-horn would make a very suitable gift and there are numerous references in the Irish annals to the gift of decorated horns by Irish kings to the Church[13] and the giving and exchange of luxury items, including drinking horns, was widespread in Ireland as a means of affirming political alliances.[14]

Around the time that Thangmar was writing in praise of Insular metalwork, the Annals of Ulster record in 1023 (recte 1024) the death of Emperor Henry II "king of the world" and the accession of Conrad II as his successor. The same annals also chronicle a battle between the Emperor Conrad and the Franks in 1038. References to contemporary events on the continent are unusual in Irish annals and it is possible that these entries may reflect a particular alliance, otherwise undocumented, between an Irish king and Imperial Germany in the early eleventh century which was sealed by the gift of an item of precious metalwork. Such diplomatic gifts were not unusual in medieval Europe.[15] There is one other recorded instance of diplomatic gift-giving by an Irish king to a foreign monarch: the Frankish *Annales Bertiniani* record a legation from *Rex Scottorum*—perhaps the high king, Maelsechlainn, or the king of Cashel—which came with gifts to the court of Charles the Bald announcing the defeat and expulsion of the Norse from Ireland.[16] It is possible that the so-called Book of Macdurnan, associated with Macdurnan (+927), Abbot of Armagh and Kells, which was given to Christ Church, Canterbury by King Æþelstan (+939) may also originally have been a royal gift from an Irish king.[17]

There are a few references to precious objects which may have been brought to Ireland as gifts from Scandinavian, Saxon, or continental rulers and which could in turn have inspired native goldsmiths. It has been suggested that the "Sword of Carlus," which along with the "ring of Tomrar the Earl" was one of the treasured possessions of the Viking kings of Dublin in the tenth and eleventh centuries, may have been a gift from Charlemagne ("Carlus") to a Scandinavian chief.[18] However, it is more likely that the Carlus in question was Carlus Mac Conn, the Clann Colmáin king of Meath who was slain in Dublin in 960.[19] Both the Annals of Ulster and the Annals of the Four Masters record the gift in 1165 of a sword called "the Sword of the son of the Earl" by Eochaidh Mac Duinnsléibhe, King of Ulster to the High King Muirchertach Mac Lochlainn as part of his tribute. The word "earl" at this time is usually applied to Viking rulers and suggests that its original owner was of Scandinavian origin. Another diplomatic gift may have been the "standard of the king of the Saxons"—*merrge ríg Saxan*—which, along with the sword of Brian Ború was one of the treasures of the kings of Leinster bestowed by Diarmait, king of Leinster on his ally Toirdelbach Ua Briain, king of Munster, in 1068.[20] The most important of these gifts is, of course, the gift of a portion of the True Cross to Toirdelbach Ua Conchobair, king of Connacht in 1123[21] while surely one of the most bizarre was the camel presented by the king of Scotland in 1105 to Muirchertach Ua Briain, king of Munster.[22]

It should therefore not come as any surprise that Insular metalwork would be praised in a text written in lower Saxony in the early eleventh century. Apart from the exchange of gifts, continental influences could have reached Ireland through contacts established through the foundation of new Irish monastic communities on the continent from the mid-ninth century and through pilgrimages, especially in the eleventh and twelfth centuries.

Although they have received less attention in the literature the *Scotti vagantes* were, at this time, still to be found on the continent in the great centers of the Frankish empire and from the mid-tenth century a new phase of Irish monastic foundations had begun: St. Cadroe of Armagh founded a monastery at Waulsort in Lorraine in 946 and established another community at Metz in the 970s.[23] An Irishman, one Israel Scottus, was tutor and confidant of archbishop Bruno of Cologne (953–965), brother of Otto the Great. Later, the Abbey of Gross Sankt Martin in Cologne was assigned to Irish monks by archbishop Gero in 975 and early in the eleventh century this foundation and also that of St. Panthaleon were under the rule of Abbot Elias, otherwise Ailill, an Irish monk from Mucknoe, County Monaghan whose death as "head of the Irish monks in Cologne" is recorded in 1042.[24] It is perhaps at one of these monasteries that Donnchad, abbot of Dunshaughlin, died "in Colonia" in 1027. Broen, the former king of Leinster, who was deposed in 1015 retired to Cologne where he died in 1052 "*do ec i Colanea.*"[25]

In the late-eleventh century Marianus Scottus (Muiredach Mac Robartaigh) set out from Ulster on a pilgrimage to Rome and was forced to remain in Regensburg (Ratisbon) on his way back, thus beginning the foundation of a series of *Schottenklöster* throughout Southern Germany and Central Europe which extended as far east as Kiev.[26] While the earlier continental foundations of the tenth and eleventh centuries appear to have been associated with the north and east of Ireland, the *Schottenklöster* movement seems to have had close connections with Munster.[27] In the twelfth century, Irish scholars and intellectuals continued to study on the continent. The Annals of Ulster record the death in 1174 of Flann Ua Gormain, *fer léigind* or lector, of Armagh who had spent "a year and twenty learning amongst the Franks and Saxons."[28]

Allied to this later movement of churchmen on the continent was the upsurge in pilgrimage to Rome from Ireland in the eleventh century. From 1024 onwards, a number of pilgrimages of prominent kings and churchmen from Ireland to Rome are recorded. There is a particularly large number of entries in the period 1024 to 1064 and A. Gwynn suggested that the reason for this was the reopening of the pilgrim route to Rome in 1027 after a treaty ensuring safe conduct was signed between King Canute on the one hand

and the German Emperor, Conrad and the king of Burgundy, Rudolf II on the other.[29] Gwynn's suggestion has been accepted by subsequent writers but the Irish pilgrimages had started three years earlier, in 1024, when Fachtna, *fer léigind* or lector of Clonmacnois, died at Rome, whither he had gone on pilgrimage.[30] Is it possible to see in the annalistic reference of the same year to the death of the German Emperor Henry II and the accession of Conrad coupled with the mention of gifts of Irish metalwork to the Emperor in the *Vita Bernwardii*, dating as early as 1022, the seeds of a separate and earlier agreement concerning pilgrims between an Irish king and the Emperor which was sealed by diplomatic gifts of fine metalwork?

The list of royal pilgrims during this forty year period in the mid-eleventh century includes a king of Cenél Conaill; a king of Cenél Eógain; a king of Brega; two Scandinavian kings of Dublin, a king of Munster, and a king of Gailenga (in Meath). Among the ecclesiastics are listed abbots of Cork and Aghaboe and the lector of Clonmacnois. Their route, in so far as we can tell, lay through the west and south of England and on to Rome, probably via the Irish foundations in Cologne.[31] There is evidence that the monastery of S. Maria in Palladio in Rome housed a community of Irish monks at the end of the eleventh century and the death of its Abbot Eogan "head of the Irish monks in Rome" is recorded in 1095.[32] While attention has focussed on the royal pilgrimages of the mid-eleventh century, pilgrimages to Rome continued throughout the twelfth century.[33]

It is clear from the annalistic entries that large parties were involved in these pilgrimages consisting of kings, clerics, members of their families, and other followers. No doubt the opportunity was taken to collect relics and other souvenirs along the pilgrim route to be enshrined on their return. Such may be the origin of the contents of the Breac Maodhóg shrine, dating to around 1100, which contained we are told, among other things, the relics of the martyrs Stephen, Lawrence, and Clement, the ankle bone of St. Martin and some of the hair of the Virgin.[34] The shrines and reliquaries seen by these pilgrims would have been described on their return and copies could have been commissioned from Irish craftsmen. It is also possible that complete reliquaries were brought back which could then, in turn, have been copied by Irish craftsmen.

It has been suggested that the large numbers of fragments of imported green porphyry (*verde antico*) quarried in Laconia, Greece and originally used in Roman imperial buildings, which have recently come to light in large numbers on Irish excavations may be related to this Roman pilgrimage.[35] Most consist of small fragments and are variously interpreted as keepsakes or souvenirs, as raw material for jewelers or for the decoration of shrines or altars but an alternative theory is that some may once have formed part of portable altars. Of importance here is the fact that "the main date of importation of porphyry in Ireland was the eleventh century or a little later."[36] C. J. Lynn rightly argued that the sheer quantity of finds made it unlikely that all these fragments of exotic stone came from portable altars. Three new finds from ecclesiastical sites, two from Scotland (Whithorn and Barhobble in Galloway) and one from Ireland (Skeam West, County Cork) were found in the fill of graves and tend to support the hypothesis that these fragments were keepsakes or souvenirs.[37]

No elaborate Irish portable altars have survived and Lynn[38] was unable to cite any references to their use in Ireland in the medieval period. However, portable altars containing relics, including altars of marble, were known in Ireland at this time. Among the objects described as the guarantees of Ireland used to conclude a peace between the kings of Meath and Connacht in 1143 was the "altar of Ciarán [of Clonmacnois] and its relics."[39] In a list of relics preserved in Dublin's Christ Church Cathedral compiled in the fifteenth century, the relic listed as third in importance is a marble portable altar of St. Patrick—*superaltare marmoreum Sancti Patricii*— which was kept in Armagh until it was removed, probably around 1180 along with other relics of St. Patrick, to Dublin.[40] This portable marble altar is not mentioned in the earlier Patrician texts and only appears in later lives such as the Vita Tertia,[41] Jocelin's Life,[42] and the Leabhar Breac homily on St. Patrick in which it is stated that the saint left his portable altar to the church of Donaghpatrick, County Meath.[43] This would suggest that the object was a late addition to the relic cult of Patrick, certainly no earlier than ca. A.D. 800 and probably much later.

Relic lists, which are preserved in Irish and Anglo-Norman documents, give us a tantalizing glimpse of object types such as portable altars which are now lost, some of which may have been imported or based on imported models. Did the "model of the Temple of Solomon" which was stolen from the altar at Clonmacnois in 1129[44] resemble reliquaries in the form of an Early Christian church such as those now in the cathedral treasuries of Aachen and St. Mark's, Venice,[45] or was it perhaps a censer representing the Temple of Solomon such as that in the Cathedral Treasury at Trier?[46] The most prized relic in Christ Church Cathedral in the twelfth century was not the Crozier of St. Patrick or "Staff of Jesus" but a miracle-working speaking cross adorned with the figure of the crucified Christ,[47] perhaps not unlike the altar crosses at Essen.[48] The moulded terminals of the stone cross at Glendalough, County Wicklow are clearly based on a metal prototype such as the Lothar cross at Aachen or the cross of Mathilde and Otto at Essen, as pointed out by S. McNab,[49] and demonstrate that such jeweled wooden crosses were known in Ireland by the twelfth century.

We cannot say whether any of the above objects were imported or of native manufacture. Imported objects of the period from Ireland are rare but are more common than one would have imagined and more imports of eleventh and twelfth-century date can be cited than for the eighth and ninth centuries. These include a pair of silver drinking bowls from Taghmon, County Westmeath (pl. 13.1) which may now be considered of Rhenish workmanship of the twelfth century;[50] a filigreed gold pendant cross from Mellifont, County Louth, possibly of twelfth-century Cologne workmanship,[51] and a gold finger ring with cloisonné enameled bezel possibly of tenth- or eleventh century date from Ireland.[52] Two engraved bronze bowls of late-eleventh- or early twelfth-century German or English manufacture are known. One of these is from a crannóg at Cloonfinlough, County Roscommon,[53] the other from the River Blackwater at Charlemont, County Armagh was adapted by an Irish craftsman as a hanging bowl by the addition of escutcheons.[54] This small group of objects suggest northern Germany and England as a source for imported, prestige, metalwork objects. Apart from the Blackwater bowl, further evidence for the reuse of an imported piece of fine metalwork is to be found on one of the most important reliquaries of the period—the Shrine of St. Patrick's Bell made around 1100 (pl. 13.2). In the center of the front of the crest of the shrine is a small stud of blue glass inlaid with a four-petalled flower in cloisonné enamel, the cloisons being of gold and the petals of red and white enamel.[55] Françoise Henry believed that this stud along with related examples on an unprovenanced Irish crozier were unique examples of the use of a version of cloisonné enameling in Ireland.[56] The stud is, however, an import and it is paralleled *exactly* in its size and decoration on the decorated rim of the agate navette from the treasury of Saint Denis.[57] The rim mounts of the latter are considered to be of Ottonian manufacture of the early eleventh century and are similar in style to the enamels on the Nail Reliquary from the Egbert Shrine at Trier, dating to the close of the tenth century. Does the presence of this stud indicate the recycling of an older, damaged imported object or were individual decorative elements imported for use as inlays on Irish objects? Whatever its origin, the stud was considered of sufficient value to be mounted in the center of the front of the bell shrine.

The Shrine of St. Lachtin's Arm—the product of a Munster workshop of ca. 1120—shows in its form and in elements of its decoration strong influences from continental Europe. It is one of two surviving Irish examples of an arm reliquary (the other being the fifteenth-century Shrine of St. Patrick's Hand) but there is evidence that the type was once common—the arm shrines of St. Ruadhán of Lorrha and St. Ciarán of Clonmacnois survived until the late Middle Ages.[58] The Shrine of St. Lachtin's Arm is, in fact, one of the earliest surviving European arm reliquaries as most date to the later twelfth and thirteenth centuries.[59] Their form is standard, a clothed arm with the fingers of the hand fully extended or raised in blessing. The cuff and

Pl. 13.1. Pair of silver bowls from Taghmon, County Westmeath. Photograph by permission of National Museum of Ireland.

folds of cloth are clearly delineated and the decoration is confined to discrete border panels on either side. The Shrine of St. Lachtin's Arm belongs to an earlier tradition in which the arm is cylindrical in shape, the cuff and sleeve are not shown and the decoration covers the whole surface of the arm. Similar arm shrines on the continent are dated to the late-eleventh century and the type is regarded as of Byzantine origin.[60] A particularly close example is the arm reliquary of St. Anne in Genoa Cathedral, considered to be of Byzantine workmanship of eleventh- or twelfth-century date. Like the Irish arm reliquary, the arm is cylindrical, with jeweled bands above and below; the arm is decorated with vertical panels of incised ornament. It also has a truncated cylindrical cap identical to that

Pl. 13.2. Cloisonné enameled stud on the crest of the Shrine of St. Patrick's Bell. Photograph by permission of National Museum of Ireland.

fitted to the base of the Shrine of St. Lachtin's Arm.[61] The early date of the latter shows how soon new forms, brought from the Byzantine world to Europe as a result of the Crusades, could be adopted in Ireland.

The Shrine of St. Lachtin's Arm may also serve to illustrate how imported continental manuscripts could also have been a source of inspiration for designers. Set into the palm of the hand is a triangular plate of gilt silver engraved with a pair of tightly coiled foliate scrolls with curled offshoots which end in trefoils (pl. 13.3). The manuscript affinities of this decoration are clear and foliage of an almost identical type is found on a Cologne Bible of mid-eleventh-century date preserved in the Historisches Archiv (fig. 13.1).[62] Perhaps a manuscript illuminated in this style was brought back from Cologne where we know that communities of Irish monks existed in the eleventh century.

I have argued elsewhere that the production of fine metalwork in Ireland was, by the end of the eleventh century, confined to the towns and to a small number of important monasteries and that the craft of the goldsmith was an hereditary one—at least in the monasteries.[63] Much of the surviving metalwork can be grouped into schools, some of which have distinct regional distributions. Occasionally the location of the production center can be suggested. One of these workshops I suggested, following

Françoise Henry, was located at Kells and is exemplified by the Cathach book shrine, dated by its inscription to between 1062 and 1098. Further confirmation of this has come from a recent visit to Kells which has convinced me that the sundial there is of eleventh century date and not late medieval as is usually thought. The sundial bears a closed foliate link ending in a notched lobed tendril of a type found exclusively in metalwork on objects of the Cathach group.[64] Another product of this workshop has recently come to light in Scotland on the site of the Augustinian Priory of Inchaffray in Perthshire. It is the crest of a small bell or bell shrine and its construction and decoration is paralleled by another bell crest from the River Bann. Inchaffray is known to have had a community of Culdees prior to its adoption of the Augustinian rule, and, although there is no evidence of a connection with Iona, it is possible that it was through Iona that the object was acquired from Ireland.[65] All the Irish products of the Cathach group, which can be associated with monastic sites, come from monasteries of the Columban federation and we may well be dealing here with a central workshop of goldsmiths located at Kells serving the needs of the Columban *paruchia* in the later eleventh century.

The other well-defined workshop of this period is that which produced the Cross of Cong and St. Manchan's Shrine. It was located west of the Shannon, perhaps at Roscommon or Tuam and was active in the second and third quarters of the twelfth century. The cross form on which the Cross of Cong was based was thought to have been derived from continental models.[66] The recent find of the Lough Kinale book shrine and the Tully cross shows that this form of cross with cusped arms was already established in Ireland in the eighth century. In fact the use of cast, gilt bronze openwork panels of animal ornament occurs on both objects. The positioning of the Cross of Cong's inscription on the narrow sides of the cross is found in contemporary sculpture such as on the freestanding cross of Cathasach from Inis Cealtra, erected to the memory of an ecclesiastic who died in 1111.[67] The positioning of a beast head gripping the base of the cross of Cong may, however, have been inspired by German Romanesque altar crosses which have a gripping lion head in the same position.[68] An imported cross- or candlestick-base was undoubtedly the model for a small three-legged stand from County Galway, also a product of the Cross of Cong group.[69]

The gabled form of St. Manchan's Shrine is paralleled in tent-shaped founder's tombs of stone found at a number of monastic sites in the west of Ireland. While the latter are often presumed to be early in date, none can be dated so that one cannot say when this form began to be used. However, an antiquarian drawing of a very similar gabled wooden shrine with decorated mounts associated with St. Winifred and formerly preserved at

Pl. 13.3. Foliate ornament on the Shrine of St. Lachtin's Arm. Photograph by permission of National Museum of Ireland.

Gwytherin, North Wales, has recently come to light.[70] The style of the mounts is Anglo-Saxon, probably eighth century. The gabled form of the latter shows that the gabled form of St. Manchan's Shrine can no longer be considered to be a novel twelfth-century invention. What is innovative on the shrine is the use of separately cast appliqué figures, originally arranged in two registers (pl. 13.4). The shrine is in fact an Irish adaptation of a

Fig. 13.1. Initial P, Bible, Cologne. Drawing after *Aachener Kunstblätter* 36 (1968), pl. 107.

continental châsse. Various models have been proposed for the figures, an imported crucifix being most often suggested. The origin of this model has been sought in various parts of the continent, ranging from the Rhineland[71] to northern Spain.[72] Others have suggested that the style of the figures owes more to native sources.[73] I would like to suggest that parallels for the figures may be found in the English West Country, more specifically the lower Severn Valley. The stylistic affinities between Irish Romanesque architecture and that of the west of England have been known for some time, as

Pl. 13.4. Cast appliqué figures of saints(?) on St. Manchan's Shrine. Photograph by permission of National Museum of Ireland.

exemplified by the comparison between the facades of Roscrea, County Tipperary and Lullington in Somerset.[74] Also closely related to the style of the Manchan's Shrine figures are the sculptures at Kilpeck and others of the Herefordshire school.[75] Parallels for the kilt form of the figures on St. Manchan's Shrine can be found in late Anglo-Saxon carving such as that

Pl. 13.5. Ivory carving of the Deposition. Photograph courtesy of Board of Trustees of the Victoria and Albert Museum.

worn by the figure of Christ in a Crucifixion scene at Daglingworth in Gloucestershire.[76] It has been suggested that the Daglingworth figures are twelfth-century works of a west Mediterranean, and probably Spanish origin.[77] The figure style, including triangular faces, large bulbous eyes, and small noses, and the treatment of the hair of the figures on St. Manchan's Shrine were compared by Beckwith[78] to those on an ivory carving of the Deposition now in the Victoria and Albert Museum (pl. 13.5). Beckwith attributed the ivory to the School of Herefordshire of ca. 1150 although the origins of this piece are disputed—whether it is of Spanish or of West Country manufacture.[79] One could add to Beckwith's parallels the similarity in treatment of the accentuated rib cage of the Christ figure on the ivory and the metalwork figures. There is, however, one very specific detail that both objects share which does suggest a closer relationship. A characteristic feature of some of the St. Manchan's Shrine figures is the unexplained "fringing" of the lower arms. This takes the form of a series of parallel ribs, which follow the curve of the arms and continue onto the chest or rib cage, sometimes continuous with the latter. The figures are naked to the waist, yet the effect produced looks like a fringed sleeve. This finds its closest parallel in the pleated folds of drapery, which occur on the arms and legs of the angels on the Deposition ivory in the Victoria and Albert Museum. It has been demonstrated that the sculpture of the Herefordshire school of the 1130s owes its inspiration to a pilgrimage by a West Country sculptor to Santiago de Compostela in Spain.[80] It is not clear whether the apparent similarities in portraying human figures in West Country sculpture and ivory carving, heavily influenced by Spanish models on the one hand and Irish metalwork on the other is as a result of direct influences or of a common response to external influences (the pilgrim routes to Compostela?), but the parallels are worthy of more detailed examination than is possible here.

There is ample evidence of an historical context for direct connections between the area of the lower Severn Valley and Ireland in the eleventh and twelfth centuries. Close links were forged between Dublin and the Benedictine monasteries of Worcester and Winchcombe and there was probably a community of English Benedictines in Dublin in the 1070s and 1080s. Also close political links existed between the west of England and Ireland at this time. In the eleventh century, the sons of Godwin, Earl of Wessex took refuge in Ireland as did the sons of King Harold after the battle of Hastings.[81] Irish pilgrims went in large numbers to the shrines of Patrick, Brigid, and Indracht at Glastonbury as well as to the shrine of St. Wulfstan at Worcester. A thirteenth-century pewter ampulla from the shrine of St. Wulfstan of Worcester was found in the High Street excavations in Dublin.[82] It is from precisely this area also that many of the Anglo-Norman settlers and adventurers came. A thirteenth-century relic list of Leominster cathedral lists the relics of no fewer than twelve Irish saints, some of which may have reached the West Country before the Anglo-Norman invasion.[83]

The apparent conservative nature of Irish Romanesque metalwork is the result of the selective survival of only a limited range of object types mostly associated with the church. Moreover, these consist principally of bell-shrines, book-shrines, and croziers which of their nature would imitate earlier forms. Curved drinking horn terminals of cast bronze in the shape of animal heads are also directly descended from eighth- and ninth-century native prototypes. However, new forms such as arm shrines, cross- or candlestick-bases, crucifixes and crucifix figures, and portable altars make their appearance in the late-eleventh and early twelfth centuries. In addition a whole host of new techniques of inlaying in silver, copper and niello; glass and enamel work; gold and silver filigree, and the use of geometric openwork decoration were introduced into the repertoire of the Irish goldsmith. These cannot be discussed here but many were copied from contemporary continental European metalwork.[84] On the other hand, artefact types of eleventh- and twelfth-century date such as censers, aquamaniles, flabella, brooches, and finger-rings are so far either unknown or unrecognized in the Irish repertoire. There is annalistic and literary evidence of an increase in the translation of saints remains at this time which may well be tied in to the reforms of the Irish church in the eleventh and twelfth centuries on the one hand and the rise of ambitious dynasts on the other. The monasteries and larger churches vied with one another for powerful patrons and a secure position in the new order. In such an atmosphere, opportunities to experiment with new forms were offered to craftsmen by wealthy secular and ecclesiastical patrons seeking to model themselves on their continental European contemporaries and enrich the treasuries of their sponsored foundations.

NOTES

1. A. Hamlin, "The Archaeology of the Irish Church in the Eighth Century," *Peritia* 4(1985): 279–99, esp. p. 283 with refs.

2. F. Henry, *Irish Art in the Romanesque Period (1020–1170)* (London: Methuen, 1970), xiii.

3. R. Ó Floinn, "Irish Romanesque Crucifix Figures," in E. Rynne, ed., *Figures from the Past: Studies on Figurative Art in Christian Ireland in honour of Helen M. Roe* (Dun Laoghaire: Glendale Press; Royal Society of Antiquaries of Ireland, 1987), 168–88.

4. R. Ó Floinn, "The Soiscél Molaisse," *Clogher Record* 13 (1989): 51–63. Previously dated 1001–1025.

5. P. Ó Riain, "The Shrine of the Stowe Missal, Redated," *P.R.I.A.* 91C (1991): 285–95; P. Ó Riain, "Dating the Stowe Missal Shrine," *Archaeology Ireland* 5, no. 1 (1991): 14–15. Previously dated 1045–1052.

6. For the Lough Derg sword see R. Ó Floinn, catalogue entry no. 431 in E. Roesdahl and D. M. Wilson, eds., *From Viking to Crusader—The Scandinavians and Europe 800–1200,* 22nd Council of Europe exhibition Paris—Berlin—Copenhagen 1992 (New York: Rozzoli, 1992); the Smalls Reef sword fitting is now in the National Museum of Wales. For drinking horns see R. Ó Floinn, "Schools of Metalworking in Eleventh- and Twelfth-Century Ireland," in M. Ryan, ed., *Ireland and Insular Art A.D. 500–1200* (Dublin: Royal Irish Academy, 1987), 179–87.

7. F. Henry, *Irish Art in the Romanesque Period,* 74–75.

8. J. J. O'Meara, *Gerald of Wales: The History and Topography of Ireland* (London: Humanities Press, 1982), 116.

9. M. Lapidge, "The Cult of St. Indracht," in D. Whitelock, R. McKitterick, and D. Dumville, eds., *Ireland in Early Medieval Europe* (Cambridge: Cambridge University Press, 1982), 199, l.25.

10. The text is quoted in P. Lasko, *Ars Sacra: 800–1200* (Harmondsworth: Penguin, 1972), 260, n. 6. Lasko states that Thangmar's authorship of this version of the saint's life has been questioned and that it may represent a re-edited version dating to the late-twelfth century. Even if this were the case, the reference to Insular metalwork is still remarkable. The passage is also quoted by J. J. Buckley, *Some Irish Altar Plate* (Dublin: Falconer, 1943), 1, and is also referred to by C. R. Dodwell, *Anglo-Saxon Art: A New Perspective* (Manchester: Manchester University Press, 1982), 45, and 256, n. 13. The words *transmarinis* and *Scotticis* were translated respectively as "overseas" and "Irish" by Buckley and as "overseas" and "Scottish" by Lasko. Dodwell has shown that the former means Anglo-Saxon. The term "Scotti" still meant "Irish" until the early thirteenth century.

11. S. Youngs, ed, *"The Work of Angels": Masterpieces of Celtic Metalwork, 6th–9th Centuries A.D.* (London: British Museum, 1989), 134.

12. M. Ryan, "The Irish Horn-reliquary of Tongres/Tongeren, Belgium," in G. Mac Niocaill and P. Wallace, eds., *Keimelia: Studies in Medieval Archaeology and History in Memory of Tom Delaney* (Galway, Ireland: Galway University Press, 1988), 127–42. It is not known, however, when this object was added to the treasury at Tongeren.

13. R. Ó Floinn, "The Kavanagh 'Charter' Horn," in D. Ó Corráin, ed., *Irish Antiquity: Essays and Studies Presented to Professor M. J. O'Kelly* (Cork, Ireland: Tower Books, 1981), 268–78, esp. 271–72.

14. C. Doherty, "Exchange and Trade in Early Medieval Ireland," *J.R.S.A.I.* 110 (1980): 67–89, at pp. 72–75.

15. See D. W. Rollason, "Relic Cults as an Instrument of Royal Policy c.900–c.1050," *A.S.E.* 15 (1986): 91–103 with refs. for a discussion of the practice in Anglo-Saxon England and on the continent.

16. F. J. Byrne, *Irish Kings and High-Kings* (London: Batsford, 1973), 262; J. L. Nelson, *The Annals of St. Bertin* (Manchester and New York: Manchester University Press, 1991), 66, anno 848.

17. J. J. G. Alexander, *Insular Manuscripts 6th to the 9th Century* (London: Harvey Miller, 1978), no. 70.

18. E. Curtis, "Norse Dublin," in H. Clarke, ed., *Medieval Dublin: The Making of a Metropolis* (Dublin: Irish Academic Press, 1990), 100. A decorated sword of later-ninth-century with later additions preserved in the Kunsthistorisches Museum in Vienna is associated with Charlemagne. Jeweled swords are not unknown in church treasuries, such as that in the treasury at Essen in Germany, illustrated in Lasko, *Ars Sacra* pl. 125, and the so-called "Mauritiusschwert" of eleventh- and twelfth-century date in Vienna, illustrated in the exhibition catalogue *Das Reich der Salier 1024–1125* (Speyer 1992), p. 245.

19. S. Mac Airt and G. Mac Niocaill, eds., *The Annals of Ulster (to A.D. 1131)* (Dublin: Dublin Institute for Advanced Studies, 1983), anno 960. Hereafter *AU.*

20. S. Mac Airt, ed., *The Annals of Inisfallen* (Dublin: Dublin Institute for Advanced Studies, 1951), anno 1068.5. Hereafer *AI.* M. T. Flanagan, *Irish Society, Anglo-Norman Settlers, Angevin Kingship* (Oxford: Clarendon Press; Oxford University Press, 1989), 58 suggests that the battle standard may have been presented to the king of Leinster by one of the many political exiles from England who sought refuge in Ireland in the eleventh century.

21. W. Stokes, ed., "The Annals of Tigernach," *Revue Celtique* xvi–xviii (1895–97): anno 1123. Hereafter *ATig.*

22. *AI* 1105.

23. The literature on this subject is extensive: see especially J.F. Kenney, *The Sources for the Early History of Ireland, Vol. 1, Ecclesiastical* (New York: Columbia University Press, 1929), 605–21; and D. Bethell, "English Monks and Irish Reform," in T. D. Williams, ed., *Historical Studies VIII* (Dublin: Gill & Macmillan, 1971), 111–35.

24. *AI* 1042.

25. *AU* 1027; *AU* 1052; J. O'Donovan, ed., *Annála ríoghachta Éreann: Annals of the Kingdom of Ireland by the Four Masters* (Dublin: Hodges and Smith, 1851), anno 1052. Hereafter AFM.

26. On the *Schottenklöster* see especially A. Gwynn, "Ireland and the Continent in the Eleventh Century," *Irish Historical Studies* 8 (1953): 193–216; P. A. Breatnach, "The Origins of the Irish Monastic Tradition at Ratisbon (Regensburg)," *Celtica* 13 (1980): 58–77.

27. D. Ó Riain-Raedel, "Aspects of the Promotion of Irish Saints' Cults in Medieval Germany," *Z.C.P.* 39 (1982): 224ff.

28. For scholarly and intellectual contacts see M. Richter, "The European Dimension of Irish History in the Eleventh and Twelfth Centuries," *Peritia* 4 (1985): 336–38.

29. On pilgrimages see Gwynn, "Ireland and the Continent in the 11th Century," and Bethell, "Irish Monks and English Reform" in *Historical Studies VII.*

30. *AFM* 1024.

31. *ATig* 1026: Maelruanaid Ua Maeldoraid, king of Cenél Conaill, went to Rome via Clonfert and Iona; *ATig* 1051: Laidgnen, king of the Gailenga, died in Britain on his way back from Rome.

32. C. Lynn, "Some Fragments of Exotic Porphyry found in Ireland," *J.I.A.* II (1984): 19–32, at p. 26.

33. See the deaths of pilgrims in Rome recorded in *AU* 1098, 1103, 1118, 1122, 1123, 1168, and 1188.

34. C. Plummer, *Lives of Irish Saints*, 2 vols. (Oxford: Clarendon Press, 1922), II, 258.

35. C. J. Lynn, "Exotic Porphyry;" W. F. Cormack, "Two Recent Finds of Exotic Porphyry in Galloway," *Trans. Dumfries. and Galloway Nat. Hist. and Antiq. Soc.* 64 (1989): 43–47.

36. Lynn, "Exotic Porphyry," 29.

37. For the Scottish sites see Cormack, "Two Recent Finds," who also notes another eleventh-century find from Dublin and also one from the monastic site of Derrynaflan, County Tipperary. For Skeam West see I. Bennett, ed., *Excavations 1990* (Dublin: Wordwell, 1991), 20.

38. Lynn, "Exotic Porphyry," 25.

39. *AFM* 1143. It is described as "the alter of St. Querans shrine" in the *Annals of Clonmacnoise* for the year 1139, see D. Murphy, *The Annals of Clonmacnoise* (Dublin: Royal Society of Antiquaries of Ireland, 1896), 197.

40. J. C. Crosthwaite, *The Book of Obits and Martyrology of the Cathedral Church of the Holy Trinity* (Dublin: Irish Archaeological Society, 1844), xx–xxii, 3.

41. L. Bieler, *Four Latin Lives of St. Patrick* (Dublin: Dublin Institute for Advanced Studies, 1971), 133–34, 150. This text is dated somewhere between ca. 800 and ca. 1130, probably near its later end. Ibid. 25–26. Kenney, *Sources* 341–42 regards the *Life* as depending on an original written in Ireland "probably in the second half of the ninth century."

42. Kenney, *Sources*, 347–48, dated 1185/86.

43. W. Stokes, *The Tripartite Life of St. Patrick*, 2 vols., (London: H.M.S.O., 1887), II, 466–67.

44. *AFM* 1129.

45. *The Treasury of San Marco Venice*, exhibition catalogue, British Museum (Milan: Olivetti, 1984), 237–43.

46. J. G. Hawthorne and C. Stanley Smith, *Theophilus: On Divers Arts* (New York: Dover, 1969), pl. IX.

47. Crosthwaite, *Book of Obits*, vi–vii, 3.

48. See Lasko, *Ars Sacra*, pls. 94, 95.

49. S. McNab, "Styles used in Twelfth-century Irish Figure Sculpture," *Peritia* 6–7 (1987–88): p. 287.

50. A. Mahr, *Christian Art in Ancient Ireland* (Dublin: Stationary office of Saorstat Eireann, 1942), pl. 43. For parallels see A. Andersson, *Mediaeval Drinking Bowls of Silver Found in Sweden* (Stockholm: Kungliga Vitterhets, Historie och Antikvitets Akadimien; Almquist & Wiksell International, 1983), *passim*.

51. J. Cherry, "Medieval Jewellery from Ireland," in G. Mac Niocaill and P. F. Wallace, eds., *Keimelia*, pp. 148–49 and pls. 12, and 13.

52. M. Chauncey Ross, "An Irish Cloisonné Enamel," *Down and Connor Hist. Soc. J.* 5–6 (1933–34): 43–46.

53. W. G. Wood-Martin, *The Lake Dwellings of Ireland* (Dublin and London: Hodges, Figgis, 1886), fig. 55.

54. C. Bourke, "The 'Virtues' of a Blackwater Bowl," *Archaeology Ireland* 5, no. 3 (1991): 22.

55. Best illustrated in a lithograph in W. Reeves, *Five Chromo Lithographic Drawings Representing an Irish Ecclesiastical Bell which is supposed to have belonged to St. Patrick*, 2nd. ed. (Belfast: Marcus Ward, 1850), Pl. I.

56. F. Henry, *Irish Art in the Romanesque Period*, 78–79.

57. *Le Trésor de Saint Denis*, exhibition catalogue, Musée du Louvre (Paris: Reunion des musées nationaux, 1991), col. pl. p. 157.

58. H. S. Crawford, "A Descriptive List of Irish Shrines and Reliquaries," *J.R.S.A.I.* 53 (1923): 90–91.

59. J. Braun, *Die Reliquaire des christlichen Kultes und ihre Entwicklung* (Freiburg im Breisgau: Herder, 1940), 388–411.

60. For example, the arm reliquary of St. Blaise in the Guelph Treasure of ca. 1075, see P. M. de Winter, *The Sacral Treasure of the Guelphs* (Cleveland, Ohio: Cleveland Museum of Art; Indiana University Press, 1985), fig. 29; H. Swarzenski, *Monuments of Romanesque Art,* 2nd ed. (Chicago: University of Chicago Press, 1967), fig. 66, or that of St. Basil, of the same date, in the Cathedral Treasury at Essen, see *Ornamenta Ecclesia*, exhibition catalogue, Cologne 1985, vol. 3, 38, and fig. 5.

61. C. Marcenaro, *Il Museo del Tesoro della Cattedrale a Genova* (Genoa, Italy: Silvana Editoriale D'Arte, 1969), pl. III.

62. P. Ludwig, ed., "Grosse Kunst aus Tausend Jahren," *Aachener Kunstblätter* 36 (1968): 48, and pl. 107.

63. Ó Floinn, "Schools of Metalworking," 179.

64. Ibid., fig. 1.

65. I. B. Cowen, "Early Ecclesiastical Foundations," in P. McNeill and R. Nicholson, eds., *An Historical Atlas of Scotland c400–c1600* (St. Andrews: University of St. Andrews, 1975), 17–19, and map 15.

66. F. Henry, *Irish Art in the Romanesque Period,* 109–10.

67. P. Harbison, *The High Crosses of Ireland,* 3 vols (Bonn: R. Halbelt, 1992), no. 119, figs. 317, and 1015.

68. P. Springer, *Kreuzfüsse—Ikonographie und Typologie Eines Hochmittelalterliches Gerätes,* Bronzegeräte des Mittelalters 3 (Berlin: Deutscher Verlag fur Kunstwissenschaft, 1981). See also P. M. de Winter, *The Sacral Treasure of the Guelphs,* figs. 118, 119.

69. Ó Floinn, "Irish Romanesque Crucifix Figures," 177, and illus. 10.16.

70. L. Butler and J. Graham-Campbell, "A Lost Reliquary Casket from Gwytherin, North Wales," *Ant.J.* 70 (1990): 40–48.

71. T. D. Kendrick and E. Senior, "St. Manchan's Shrine," *Archaeologia* 86 (1936): 114–15, and R. Stalley, "Irish Art in the Romanesque and Gothic Periods," in P. Cone, ed., *Treasures of Early Irish Art 1500 B.C. to 1500 A.D.* (New York: Metropolitan Museum of Art; A. A. Knopf, 1977), 190.

72. Henry, *Irish Art in the Romanesque Period,* 113.

73. C. Bourke, "Three Twelfth-Century Appliqué Figures," 112–26 in G. Mac Niocaill and P. F. Wallace, eds., *Keimelia,* p. 120; S. McNab, "Styles used in Twelfth Century Irish Figure Sculpture," 280–81; Ó Floinn, "Irish Romanesque Crucifix Figures," 179–80.

74. R. Stalley, "A Twelfth-Century Patron of Architecture: A Study of the Buildings Erected by Roger, Bishop of Salisbury," *J.B.A.A.* 34 (1971): 79–80.

75. L. Stone, *Sculpture in Britain, the Middle Ages* (Harmondsworth: Penguin, 1955), 244, n. 8.

76. Illustrated in C. Heighway, *Anglo-Saxon Gloucestershire* (Gloucester: Sutton and Gloucestershire County Library, 1987), 143.

77. T. D. Kendrick, *Late Saxon and Viking Art* (London: Methuen, 1949), 51.

78. J. Beckwith, "An Ivory Relief of the Deposition," *Burl. Mag.* 98 (1956): 228–35.

79. For full references to this piece see D. Gaborit-Chopin, *Elfenbeinkunst im Mittelalter* (Berlin: Mann, 1978), Catalogue No. 110. Gaborit-Chopin accepts Beckwith's Herefordshire provenance. The West Country origin of the piece has been disputed and the ivory was omitted from the exhibition *English Romanesque Art 1066–1200* held in the Hayward Gallery, London, in 1974 because of the conflicting attributions.

80. G. Zarnecki, "Sculpture," in G. Zarnecki, J. Holt, and T. Holland, eds., *English Romanesque Art 1066–1200* (London: Arts Council of Great Britain, 1984), 148.

81. Flanagan, *Irish Society, Anglo-Norman Settlers, Angevin Kingship*, 57–58.

82. B. Spencer, "Pilgrim Souvenirs," in *Miscellanea* 1, Medieval Dublin Excavations 1962–81, ser. b, vol. 2 (Dublin: Royal Irish Academy, 1988), 33–48.

83. O. Lehmann-Brockhaus, *Lateinische Schriftquellen zur Kunst in England, Wales und Schottland vom Jahre 901 bis zum Jahre 1307*, 6 vols. (Munich: Prestel, 1955–60), 2, no. 2301. The text—a Register of Richard de Swinfield, Bishop of Hereford, dated 1286—purports to list those relics which have been at Leominster *ab antiquo*. Of course, it is possible that these relics arrived in Leominster subsequent to the Anglo-Norman conquest.

84. The best summary of the techniques used in eleventh- and twelfth-century Irish metalwork is still Henry, *Irish Art in the Romanesque Period*, 74–122.

CHAPTER FOURTEEN

Rosemary Cramp

THE INSULAR TRADITION

An Overview

When I was asked to provide an overview of the tradition with which this series of essays is concerned, it was obvious that I could not cover all of the field of study reflected in the other contributions. Since I am an archaeologist, I have concentrated therefore on new research and new discoveries which have contributed, in my own field, to an increased understanding of the social and technological processes which formed and developed the Insular traditions. Although the term "Insular" has a very wide semantic field in modern scholarship, I shall try to use the term with as radical a meaning as possible, referring to the distinctive cultural traditions of that group of islands to the west of the European and Scandinavian land masses, occupied by those peoples who today call themselves English, Irish, Scots, and Welsh, or sometimes Irish and British. It is, as I see it, the distinctiveness of the material culture of these islands rather than a consideration of every type of activity which occurs in these islands which is the concern of this overview.

We might do well to note at the outset that the term "Insular" in relation to art, was coined to avoid the ethnic wars of the books between those who wished to associate certain styles of art with major tribal groups. The disputed places of origin of such complex masterpieces as the Book of Durrow, the Lindisfarne Gospels, or the Book of Kells (to give them their common names), and other manuscripts, which may be their progenitors or imitators, has been a major source of scholarly preoccupation for over a hundred years.[1]

I am not proposing to enter the manuscript debate in this chapter but to consider further the contacts which brought about the production of such work. These contacts were already long established by the time the great manuscripts were produced and are manifested in other media. Material evidence for the production of metalwork is more durable in the archaeological record than that for the production of books, or indeed any object formed from organic materials, and thus the centers of production are better known. It should also be noted that the distinctiveness of Insular work has mainly been seen in metalwork and manuscripts rather than in sculpture and architecture.[2] Metalwork was the craft most prized by native Insular patrons,[3] and the craft had a long secular tradition before Christianity was accepted, even though the Roman intervention fragmented the native tradition. The production of fine metalwork, and with it production of portable wealth, was a common factor which united the interests of the native tribes and the Anglo-Saxon invaders, but the response of the different groups to the more rooted arts of sculpture and mortared stone architecture was diverse. In fact I would go so far as to say that, save on the modern border regions of England and Scotland or England and Wales/Cornwall, there is little chance of confusing the country of origin if one were asked to identify from a photograph a piece of sculpture or a stone building of the period ca. A.D. 650–1050. I will discuss this further, but, one should also note, that there is very little chance of confusing the sculpture and architecture in the British Isles and Ireland with anything on the continent of this date. There is a sea change in the transmission. That change and our understanding of it is the subject of this chapter.

I will consider first some of the circumstances which produced Insular culture, then some of its manifestations, finally some surviving problems. My initial assumption is that Insular culture was formed in the islands of Britain by a variety of contacts—military, diplomatic, social, religious—between the peoples who inhabited these areas in the period fifth through eighth century, but, since that is a period nearly as long as the Roman occupation of Britain or from the early seventeenth century to today, and since the contacts vary in type and intensity, one should not expect to find the cultural expression consistent or unchanging in time and place. There was likewise a widespread culture change both amongst the indigenous Britons and Irish as well as the invading Anglo-Saxons, and it may have been relatively swift, although we have not the evidence to prove that. In art, what we think of as the heyday of the Insular achievement is between ca. A.D. 650 and 750, but there may have been a short or long process of definition before that date, and there were certainly regional and temporal variations within that century. I will not consider the period after the middle of the ninth century for two reasons, first because of the important influences which the Carolingian renaissance brought to Anglo-Saxon England, which produced a transformation of the art, (and in particular the stone architecture), of the English kingdom, and second because the Viking invasions and settlements formed new enclaves and relationships. In England this drove a wedge between the northern and southern English, which altered not only the economy but also the cultural contacts of the two parts of the island. From that time onwards the highland north, which had been the most fruitful forcing house for Insular culture, became, as it was in Roman Britain, a marginalized military zone.

This is perhaps a reversion to a basic role dependent on geographic considerations, but for a time in the fifth to seventh centuries there was a more uniform cultural level in the British Isles. As an urban economy reasserted itself by the ninth century, the old division between north and south reemerged in Britain. The received assumption that in western Europe there is a northern zone which includes north Britain, Ireland, and Scandinavia, while the south of Britain belongs to an intermediate zone, remains valid throughout much of the first millennium A.D. The Insular tradition or traditions emerged then in the process of forging new and acceptable identities, particularly amongst the peoples in the northern zone. I would indeed maintain that much of the art of the sixth and seventh centuries, is a visible manifestation of distinction from, or affiliation to, certain secular or religious groupings.

Such a "language" of style has been much discussed over the last decade by ethnographers in relation to contemporary tribal societies, and has been increasingly applied to the study of Anglo-Saxon burials.[4] The studies nevertheless produced no simple blueprints, although some of the work concerned with the identification of those circumstances in which style plays an important role in distinguishing one individual or group from another suggest new ways of looking at Insular art.

We are slowly learning more about the life-styles of the peoples with whose interactions we are concerned, although not all are equally visible in the archaeological record. The Picts seem to have formed their identity in response to the pressures of Late Roman Britain,[5] while the Irish/Scots maintained their distinctive traditions largely because there was no Roman occupation of their island. Both peoples, as early as A.D. 387, were sufficiently in contact to join with invading Germanic tribes in attacks against the Roman Britons.

It is still an open question as to how like other Roman provinces Britain was in its response to barbarian attacks and invasions, and some attempts to fit events into a continental pattern are not convincing. The difference between Insular and continental response to the barbarian invasions is quite apparent in the early fifth century.[6] The Roman acceptance of the loss of legal control of Britain by A.D. 410 meant that the legal arrangements for settling Germanic mercenaries in the eastern part of the main island need not have been the same as those which have been adduced by Goffart for continental provinces.[7] It is also clear from contemporary documents that while some of the British leaders felt themselves to be the heirs to the traditions of the Roman Empire, others did not and identified with the traditions of their Celtic neighbors. I shall be focusing on the Insular cultures of that area of Britain which came under the rule of the Anglo-Saxon tribes, but, despite the dominance of their language and legal organization, we now can see that many of their social customs—including their art—were shaped by contact with the people whom they conquered, or lived alongside. In their turn, these native peoples of Britain or more recent settlers such as the Dalriadic Irish had to accommodate themselves to the dominant Germanic group.

All dated records of events in the first half of the fifth century in Britain have been recently subjected to reevaluation,[8] and since this is not the subject of my study I will have to simplify the issues here. Nevertheless I think that there is general agreement that, in the first half of the fifth century, mainland Britain was still considered to be within the Roman orbit, despite the differences between north and south or east and west. But, one major problem of this period remains the invisibility of the Britons in the archaeological record. This may be because the rural populations seem to follow a life-style indistinguishable from those of the pre-Roman Iron Age, and the aristocracy may have imitated the pattern of the Romans, so both sections of society were for a time chronologically indistinguishable from what had gone before. The evidence for comparing the life-style of the Britons, Anglo-Saxons and Irish or Picts in the fifth to seventh centuries is not of the same type, and this no doubt invalidates comparisons, and renders an attempt to put together the activities of the different peoples under the heading of Insular more suspect.

One common factor in the making of a common civilization for the disparate groups of western Europe in the early Middle Ages was of course the Christian church, but how much was the church in Britain the preserver and transmitter of the traditions of the wider Late Antique world? Elsewhere in the old Roman provinces of Europe the well established structures of the church survived in some measure, and clerics and bishops took over influential state positions.[9] In Merovingian Gaul—an area which maintained a contact with and influence on Britain—it has been noted that "ecclesiastics had become accustomed to fend for themselves." "There was less sense of separation between sacred and secular roles to the point at which ecclesiastics were asked to wear their distinctive dress in order to be identifiable."[10] The Christian church in Britain seems to have been even less firmly established than in Gaul, and one of the major problems in discussing the relative influence of the Christian church established in Roman and sub-Roman Britain and the new influences which were introduced under the Anglo-Saxon regime is that the rich areas of the south and west, where Christianity obviously flourished most strongly in the Roman period, were those of the earliest English pagan settlement, and consequent destruction of Christian continuity.

We now know from recent excavations in sites such as Icklingham Suffolk, Witham Essex, Uley Gloucestershire, or Wells Wiltshire[11] that some Roman British baptisteries, churches, or mausolea were built on earlier native pagan sites. We know also that, although there is evidence for destruction of the structures on these sites, a significant number of them were revived as Christian centers by the Anglo-Saxons at a later date. It is therefore sometimes difficult to know whether we are looking at a survival or revival of influences. The vestiges of Christianity which survive in the archaeological record, do not in any way match the continental evidence. Charles Thomas' heroic efforts to clarify or even to maximize the evidence have not really done so. He attempts to use a combination of place name evidence and material remains to produce a picture[12] and also to chart what for the development of Insular culture is also important: the potential contacts between the sub-Roman population of Britain and the invading Germanic groups.[13] This does not really produce a coherent picture, largely I suspect because we have not yet fine enough instruments for close dating. Yet the interaction between the British and the Anglo-Saxons in the southern and western zones of Britain can easily be underestimated, influenced as we tend to be by Bede's view of the intransigence of the Britons in sharing their culture and religion with the Anglo-Saxons, and the undoubted truth that in North Britain the influence of the Irish church was profound.

Recently, however, the nature of the survival of a British way of life at the margins of Anglo-Saxon England is being illuminated by excavations at Whithorn, Galloway, and Tintagel, Cornwall.[14] I refer further to the former site later, but it is important here to stress the continuity of the sites from the fifth century onwards, and the important links which both have with the western seas. Both have produced evidence for trading contacts with the Mediterranean in the fifth and sixth centuries. Preliminary excavations at the Tintagel site of the headland/island indicate that this was an important fifth/sixth-century citadel, and other excavations in the churchyard on the mainland have produced burial mounds with cist burials perhaps of the inhabitants of the headland. The burial pattern is very like the early burials at Whithorn, and may well demonstrate the existence of private churches founded to maintain a particular tomb or to serve an important local family. It is possible that sites like these will eventually illuminate how the British church survived under the protection of secular potentates, and suggest a scenario for the development from independent bishops based on urban communities to the "proprietary" bishops of each major tribe. This seems to be the pattern which the Anglo-Saxons also adopted later.

In summary then, despite the fact that we still have much to discover concerning the way of life of the Britons in the fifth/sixth centuries in comparison with the Irish or the Anglo-Saxons, it is plausible that like other native tribes, such as the Picts, the need to establish a distinct identity was forced upon them as a response both to the power vacuum left by the withdrawal of Roman power and the threat of the Anglo-Saxon settlers and new invaders. (The fifth and sixth centuries also saw the "making" of the distinct English tribes from hybrid groups of immigrants.)[15] The common Insular styles then arose from the contacts and conflicts of peoples all of whom were experiencing some process of change.

As far as the Anglo-Saxons were concerned, the current evidence of archaeology suggests that they were significantly influenced by the art and customs of their new land, even though they retained and indeed imposed a very distinct identity on it. There are special characteristics which inform maritime migration, which perhaps make the people who undertake such a hazardous operation more receptive to new influences. There is disruption of social structure, and disruption of religious structure, especially if it is, as the Germanic beliefs seem to have been, associated with specific locations, such as woods, groves, lakes, and sources of springs.[16] Place names show that new religious sites were found,[17] and that these were often prehistoric, although it is not clear how some sites were recognized in the landscape. There is now a significant body of evidence for the use of old pre-Christian locations, for example, barrows, stone or wood circles, and henge monuments. (For Saxon burial grounds, see, for example, Mucking, Heslerton, Yeavering, or Thwing which are discussed below.) This practice has been seen by some as an attempt by the newcomers to assert power and authority by making ancestral links in a new land—not as a sign of continuity of use of the site—and certainly, for some places, there is a clear gap between the prehistoric past and first millennium use of the site. But the Britons may have already shown the way in this practice,[18] and it could denote evidence for contact between the invaders and the indigenous groups. Not only secular rulers but also the sub-Roman Christian church had taken over cult sites such as springs and wells, as, for example, recent excavations at Wells have demonstrated.[19]

The religion of the pagan Anglo-Saxons has traditionally been demonstrated through their burial rites, although increasingly these have been perceived as influenced by social as much as religious custom.[20] The more elaborate depositions of the seventh as opposed to the sixth century have been interpreted plausibly as a reaction by some of the members of the ruling elite to the growing acceptance of Christianity. We might neverthe-less consider that not all the Anglo-Saxons practiced the same religious rites and that this could be reflected in variations of burial practice not only in the simple variation between cremation and inhumation, but also in the deposition of goods and animals.[21] The recent excavations at Sutton Hoo have, however, demonstrated that significant variations in burial practice can occur even in what seems to be the graveyard of one defined group.[22]

The sixth century seems to have been an age of fluid social practice in the British Isles and there is now some evidence, as at Catterick,[23] that some Britons may have adopted the Anglo-Saxon practice of clothed burials. It is difficult to distinguish a dead Briton from a dead Saxon unless they have been buried clothed. Under Roman rule no doubt, the wearing of dress fastenings, which proclaimed tribal or family affiliations, was discouraged, and we know that the great tribal centers, where gold-smiths produced "Native" types of brooch, were closed down in the second century A.D. although there was a revival of native art in the fifth century.[24] At the end of the Roman period tribal groupings were swiftly formed. A return to the social structures still maintained by the Celts of Ireland including the adoption of their styles of dress would be a plausible development.

Whether in social or ethnic terms, clearly dress fashions reflect the need or the aspiration to belong to a group.[25] The swift changes in Kent from long brooches to the round continental aristocratic type of ultimately Byzantine derivation, bears this out. If anything supports the thesis that Francia claimed some sort of autonomy over Kent in the early sixth century,[26] it is the way in which the Kentish elite adopted Frankish types of dress fastenings. On the other hand, all of the Celtic neighbors of the Anglo-Saxons retained their traditional ring brooches, and thereby asserted their common identity, although perhaps the new ostentatious forms of the late-seventh and eighth centuries[27] reflect the influence of the showy Anglo-Saxon brooches. The ornament of these Celtic brooches was a fusion of motifs derived from several Insular sources, and the discovery of work-shops such as those of the Mote of Mark or Dunadd[28] indicate how native smiths copied Anglo-Saxon techniques and ornament. On the other hand, the contents of rich Anglo-Saxon graves, such as not only Sutton Hoo, mound one, but also the recently published satchel from the grave at Swallowcliffe Down, Wiltshire[29] indicate the range of Anglo-Saxon contact with the traditional arts of the Celtic smiths.[30] On the Swallowcliffe mounts, we find spirals and trumpet scrolls combined with Germanic animals and a close meshed type of interlace, which is one of the elements of early Insular art found throughout Britain from Kent to southwest Scotland.

The first development of Insular ornament is then to be found in lay patronage and lay emulation, although we still are not clear how the production and distribution of such material was organized. We lack the evidence from the early Anglo-Saxon sites of fine metal work production, although rural sites such as Heslerton are producing evidence for lay iron working on quite a large scale.[31] We also do not have the evidence for the training of metal workers and the models for the transmission of ideas which the motif pieces from Ireland provide.[32] Unfortunately the independent dating of fine metal objects is not precise enough to chart the speed of stylistic change and we can only see the defined end of a process of assimilation.

Divisions, whether social or ethnic, are manifested amongst peoples not only in language, physical appearance, and dress, but also in the forms of their settlements and houses. With improved archaeological techniques and large scale excavations, we are beginning, in a very exciting way, to see characteristic architectural forms for timber buildings. Although there are areas of Britain and Ireland where dry stone architecture was the norm, the Irish and the Anglo-Saxons both built in timber, and whether it was the construction or the decoration which made the difference between their architecture which Bede noted,[33] we now know that there is a common Insular style of building layout which seems to develop in Britain and to be the fusion of late Romano-British and Anglo-Saxon traditions.[34] The lowest common denominator of the Anglo-Saxon house type: rectangular half-timbered buildings, often with a division at one end, have been found throughout England on sixth- to eighth-century settlements from Mucking in Essex[35] to Heslerton in Yorkshire (where the extensive excavation has revealed zones of specialized activities), or to the Northumberland site of Thirlings.[36] These are sprawling sites without a clearly defined focus, but on sites of a higher social level such as Yeavering, Northumberland, or Cowdery's Down, Hampshire[37] a focus does seem to be provided by a large building, the hall (?), which is built and rebuilt on the same spot. B. Hope-Taylor, many years ago, felt that the changing architecture of the great halls of Yeavering could be explained first as an assimilation of Romano-British traditions, and second by the contacts of the Northumbrian kings with the Irish at Iona.[38] More recent excavations have provided parallels for the Yeavering house plans in other centers, and the idea that their architectural forms may have developed from a combination of influences from Romano-British and Anglo-Saxon traditions, has been reinforced, although the buildings with annexes which Hope-Taylor considered were derived from contact with the Dalriadic Irish, appear on other sites such as Cowdery's

Down in Hampshire, and Sprouston in Berwickshire[39] to be part of the same sequence, and not a new development. By the later phases of Yeavering and apparently also at Sprouston, the proprietary church with its graveyard is part of the settlement complex and there seems to be no difference in form and construction between the church and the domestic buildings.

If the first coming together of craftsmen and patrons to produce characteristic Insular art was in the royal and princely centers where the moulds and motif pieces have been found, the second was in the monastic centers where, as contemporary writers tell us, communities were drawn not only from the Irish and Anglo-Saxon peoples but also from a wider continental network; in these sites, we are beginning also to find evidence for production of fine metalwork in an Insular manner.[40]

The evidence for the production of metal work in the seventh and eighth centuries on monastic sites in Northumbria is not extensive, and both at Hartlepool[41] and Jarrow the excavated evidence is no more than that which might be expected for the uses of the community, which, like any other substantial group, could have retained a resident smith and could have used the services of itinerant smiths. There is some difficulty in relating the recently excavated areas of extensive and intensive craft work at such sites as Brandon and Flixborough,[42] (which have been assumed to be monastic), to comparable evidence in monastic communities elsewhere. The assumption that only the monastic workshops produced liturgical or "literate" evidence such as styli or inscriptions, may or may not be correct. It is true that there is a close parallel between some of the objects found at Flixborough and those found at Whitby or Barking,[43] which are documented monastic sites, but were the circumstances in which the objects were deposited the same? Swan and Ryan have pointed out how recent excavations at Armagh and aerial surveys of other sites demonstrate the large scale of Irish monasteries in which the inner enclosure contained the buildings for the use of the religious community and the outer enclosure the craft or industrial zone.[44] This pattern is repeated at Hoddom, Dumfriesshire, where the 1990–1991 excavations have revealed the extent of the enclosure and the fact that the church and cemetery is far distant from the large scale domestic complex on the periphery.[45] These "productive sites" such as Flixborough and Brandon with their timber buildings, which are no different from any other domestic site, and their dirty floors littered with animal bones and pottery could be part of the outer periphery of monastic houses whose cult centers are yet to be discovered, but it should be remembered that the styli and pins from Whitby possibly, and from Jarrow certainly, were found in the cult center itself and were presumed to have been lost while in use. In neither of these two centers was there the same intensity of evidence for craft work as at Flixborough, but at Jarrow at least, the evidence for craft activity increased in the ninth-century occupation deposits and in places overlaid a burial ground, and the same can be said for the monastery of Dacre.[46] The current excavations at Whithorn have demonstrated very clearly the changes of use and of emphasis between lay and religious activities that can take place on a single site,[47] and we have still a lot to learn about the nature of these early communities.

The acceptance of Christianity by the Anglo-Saxons encouraged a new network of contacts, not least, by the early eighth century, with the Picts, as is most notably reflected in the surviving Insular manuscripts. While the earliest churches in the north conformed to a timber type, a series of initiatives in the late-seventh century by notable clerics such as Wilfrid of Hexham or Benedict Biscop of Wearmouth/Jarrow, produced new models. We can now begin to see how the continental ideas, which they introduced to Britain, may have revived interest in the monuments and buildings still surviving in Roman Britain, and also how they interacted with the newly formed Insular art styles.

The first mortared stone buildings at Monkwearmouth, which, our texts tell us, were built by Gaulish masons in 674, employed Roman poured concrete constructions, both in the church and monastic buildings, and the orderly layout linked by a long passage could well be inspired by continental models. But by the time the twin foundation of Jarrow was built, in 685, possibly by Anglo-Saxon monks, the large public buildings from the site were laid out in strings like the Yeavering royal halls, and they are very much of the same scale and appearance, although they are not in wood but in mortared stone. Recently, the excavations at Whithorn have demonstrated, in the Northumbrian phase, how Anglo-Saxon architectural styles were translated into the old territories of the Britons, and in the process were subtly transformed.

I argued many years ago,[48] and, incidentally, still believe, that it was the introduction of continental traditions of stone building and carving which reintroduced the art of low relief stone carving into these islands and with it the remarkable variety of Insular monuments. The great stone crosses or upright slabs which must once have existed in tens of thousands in the countryside and in the churches and churchyards of Britain and Ireland are the Insular field monument par excellence. It is true that there are plain incised stele in northern France which, as I have discussed elsewhere, had an influence on the monuments of York and Whitby,[49] and there are simple stone crosses in Brittany which are closely linked with the granite crosses of Cornwall, but there is nothing on the continent to match the variety of decorated stone crosses which we find in the British Isles.

The precursors for these monuments were the upright incised stele of Early Christian Gaul, western Britain, and Ireland with their inscriptions and Christian symbols of the Chi-Rho or crosses of arcs.[50] This form and the cross of arcs continues in the Celtic west through the seventh century, alongside the newer stone crosses.

The early incised stele may well have had an influence on the earliest Pictish monuments. The origins of Pictish Style 1 monuments, which consist of rough hewn boulders decorated with abstract ornament, has been much debated and it would be impossible for me to attempt even to summarize recent discussion here. Nevertheless, as a contribution to the debate, one may note that there is in Scotland a tradition of rock art, which seems to have been continuous from the Bronze Age into the first millennium A.D. Recently many examples of rock art have been discovered in Galloway with spirals, hand and foot prints and animals incised on the stone, while in the Northern Isles, similar proto-Pictish incised carvings have also been discovered.[51] The combined influence of the incised art of what appear to be ancestral holy places and the incised monuments of the centers of Christian Roman power could have inspired the Pictish rulers, who wished to define their own identity, to produce public monuments which spoke their own language in an ornamental alphabet which seems, like other alphabets, to have been brought together at one time and in one form and developed by small additions later. The Southern Picts were traditionally first Christianized by the Briton, Ninian of Whithorn, and the northern group by the Irish monks from Iona but, in 716, they requested theological and architectural help from the Saxon monastery of Monkwearmouth and Jarrow and this seemingly also provided a new inspiration for their stone carvings. Their class 2, Christian, monuments are clearly influenced in form by Northumbrian memorial slabs with bold crosses in high relief,[52] and their decoration by Insular manuscript art. The Picts' absorption of so many influences and their contribution to the synthesis of Insular art is difficult to quantify but it is an essential element.

The stone crosses of the Northumbrians may have derived from a variety of influences and models provided by both continental and Insular sources which need not have been adopted at the same time but as part of a continuous process of absorbing Christian art. Wooden crosses were introduced from Dalriada by King Oswald as a focus for prayer and standard of victory before the battle of Heavenfield.[53] Such crosses would have reminded the learned of Constantine's *labarum*, and indeed this reminiscence is clearly indicated in an inscription in honor of the cross, on a cross-bearing slab at Jarrow.[54] This association could well have prompted a greater interest for patrons and carvers in the stone monuments surviving from the Roman occupation, which would still have been visible in the

British landscape, and once the art of stone relief carving had been rein-troduced into the island, would have seemed more relevant. The impres-sive jeweled altar crosses, such as the first southern missionary Paulinus brought back from Northumbria to Kent[55] likewise could have served as models, as is apparent in some of the fine chevron or pelleted ornament, which appears to translate the mode of metalwork on the carvings of the Ripon and Hexham schools.[56] Ann Hamlin has, however, recently reminded us that clearly "crosses did fulfill a wide variety of functions and were put up for many different reasons, and it is surely important to bear that range in mind when studying material, for example, the whereabouts of crosses, their relationship to one another and to other features, as well as their decoration and iconographic sources."[57] Sometimes it must have been the different functions, and sometimes the local traditions which produced such marked variations in form and ornament in the crosses of Britain and Ireland.

It is arguably easier to discuss differences of function than of signifi-cance for these monuments. The pagan Germanic traditions which would have invested the wooden crosses with a deeper significance are explored elsewhere by Douglas Mac Lean (see pp. 83–88), and no doubt there were explicit contrasts to be drawn, when looking at crosses, between the world view of the pagan and the Christian eras. The placing of the image of the inhabited tree on the narrow faces of crosses with important figural programs such as at Bewcastle, Ruthwell, or Otley may mean that the image also had a strong didactic function. There has recently been a deeper exploration of the liturgical and devotional content of crosses within the Christian tradition,[58] but, the few important figural monuments, which have attracted so much attention, should not blind us to the fact that the majority of crosses are covered with non-figural ornament and that the figural repertoire is not large—mainly the life and miracles of Christ. This is a more limited repertoire than that of the icons which Bede describes as hanging around the churches of Wearmouth and Jarrow, or the range of Old Testament scenes such as decorate the "scripture crosses" in Ireland. Old Testament scenes such as Samson bearing off the Gates of Gaza, David playing the harp, or the Sacrifice of Isaac, become more popular in all areas of Britain in the ninth and tenth century, and this may reflect some adherence to the traditions of iconoclasm, elsewhere in the Christian world. By the time that we get to the late-ninth century, the different ethnic groups in the British Isles were accepting and developing different traditions. Political power and cultural influence had passed to the kingdoms of Mercia and Wessex, but in the remote places of British and Anglo-Saxon Cumbria the old Insular love of abstract ornament survived until it was absorbed and transformed by the new Scandinavian settlers.

I have tried to show how the political and social contacts of the sixth to seventh centuries encouraged an assimilation of traditions, but that distinctive idioms remained. The Insular tradition is not monolithic, there are perceptible regional and cultural differences, particularly between those who did and those who did not accept without adaptation Mediterranean traditions. This is a period of swift assimilation, which produces an art which is patternmaking and motif making, breaking the flowing repetitive rhythms of classical art into isolated densely packed elements, and this remains an important aspect of Anglo-Saxon art right up to the Conquest.

Our increasing knowledge of production centers has helped to define foci of influence, but has not so far aided us in following up distribution or indeed in helping us to understand the significance of the art of the pagan peoples to themselves.

When we reach the period of Christian iconography, even with the important new insights into the liturgical meanings of the material, which have been so important a feature of recent research, can we ever know that interpretations did not differ from one background to another informed by a substratum of belief which we have not been able to retrieve?

NOTES

1. C. Nordenfalk, "One Hundred Years of Varying Views on the Early Insular Gospel Books," in M. Ryan, ed., *Ireland and Insular Art A.D. 500–1200* (Dublin: Royal Irish Academy, 1987), 1–6.

2. M. Ryan, "Links between Anglo-Saxon and Irish Medieval Art: Some Evidence of Metalwork," in C. Karkov and R. Farrell, eds., *Studies in Insular Art and Archaeology*, A.E.M.S. 1 (Oxford, Ohio: American Early Medieval Studies, 1991), 117–26.

3. C. Dodwell, *Anglo-Saxon Art a New Perspective* (Manchester: Manchester University Press, 1982).

4. J. D. Richards, "Style and Symbol: Explaining Variability in Anglo-Saxon Cremation Burials," in S. T. Driscoll and M. R. Nieke, eds., *Power and Politics in Early Medieval Britain and Ireland* (Edinburgh: Edinburgh University Press, 1988), 145–61.

5. This view is most cogently discussed by J. C. Mann in "Hadrian's Wall: The Last Phases," in P. J. Casey, ed., *The End of Roman Britain*, B.A.R. Brit. ser. 71 (Oxford: British Archaeological Reports, 1979), 148–51. For a survey of the later development of Pictish culture see S. M. Foster, "The State of Pictland in the Age of Sutton Hoo," in M. O. H. Carver, ed., *The Age of Sutton Hoo* (Woodbridge and Rochester, N.Y.: Boydell Press, 1992), 217–34.

6. R. S. O. Tomlin, "Meanwhile in North Italy and Cyrenaica," in P. J. Casey, *End of Roman Britain*, 253–70.

7. W. Goffart, *Barbarians and Romans A.D. 418–584: The Techniques of Accommodation* (Princeton: Princeton University Press, 1980).

8. See in particular, M. Lapidge and D. Dumville, eds., *Gildas: New Approaches* (Woodbridge: Boydell Press, 1984).

9. Goffart, *Barbarians and Romans*.

10. J. Herrin. *The Formation of Christendom* (Oxford: Basil Blackwell, 1987), 115.

11. C. Thomas, *Christianity in Roman Britain to A.D. 500* (London: Batsford, 1981), 202–27.

12. Ibid., fig. 49.

13. Ibid., fig. 47.

14. C. Morris, "Tintagel Island," *Universities of Durham and Newcastle upon Tyne Archaeological Reports for 1990* (1991): 42–44; J. Nowakowski and C. Thomas, *Excavations at Tintagel Parish Churchyard, Cornwall Spring 1990* (Truro: Cornwall Archaeological Unit, 1990); P. Hill, *Whithorn 4. Excavations at Whithorn Priory, 1990–91* (Whithorn: Whithorn Trust, 1992); P. Hill, *Whithorn and Saint Ninian: Excavations of a Monastic Town* (forthcoming).

15. S. Bassett, ed., *The Origins of the Anglo-Saxon Kingdoms* (London and New York 1989); M. O. H. Carver, ed., *The Age of Sutton Hoo* (Woodbridge and Rochester, N.Y.: Boydell Press, 1992).

16. H. R. Davidson, *Myths and Symbols in Pagan Europe* (Manchester: Manchester University Press, 1988), 13–35.

17. M. Gelling, *Signposts to the Past: Place-Names and the History of England* (London: Dent, 1978), fig. 11.

18. B. Hope-Taylor, *Yeavering: An Anglo-British Centre of Early Northumbria*, Dept. of Environment Archaeol. Reports, No. 7 (London: H.M.S.O., 1977), 154–64 and figs. 74–78.

19. W. Rodwell, "Churches in the Landscape: Aspects of Topography and Planning," in M. Faull, ed., *Studies in Late Anglo-Saxon Settlement* (Oxford: Oxford University Dept. for External Studies, 1984), 13–14; R. K. Morris, *The Church in British Archaeology*, C.B.A. Research Report 47 (London: Council for British Archaeology, 1983), 23–28.

20. J. Shepard, "The Social Identity of the Individual in Isolated Barrows and Barrow Cemeteries in Anglo-Saxon England," in B. Burnham and J. Kingsbury, eds., *Space, Hierarchy and Society*, B.A.R. Int. ser. 59 (Oxford: British Archaeological Reports, 1979), 49–80.

21. A. Meaney, *A Gazetteer of Early Anglo-Saxon Burial Sites* (London: Allen & Unwin, 1964).

22. M. Carver, "Kingship and Material Culture in Early Anglo-Saxon East Anglia," in S. Bassett, ed., *The Origins of Anglo-Saxon Kingdoms*, 141–58; M. Carver, "The Anglo-Saxon Cemetery at Sutton Hoo: An Interim Report," in Carver, ed., *Age of Sutton Hoo*, 343–71. A full account of the burials including the intact inhumation of the youth with his horse, discovered in 1991, is forthcoming. This discovery adds, however, to the variety of burial rites from this site, both in the mode of cremation and imhumation.

23. P. Wilson, et al., "Early Anglian Catterick and *Catraeth*," M.A. (forthcoming). Also R. White, "Scrap or Substitute, Roman Material in Anglo-Saxon Graves," in E. Southworth, ed., *Anglo-Saxon Cemeteries: A Reappraisal* (Stroud 1990; Dover, N.H.: A. Sutton, 1991).

24. H. Kilbride-Jones, *Celtic Craftsmanship in Bronze* (London: Croom Helm, 1980).

25. M. R. Nieke and H. B. Duncan, "Dalriada: The Establishment and Maintenance of an Early Historic Kingdom in Northern Britain," in S. T. Driscoll and M. R. Nieke, eds., *Power and Politics*, 14–15.

26. I. Wood, "The End of Roman Britain: Continental Evidence and Parallels," in Lapidge and Dumville, eds., *Gildas*, 1–25, especially 23–24.

27. R. Ó Floinn, "Secular Metalwork in the Eighth and Ninth Centuries," in S. Youngs, ed., *"The Work of Angels": Masterpieces of Celtic Metalwork, 6th–9th Centuries A.D.* (London: British Museum, 1989), 72–91.

28. A. Curle, "Report on the Excavation, in September 1913, of a Vitrified Fort at Rockcliffe, Dalbeattie, known as the Mote of Mark, *P.S.A.S.* 48 (1913–14): 125–68; L. Laing, "The Mote of Mark and Celtic Interlace," *Antiquity* 49 (1975): 98–108; Nieke and Duncan, "Dalriada," 14–21; E. Campbell and A. Lane, "Celtic and Germanic Interaction in Dalriada: the 7th-Century Metalworking site at Dunadd," in R. M. Spearman and J. Higgitt, eds., *The Age of Migrating Ideas: Early Medieval Art in Northern Britain and Ireland* (Edinburgh: National Museums of Scotland, 1993), 52–63.

29. G. Speake, *A Saxon Bed Burial on Swallowcliffe Down*, English Heritage Archaeol. Rep. 10 (London: English Heritage, 1989).

30. S. Youngs, "Fine Metalwork to c. A.D. 650," in Youngs, ed., *"Work of Angels,"* 53–63.

31. D. Powlesland, C. Houghton, and J. Hanson, "Excavations at Heslerton, North Yorkshire, 1978–82," *Arch.J.* 143 (1986): 53–173. A report of the settlement excavation is forthcoming.

32. U. O'Meadhra, *Early Christian, Viking and Romanesque Art: Motif-pieces from Ireland* (Stockholm: Almquist & Wiksell International, 1979).

33. C. Plummer, ed., *Venerabilis Bedae Opera Historica* (Oxford: Etypographeo Clarendoriano, 1896), 3, 25; B. Colgrave and R. Mynors, eds., *Bede's Ecclesiastical History of the English People* (Oxford: Clarendon Press, 1969).

34. P. Dixon, "How Saxon is the Saxon House?" in P. Drury, ed., *Structural Reconstruction*, B.A.R. Brit. ser. 110 (Oxford: British Archaeological Reports, 1982), 275–87; S. James, A. Marshall, and M. Millett, "An Early Medieval Building Tradition," *Arch.J.* 141 (1984): 182–215.

35. H. Hamerow, *Excavations at Mucking*, vol. 2, *The Anglo-Saxon Settlement*, English Heritage Archaeol. Rep. 21 (London: English Heritage, 1991).

36. C. O'Brian and R. Miket, "The Early Medieval Settlement of Thirlings, Northumberland," *Durham Archaeol. J.* 7 (1991): 57–91.

37. Hope-Taylor, *Yeavering*, and M. Millet and S. James, "Excavations at Cowdery's Down, Basingstoke, Hampshire, 1978–81," *Arch.J.* 140 (1983): 151–279.

38. Hope-Taylor, *Yeavering*, 205–75, 313–24.

39. I. Smith, "Patterns of Settlement and Land Use of the Late Anglian Period in the Tweed Basin," in M. Faull, ed., *Studies in Late Anglo-Saxon Settlement* (Oxford: Oxford University Dept. for External Studies, 1984), 177–96; I. M. Smith, "Sprouston, Roxburghshire: An Early Anglian Centre of the Eastern Tweed Basin," *P.S.A.S.* 121 (1991): 261–94.

40. M. Ryan, "Fine Metalworking and Early Irish Monasteries: the Archaeological Evidence," in J. Bradley, ed., *Settlement and Society in Medieval Ireland* (Kilkinny, Ireland: Boethias Press, 1988), 33–48.

41. R. Cramp and R. Daniels, "New Finds from the Anglo-Saxon Monastery at Hartlepool, Cleveland," *Antiquity* 61 (1987): 424–32.

42. R. Carr, A. Tester, and P. Murphy, "The Middle Saxon Settlement at Staunch Meadow, Brandon," *Antiquity* 62 (1988): 371–77; B. Whitwell, "Flixborough," *Current Archaeology* 126 (1991): 244–47. Many of the finds from these sites were published in L. Webster and J. Backhouse, eds., *The Making of England: Anglo-Saxon Art and Culture A.D. 600–900* (London: British Museum, 1991).

43. L. Webster and J. Backhouse, eds., *The Making of England*, 88–101.

44. D. L. Swan, "Monastic Proto-towns in Early Medieval Ireland: The Evidence of Aerial Photography, Plan Analysis and Survey," in H. B. Clarke and A. Simms, eds., *The Comparative History of Urban Origins in Non-Roman Europe*, B.A.R. Int. ser. 255 (Oxford: British Archaeological Reports, 1985), 77–102; Ryan, "Fine Metalworking and Early Irish Monasteries."

45. C. E. Lowe, "New Light on the Anglian 'Minster' at Hoddom," *Trans. Dumfries. and Galloway Nat. Hist. and Ant. Soc.* 3rd ser. 66 (1991): 11–35.

46. R. Newman (forthcoming); R. Cramp, "A Reconsideration of the Monastic Site of Whitby," in R. M. Spearman and J. Higgitt, eds., *The Age of Migrating Ideas: Early Medieval Art in Northern Britain and Ireland* (Edinburgh: National Museums of Scotland, 1993), 64–73.

47. P. Hill, *The Whithorn Excavation: 1990 Supplement* (Whithorn: Whithorn Trust, 1991), and see note 14.

48. R. Cramp, "Early Northumbrian Sculpture," *Jarrow Lecture* (Jarrow: Rev, H. Saxby, 1965).

49. R. Cramp, "A Reconsideration of the Monastic Site of Whitby," in Spearman and Higgitt, eds., *Age of Migrating Ideas*, 68–70.

50. A. C. Thomas, *The Early Christian Archaeology in North Britain* (London, Glasgow, and New York: Oxford University Press, 1971), 91–131.

51. J. Hunter, "Pool, Sanday: A Case Study for the Late Iron Age and Viking Periods," in L. Armit, ed., *Beyond the Brochs* (Edinburgh: Edinburgh University Press, 1990), 175–93; R. W. B. Morris and M. van Hoek, "Rock Carvings in the Garlieston Area, Wigtown District," *Trans. Dumfries. and Galloway Nat. Hist. and Ant. Soc.* 3rd ser. 62 (1987): 32–39.

52. R. Cramp, *Corpus of Anglo-Saxon Stone Sculpture in England*, vol 1, *Co. Durham and Northumberland* (Oxford: Oxford University Press, 1984), 124, ill. 604.

53. Bede, *Historia Ecclesiastica* 3.2. Plummer, *Bedae*, 128–29.

54. Cramp, *Corpus*, vol. 1, 112–13, pls. 95–97.

55. Bede, *Historia Ecclesiastica*, 2.20. Plummer, *Bedae*, 126.

56. W. G. Collingwood, *Northumbrian Crosses of the Pre-Norman Age* (London: Faber & Gwyer, 1927), 27–39, 119.

57. A. Hamlin, "Crosses in Early Ireland: The Evidence from Written Sources," in M. Ryan, ed., *Ireland and Insular Art*, 138–40.

58. See for example, É. Ó Carragáin, "Christ over the Beasts and the Agnus Dei: Two Multivalent Panels on the Ruthwell and Bewcastle Crosses," in P. E. Szarmach and V. D. Oggins, eds., *Sources of Anglo-Saxon Culture* (Kalamazoo, Mich.: Medieval Institute, 1986), 377–403; P. Meyvaert, "A New Perspective on the Ruthwell Cross: Ecclesia and the Vita Monastica," in B. Cassidy, ed., *The Ruthwell Cross* (Princeton: Index of Christian Art; Princeton University Dept. of Art and Archaeology, 1992), 95–166.

CONTRIBUTORS

Shirley Alexander
Department of Art, University of Texas at Austin, emeritus

Rosemary Cramp
Durham University, emeritus

Carol A. Farr
London, England

Robert T. Farrell
Department of English, Cornell University

Jane Hawkes
School of English, University of Newcastle upon Tyne

Isabel Henderson
Newnham College, Cambridge University

Catherine E. Karkov
Department of Art, Miami University

James Lang†
University of York

Douglas Mac Lean
Northfield, Minnesota

Carol Neuman de Vegvar
Department of Fine Arts, Ohio Wesleyan University

Raghnall Ó Floinn
Irish Antiquities Division, National Museum of Ireland

Michael Ryan
Chester Beatty Library, Dublin

Roger Stalley
Department of History of Art, Trinity College Dublin

Niamh Whitfield
London, England

Susan Youngs
Department of Medieval and Later Antiquities, British Museum

† deceased

INDEX

Note: The page numbers of illustrations are given in *italics.*